I can look into the valleys or the whole countryside,
even look at the beautiful birds as they fly by.

I watch the deer drink from a kid's swimming hole,
all God's works I can see from a hi-line pole.

I have seen the beautiful pictures frosty morn will bring,
can hear the clear songs that the winter birds sing.

Lucky is the man to see a fresh fallen snow,
from top of a power pole only he will know.

My work is not all dreary, neither is it sad,
I have seen more beauty than most men ever had.

As nature covers her colorful leaves, I feel a winter freeze,
yet I recall spring's warm gentle breeze.

I see her beautiful kingdom up here in the sky,
I have learned of answers to some of nature's whys.

Yet to see her beauty is a scene to behold
from my perch on a fifty-five-foot power pole.

by Ted Aldridge

Hillbilly Poet

Gordon Galloway

DEERFIELD PUBLISHING
1994

Library of Congress Catalog Card Number: 95-68364
Copyright © 1995 by Gordon L. Galloway
All rights reserved
Printed in
The United States of America
Published by Deerfield Publishing Company
1613 130th Avenue
Morley, MI 49336
ISBN 0-9644077-1-X

The boy was half Cherokee. He was raised by his blind grandmother until he was sent to an Episcopal boys' home. Ambitious and rebellious, he knew what he wanted out of life and when the system wouldn't react to his needs, he simply bypassed it.

The mountains and rivers were his refuge and constructing power lines across this country became his vocation. A crumbling marriage brought turmoil to his life, but stability returned with a woman who was also half Cherokee.

A TRUE STORY

ACKNOWLEDGMENTS

Julie Martin designed our cover and we wish to thank her for a job well done. It was based on the poem Ted wrote while on the job near Grayling, Michigan. Julie received a Bachelor of Science and Masters of Arts Degree from Central Michigan University and teaches art at Morley Stanwood High School. One of Julie's students was my daughter Jeanne, who recently provided Deerfield Publishing with a fine logo that she designed.

My wife, Mary Ann, deserves great credit for bringing order to a disorganized manuscript and we all sincerely thank Ted and Mary for sharing their story with us.

Robert Ted Aldridge: age 17

Contents

Back Roads

For many years the main highway out of Grand Rapids, Michigan was just a two lane road that threaded its way through several small towns and villages on its way north. Now, most of the traffic has bypassed the small communities by using the new expressway to the west. Although each community along old US-131 is in some way unique, a traveler exiting the expressway for gas would probably not notice much difference between them.

At Exit 125, Jefferson Road east will bring you to a stop right across from the fire barn on Main Street in Morley. A quiet community now, Morley had once been a bustling village whose economy was fueled by the timber operations in the surrounding countryside. The majestic white pine covered this area in the 1870's and the Little Muskegon River provided the avenue for the large logs to reach the sawmill in town. For a few years the railroad from Grand Rapids ended in Morley. It brought settlers and supplies in, and hauled the lumber out.

On the south edge of Main Street a single dam remains on the river. The water passing over it does not generate electricity, power the saws or grind the grain as it once did. The dam does back up enough water to form a peaceful fishing pond and to provide folks here with some pleasant scenery.

Morley's population is about 500 people now. The towering white pines are gone and the trains don't pass through town anymore. The expressway robbed it of the volume of traffic it once knew, but still it seems to be healthy and surviving. It has a small bank, gas station, grocery store, restaurant, post office and sports shop.

If you arrived in Morley for gas or a bite to eat, unless you were headed up to Big Rapids where Ferris State University is, you'd probably go back to the expressway to continue your journey. Old 131 just doesn't receive the care it once did and is a little rough now.

Not too far north of Morley the old highway does an S turn where the railroad tracks once crossed on the bridge above. We turn right there on a gravel road going east. For the first part of the road we have to slow down because it's so bumpy.

We're on Four Mile Road now, traveling up and down some small hills through a semi-scenic non-farming countryside. If you have one particular feeling as we go along it's probably going to be that all of a sudden you're out in the sticks. In this part of Mecosta County there's just not too much to stir the curiosity.

A couple miles down the road and at the top of another hill, a road intersects from the south. A yellow DEAD END sign on the corner indicates limited travel in that direction. We make the turn anyway, and follow the road over a small hill and down to where it ends beside some old farm machinery. On the left there is a cleared out area and beside the narrow driveway is a row of tree stumps turned on edge. A sign tacked on the power pole says ALDRIDGE.

On the left of the driveway is a fairly large unpainted house and at the end of the driveway is a smaller cottage that looks as if it should be perched on the shore of some scenic lake. There is a barn and other various sized farm buildings, and more machinery lined up in the back. A few chickens stroll around in the front yard of the cottage and an old bright red GMC truck sits in the driveway. A wisp of smoke is noticeable from the chimney. Ted and Mary Aldridge live here. Follow me in and I'll introduce you to them.

After a couple of raps on the door we hear a, "Come on in!" As we enter Mary is stretched out on her sofa with a novel in her right hand and the other on the back of her little dog, a chihuahua, that's curled up beside her.

Mary is all smiles, and lets out a, "How ya doin?" Ted sits at the kitchen table with a stack of papers beside him, a cup of coffee, and a cigarette trailing smoke from an ash tray. For a 60 year old he still looks lean and rugged as he peers over his half-glasses with a grin.

We're standing in a kitchen and living room combined. Two walls are covered with shelves full of books and over the kitchen counter there are more shelves with numerous jars full of herbs that Mary has gathered from the woods. A barrel wood stove makes the temperature inside real cozy.

You probably wonder why I brought you all the way out here to meet these folks. I suppose you will also expect something sensational to be convinced that they have anything to say that you'd be interested in hearing. If you'll trust me on this one, I think you will discover that their story and Ted's poetry add lots of color and meaning to the fabric of our generation. I am also sure that when you have finished listening you will have laughed a little, had a few tears in your eyes, and will have developed a respectful appreciation for these two fine people.

Pull up a chair and sit down. Let them tell you their story as they told it to me.

Ted and Mary Aldridge at home: a little corner of Mecosta County and Deerfield Township.

Starting Out

About the only thing I can remember about my father was the time he carried me down the street to Ramsey's store. There, he bought me some candy called KITS. After my first bite into that delicious caramel peanut butter mix, he took it away. "That's got worms in it boy!" In those days when times were hard, candy was sold as is. If you didn't like the worms, you didn't have to buy it, and if you didn't notice them, no big deal.

Now some might be kind of ashamed to tell these things, but I don't care what people think, so I'll tell you about my real father. Although I never really knew him, other than the candy incident, stories handed down through the family provided me with some information about him. There is no way that you'd be able to untangle accurate details from all those old women talking, however as I understand it my real father was Robert Ward. He was a full-blooded Cherokee Indian off of the reservation at Ashville, North Carolina. At the time, he was in the Navy stationed at Norfolk. On leave he came to Petersburg, Virginia with a friend and met my mother, who was white. They must have gotten along pretty well, because at 15 years old she was pregnant. My grandfather was pretty upset and said that no way was she going to marry a damned Indian.

Now in the early 1930s Indians were not held in high esteem, and were not even encouraged to enter the military. I suppose it was an attractive alternative to reservation life and in the depression days it at least provided good meals, pay, and a change in social status. Anyway, he must have been pretty intelligent as he passed the entrance exams and was enlisted.

I guess Granddad was successful in running my real father off and in the meantime some friends introduced my mother to Stanley Aldridge and they married.

Stanley accepted me as his child. Unfortunately they did not get along and that ended up in a divorce in 1933.

I was less than two years old at the time of the divorce, and my grandma was providing most of my care and really the influence of a mother. To outsiders it probably seemed like a mixed up situation. My mother always called Grandma Mama, and Grandma called her Helen, so that's the way I referred to them. Calling Mother Helen created a distant-looking relationship. That was not the truth of the matter because we were close, but at times she seemed more like a sister.

Grandpa was a mechanical engineer. He worked at installing ice companies up and down the East Coast. He was away from home a lot, but was a good provider, especially considering those deep depression years. Certainly he was a self-made man and had led an interesting life since running away from home at the age of 12.

I never knew exactly why Grandpa left his home in Charleston, S.C. It was probably a combination of an unhappy home, maybe the idea of an adventure fueled from the tales of that seacoast city. He became a cabin boy on an ocean freighter and remained on the sea until he was about 26 years old.

As a cabin boy, he received no wages, but was well-fed. The first mate took him under his wing, and he was also well liked by the captain. I also remember him telling me how important it was to get along with the cook.

His philosophy was, "I don't care where you go, get in good with the cook. The woman of the house don't mean anything unless she's the cook. The cook is the one that's going to feed you." The other thing I remember him saying was, "Whenever you go in the front door of a place, make sure you know where the back door is because you may have to get out in a hurry." I guess that was a sailor's survival message when on shore leave.

From the first mate, the captain, and the cook, he received his education. By the time he was 18, he was a qualified seaman by company standards and now second mate. His promotion to first mate came quickly that same year when his friend, the first mate, got killed on shore leave in Italy. Fate took another twist when the captain died at sea on the return voyage. Now approaching the age of nineteen, he found himself captain of the ship. His qualifications for the job, along with reputation and performance, must have been enough to satisfy the company. When he returned, they kept him as captain for the next nine years.

In those days, the cargo that went below deck belonged to the company. The cargo that could be piled on the top deck was the captain's. Grandpa made lots of money as the top deck was piled to capacity whenever possible. The Spanish American War was on and he made runs from Charleston and New Orleans to support Teddy Roosevelt's war effort in Cuba. The captain also had the authority to determine different routings, if he deemed it more profitable for the company. One thing that Grandpa learned at an early age was that most sailors came back from shore leave with empty pockets, and he was determined not to waste his earnings.

Sometime in the 1920s, Grandpa decided to leave the sea and get a formal education. It was possible to enter a university by passing an entrance exam, even if a high school diploma was not in hand. Grandpa passed the exam at Georgia Tech and graduated as a mechanical engineer specializing in refrigeration.

My grandma grew up on the banks of the Neuse River in North Carolina. The Neuse flows to Pamlico Sound, and on into the Atlantic Ocean. She lived close to a little town called Arapahoe. Her family not only farmed, but were fishermen too. The Neuse River and coastal bays provided a variety of food and extra income. There were the herring and shad runs, plus the oysters to harvest.

Somewhere along the line she met Richard Poole, who was a native of that area. He was a hard working man that later founded Poole Trucking and became very wealthy. He married Grandma, but when he tried to move her to Greenville, N.C., to expand his trucking company, she refused to go. After three years of marriage they were divorced. She and my mother moved to Virginia to live with her mother Sarah. There Grandma met and married Bill Thomas who adopted my mother. I never met my mother's real father, Richard Poole, but have always referred to Bill Thomas as Grandpa. Unfortunately, Grandpa Bill did not have much luck with my grandmother's stubbornness either, and they started having problems about where they were going to live.

Grandpa had more than two nickels in his pocket. He owned two houses in Petersburg, and two or three vacant lots which were rented to the city for recreation. Trouble started when he bought this 400 acre farm 15 miles out of town and tried to move Grandma out of the city to the farm. Although Grandma had simple beginnings, between Richard Poole and Grandpa Bill, Grandma had acquired a taste for the city and its social life. Grandpa, on the other hand, was tired of traveling and wanted to assume the role of a gentleman farmer.

I do remember my grandfather telling me of one funny thing that happened when things started going bad between them. When he came from the sea, he brought his old captain's parrot. One day he happened to be home when the preacher and the social ladies came to call. Now Grandpa was pretty bald, and the preacher, who was also bald, arrived at the house about the same time that Grandpa usually came home from work. The parrot announced the preacher's arrival with, "Here comes that old bald-headed son of a bitch." Well this certainly upset the social ladies and the preacher. Grandma went into hysterics. She threatened afterwards that she was going to kill that bird. Grandpa said, "Nobody's going to kill that parrot for telling the truth."

A not so funny thing happened in 1933, that people said led to Grandma's blindness. Grandpa had cut his finger badly, and Grandma intended to treat it with iodine. She removed the cork and as she started to apply it to the wound, Grandpa jerked from the pain. He hit the bottle and the solution splashed out into Grandma's eyes. Grandpa put her head in the sink and flooded her face and eyes with water, but the damage apparently was already done. It was my understanding that the iodine triggered a protective growth on the eyeballs that eventually produced her blindness. I'm not sure if it really did or not, but that's what we thought caused it at the time. Their marriage deteriorated rapidly after the accident, and the farming venture.

Grandma and Grandpa didn't divorce, they just split up. Grandpa gave Grandma the two houses and four vacant lots. The city paid rent on the lots, and we rented the house we weren't living in. This income was sufficient for her, or at least Grandpa thought it was.

Grandpa sold the farm and afterwards some kind of a deal supposedly fell through and Grandpa lost $43,000. At least that's what he wanted people to believe. I found out later that Grandpa had pulled that deal to get the government off his back. The money was slowly drawn out of the bank and later declared a loss on paper.

Grandpa returned to the Atlantic Ice Company in Atlanta, Georgia. Some time later he had a chance to work for a big company in Chicago called Crown and Croft, but instead went to work for Sealtest Ice Cream Company in Richmond, Virginia. There he helped set up an automatic ice cream plant.

In 1938 Sealtest opened a plant in Petersburg, Virginia and Grandpa settled into a semi-retirement there.

It was about a year later when he came home to Grandma's house with two big boxes containing his engineering tools and instruments. He told Grandma that they were for me when I grew up and proceeded to have the heavy boxes hauled up to my room, by two able men. One box was locked, but I managed to get into the other and got out a set of micrometer calipers, which I hid under my bed. Shortly after that, Grandma sold both boxes to Grandpa's apprentice, Odis Baughan for $10. I still had the calipers and kept them for many years.

Grandpa and I had really never been close. In the early 40s I wanted to know him better and hear his stories. He seemed to feel the need for me to know more about his life too. He lived in a rented house, but I don't remember ever going there. Instead we talked while he was on the job at Roper Lumber Company. He had just gone to work there and I remember him telling me how old man Roper had asked him to overhaul a large diesel engine that ran all the mill saws and planers. It seemed that no one else could keep it running very long. I can remember seeing Grandpa standing there in his greasy overalls, with that engine, yet for some reason at that time I wasn't impressed. In the 60s, when I came back to visit, 20 years after Grandpa had died, I found the diesel was still going strong. I was impressed with what Grandpa had done with it.

When the sawmill management passed from old Henry Roper to

his son, the elder Roper instructed his son to always have a job for Bill Thomas. Eventually before his death, they fixed a place for him to sleep at the mill, and he just lived right there.

I'm not sure what happened to all of Grandpa's money. Guess he just spent it as he went along. He did have a drinking habit. Not a drunk, but alcohol was a companion in his loneliness. I did hear that at one time he had something going with a lady of the evening called Sarah Woodard, but that was just gossip. As far as I know, Grandpa never did have any other women.

Our lives changed drastically during the Great Depression. When Grandpa moved out, he had left Grandma with the capability to support herself from the one rental house and the rent the city paid on the four vacant lots. Grandma was a little too generous with friends and relatives during those times, and eventually she had to sell everything. Now we were paying rent.

One of the first houses we rented was on Wesley Street which was in the north central part of Petersburg. I can still remember an event that happened there that shook the whole neighborhood. We were renting from Thorton and Nellie McGee. Thorton was good-natured and a happy-go-lucky fellow. I was $3\frac{1}{2}$ years old and always looked forward to greeting Thorton when he came home from work. He was a brakeman on the railroad and worked a 6 p.m. to 6 a.m. shift. I used to sit on the porch or on a yard ornament and wait for him to come home, and I'd sing him a little song. He thought this was comical, and he'd always pitch me a coin, a nickel, and sometimes a quarter. With this in hand, I'd cross the street and buy a cupcake or some other treat from the grocery store.

Well, there was this nice warm morning when I was up and around, hungry as usual, with no one to get me breakfast. I decided I'd wait for Thorton and maybe I'd get enough for a treat to satisfy my hunger. When Thorton came up the walk, I was sitting on the edge of the porch, and I rattled off my little tune. He smiled and handed me a nickel. This wasn't enough to buy much, so I just decided to save it and stuck it in my pocket. It wasn't long after that, maybe twenty minutes or so, that I heard this blood curdling scream. I knew it was from Thorton and it was loud enough for the whole neighborhood to hear.

It wasn't long before an ambulance arrived. Men jumped out and carried a stretcher inside the house. Pretty soon they were coming out with Thorton on the stretcher, and off in the ambulance he went, sirens going full-blast as they headed for the hospital. After the ambulance left, Nellie came out. Helen and Grandma were there and one of them asked Nellie, "What happened?" "I cut his damn dick off," she replied. Well this didn't make a whole lot of sense to me then, but later I found out that she caught him running around, or thought she had, and cut part of his penis off. I don't know whether he was running around or not, at that time I was just interested in getting a coin for my tunes. About twenty years later, I again ran into Thorton. Fate had been unkind to him a couple more times, but I'll tell you about that later.

As I said before, things became rough for us during the Depresson, and Helen became the sole supporter of the family. Years before when she was pregnant with me Grandmother had arranged for her to live with a family in Washington, D.C. There Helen learned to become a seamstress, and when she returned Grandma again used her influence to get her a good job in a clothing factory in Petersburg. She made $15 a week which was good wages even for a man in those days.

What really put a strain on everything was when my grandmother's sister Maggie and her four children moved in with us. Maggie's husband Arthur Roberts had left on the railroad to find work someplace, and he just never returned. That was not unusual. More than one man left his family to find work, and out of frustration or whatever, many just shed their responsibilities and never returned. Maggie was left with no job and no way to feed her children. There was no welfare then.

We were renting a three bedroom house on Grove Ave. next to Cox's Alley in Petersburg. The rent was $15 a month and it was a reasonably good area. Maggie's children, Thelma, Cecil, Bill and Norman, were all older than I was. Guess I was about three at the time.

Even though we were all piled into one house with little money, as a kid I don't remember us really lacking for anything. Down Cox's Alley was the Appomattox River, which provided us fish to eat, and we spent what money we did have wisely. Maggie's boy Bill also had a job at Joe Mann's bakery for $1 a week. This job benefited the family in providing us with regular dessert, for on Saturday Bill would bring home the unsold sweetbread called slug. It was pulverized dough mixed with sugar, baked and covered with syrup. Served with the wild berries we gathered, it made us a fine treat. At Christmas there always seemed to be gifts too. The basis of your outlook on life revolved around whether or not someone in the family had a job.

It was at Cox's Alley that I began my story, with my father carrying me down the street to Ramsey's Store. It also was the place that I began my mechanical career, so to speak. Bill and Cecil's boyfriend, Wallace Edwards, had this old car that they couldn't get to run. Somehow, on a snowy day I got the engine started and the car in gear. Uncontrolled, the car and I traveled between the two houses, over a picket fence, smack into a telephone pole. When the boys came home that afternoon, they didn't seem mad about the car or fence, but rather intent on finding out how I got it started. I don't remember providing any key information, however, they were able to start it and back it off the fence. They also were able to make it run for quite awhile after that.

Maggie got a job in a clothing factory and things were going pretty well until she was laid off. Somehow, the family accumulated a debt which we couldn't pay. We couldn't continue to pay rent, have the groceries we needed, and still pay off this debt. What resulted was a move, or shuffle so to speak, to another rental. It happened a lot in those days. If you couldn't pay the rent, you jockeyed for a new place to rent. The deal was to put $5 down on the new place and promise to catch up the rest of the rent in two weeks. This gave us time to pay off the debt and then somehow we would hope to catch up the new rent.

Now, Mr. Matthew did not own the houses he collected rent for. He was simply an agent for the owners. Our next move was just three quarters of a block down on Grove Avenue. Mr. Matthew was an agent for that owner as well as the owner of our last residence, and he knew exactly why we were moving, but he knew we were trying to pay our debts so he gave us no trouble. A lot of people put him down, but he was good to us.

There was a church beside our new home on Grove Avenue, and it was of the holy roller variety. The noise on Sunday morning and evening was unbearable. Usually we would just leave until the service was over, but finally Maggie suggested to the minister that if he would close the window next to our house on Sunday, then perhaps the Lord would be able to hear our prayers too. We had some peace after that.

On Grove Avenue I learned a lot more about getting along with people. Being an only child and living with all of Maggie's family was a lot of fun. We didn't have much, and being the youngest I got kicked around a little. We did, however, learn to work together and to entertain ourselves.

It was here that I also developed my love for country music. Bill was musically inclined and was good on both the guitar and mandolin. Cecil's boyfriend, Wallace Edwards, could play the guitar. A man by the name of Eddie Crosby, who was already on his way to becoming a well-known Country artist, could play violin, piano, and about any other instrument. They were joined by Caggey Stills, a friend of Eddie's, and together on Saturday night they brought a lot of pickin' and singin' to our house. Our old piano was half-tuned, but they managed to turn out some fine music and it even sounded good. Eddie later went on to write and record a song, "Blues Stay Away From Me." It became a real popular song.

Not too long after we moved down beside the church, Maggie's boy Norman got married and moved in with his wife's family. This gave us one less mouth to feed which made it easier. Norman still kept us and his wife's family supplied with fish, as he was a real good fisherman.

One person I almost forgot to tell much about was Bertha, Grandma's oldest sister. She had lived with Maggie since Maggie's husband had run off and had been a great help to Maggie trying to raise all those kids. When Maggie and her children moved in with us, so did Bertha. She had never married and had no formal education, but she had learned a lot being brought up in North Carolina along the Neuse River. Now you've heard of people goin' out in the fields and gathering weeds and cookin' them, well she could flat do just that. Other than cabbage, we didn't grow salad greens in our garden because Bertha could find them in vacant lots and along the river. She furnished the family with everything we needed. She also was an expert at fixin' seafood. If you brought her a snappin' turtle, in thirty minutes she could have it on the stove steamin' and she knew exactly how to cut it up. She could identify and separate the many different flavored meats within the turtle. Some parts tasted like chicken, others like turkey, beef and different varieties of fish. Turtle was a delicacy where she grew up, and she had learned to treat it as such.

It was here also that I met a new friend, Jack Moore. We were about four then and hung around a lot together as he just lived down the street. One day we were playing in the backyard, and I ran through a pile of trash. Unfortunately, it was filled with broken bottles, and I really tore up the bottoms of my feet. I was kinda the apple of my grandma's eye, and she was determined that I was going to be treated at the city clinic. They carried me to the old car that I had previously learned to start, and off to the clinic we went. After another trip in the car, Grandma decided that she would rather walk than ride. She began pulling me to the clinic on a regular basis in my little wagon. She could not see well, but I would tell her when cars were coming at the street corners. This seemed to work except after several trips my feet were not getting any better. They were infected and swollen. Maggie had told Grandma in the beginning that Bertha could fix my feet, but Grandma was determined to get the best doctor the city could offer.

Each time the doctor would put on more medicine and new bandages. The only real relief for me was getting the old ones off, because of the swelling. Bertha finally put her foot down. "Those doctors are just makin' money off of that boy, and doin' nothin' for his feet. I'll heal his feet and then you can take him in the wagon to the clinic as much as you want."

Bertha didn't talk much, but when she did everyone listened. Bertha had me soak my feet in a tub of herbs and water for what seemed like a half day. She gathered more herbs and made a paste. The stuff she cooked together in the kitchen was about as foul-smellin' as you could stand. She mixed white petroleum jelly, or at times, hog lard, that had been boiled. She had an uncanny way about her that she could get you to do about anything whether you were four or fifty years old. I submitted to her treatment, and within a few weeks, I was back running around again. She told my grandma, "Now, Grace, you can pull that boy to the clinic as much as you want to."

After a year of living beside the church, financial conditions required another move. This time we didn't move together. Maggie and her family moved a block up the street, and we moved four houses down and across the street to a double tenement. It was one of the oldest houses in the neighborhood. The steps made a 90 degree turn from the street level to the porch entrance. So the house was known as Winding Steps. This is the house where Grandpa had his tools toted to my room. That evening he and Grandma traded a few choice words and I didn't see him again until 1940.

Helen was making $25 to $30 a week now, and Grandma's eyes were getting worse, so she hired a colored lady, Lulu, to help with the housework and to make sure I got off to school. Grandma could still cook, adjusting the heat in the oven by feel, and still washed dishes as she always had. Lulu did the ironing and things Grandma couldn't. My world was getting bigger now. I knew if I could slip by Grandma when Lulu wasn't there, I would be free to roam around town. This activity worried my mother and Grandma, as they thought that sooner or later I would be getting into trouble. I never looked at it that way. I can remember only one problem that brought some trouble. I was in the first grade then, and this Agree boy kept chasing me home from school each day. He was a lot bigger than I, probably two heads taller. If he got hold of me, I knew he could whip me bad 'cause he was so much bigger. With the blessing of Lulu, I came up with a plan to stop him. One evening I piled six bricks under the stairway by Huggins Store. The next day after school he came after me as usual and instead of coming down Cross Street to Grove Avenue, I took the alley behind Huggins Store. Well that was what that boy was looking for because now he could catch and whip me without anyone seeing what was happening. My plan was to gauge the speed of the chase so that I could get to the bricks before he got to me. My timing was good, but a brick in a six year old's hand is a heavy load. I really didn't swing the brick, but held it up and he ran into it. It broke his nose and bumped his forehead, and blood squirted everywhere. It scared me as much, maybe worse, than it scared him. While he was trying to figure out where he was, I was on my way out of there running for home. Grandma knew something was wrong when I got home. I told her that I had run all the way from school.

After we finished supper that evening, there was a knock on the door. It wasn't polite for kids to run to the door when someone came. I had got my butt tanned for doing that before, but I was curious when Helen opened the door. When the lady said her name was Mrs. Agree, I was filled with surprise and fear. I was trapped, and it was too late to get out the back door. We kids had heard on the radio what happened to people that killed other people and the first thing that came to my mind with all that blood was that I had killed the Agree boy and the law was coming to get me.

Mrs. Agree started the conversation. "Your boy whipped my boy today. I want you to see what he has done to him." I was somewhat relieved to learn he was still alive. I couldn't see very well because Helen stood between us. Helen listened and she called me. Well, I knew, here it comes. She had to drag me around to see Mrs. Agree. Mrs. Agree asked, "Is that your boy?"

"Yes ma'am, it's the only son I've got."

"Is he the one that did this to my boy?" Mrs. Agree inquired.

"Well, I guess he must be. Teddy had complained of some big boy chasing him home from school each day, and I asume this is the boy."

Well they got that all hashed out, and Mrs. Agree turned around and looked at her boy, and then turned his hind quarters right over the stair banister and busted his ass right there for picking on a little kid like me. When they left, that boy had both a sore ass and a busted face. Well strange things happen that you never expect, and right then I felt pretty proud of myself. I learned right then, thanks to Lulu, that I could protect myself. I had complained about this boy chasing me to Helen, Grandma, and some of my friends at school, and no one did anything to help. Now I didn't have to run home from school anymore as he and the other kids gave me a wide berth. I don't think anyone had ever stood up to him before, so I had my own reputation now.

I did enjoy my schooling. I also enjoyed sneaking off from home to play with my buddy Jack Moore. Sometimes Grandma would let me go with him, other times she would refuse. Never could figure out why she refused at times. We might get in a little mischief, but never destroyed anything. Once we did a little experimenting with cats trying to find out why when tossed up, they always landed on their feet. We carried a few up to the second floor, and even when they were flipped out the window upside down, or swung by the tail, they still landed feet first. Unfortunately we got caught and had our butts tanned good.

Probably the thing that worried Helen and Grandma the most was the trains. The tracks were only a thousand feet or so behind the house and probably like all kids, trains fascinated us. Sometimes the trains would stop to do something, and by and by we got to know the firemen and engineers. They would let us climb up and look at all the engine gadgets and instruments and a couple times when they were shifting loads, they let us ride maybe a quarter-mile. I remember the engineer would let me put my hand on the lever while he blew the whistle.

Jack's cousin Bubba was younger than us, but he also hung around the tracks with us. His dad was Paul Moore, who was a city fireman. We were interested in the things at the firehouse too, but everytime we went there his daddy would run us off. The train men were different and seemed to enjoy our company.

In the wintertime, hanging around the rail tracks brought some good to our family. I would take the wagon that Grandma used to pull me to the clinic and a couple of burlap sacks and pick up coal along the tracks. The train men would notice and after awhile there began to appear a small pile of coal next to the tracks behind our house. It was not that we were favored, for in the morning if you looked down the tracks for a mile, you could see many small piles of coal behind peoples's houses. Sometimes they would even sound a low toot on the whistle when they went by with a long line of cars. This coal furnished most of our heat for the winter. Also between the rail tracks and the river was woods. We didn't have any saw, just a single-bladed axe, but we would gather as much wood as we could. Those limbs and branches that nature had pruned off, we could chop up. I don't think we bought more than a quarter-ton of coal for the whole winter, and we kept nice and warm all the time.

After a couple years at Winding Steps, we moved across town to Washington Street. This seemed like an upper-class neighborhood compared to Winding Steps. This house was not run down and the bathroom facilities worked fine. Cecil and Wallace moved in, and helped with expenses. Hard times were behind us now, except this move made life more difficult for Grandma. In her early fifties now, her sight was about gone. With the new house and neighborhood, she had to relearn everything to get her bearings. Even the time of day was difficult for her to determine. There were no trains passing close by at different intervals, which had been her timepiece.

It didn't take me long to get adjusted to the new neighborhood and to Jackson School where I would start my second year. In fact, being over seven years old now, with Helen working and with Grandma having trouble finding her way around, it was easy for me to slip out and explore this section of town. I don't recall getting into trouble, but my freedom to roam worried both Helen and Grandma. Helen discussed her concerns with her friend Mrs. Roland, who was a probate officer, and Mrs. May Burton, a teacher. They told her about this school in Covington, called Boy's Home and the potential it might hold for me.

Now the Boy's Home idea seemed to appeal to Grandma too, and she lined up a few of her friends to use their influence to get me in the school. Mrs. Vicdodson from church provided some supplemental funds for my stay, plus Mr. and Mrs. Wells, whose family owned Wells Funeral and Wells Ice Company, put in a good word and the additional money.

They were pretty wealthy people. Some years back Grandpa had installed the ice plant for them and the freezer units at the funeral home.

The school wanted boys with the potential to make something of themselves, and these ladies figured I had it in me to become a preacher. Like it or not, that is where I found myself for the next five years.

GRANDMA AND ME

Today I took a memory trip
  I watched through tears and trembling lips,
For I was standing at Grandma's door
  looking at the love I had as a boy.
A mother's love, something I never knew,
  but I had Grandma and she loved me too.
It's no wonder her name was Grace
  it showed brightly on her smiling face,
With hard times when I was five
  her work she done without a sigh.
Evening time I'd crawl into her lap,
  she'd sing me songs while I napped.
I loved to hear Grandma's tales
  when as a girl with her daddy did sail
The Albermarle and Pamlico Sounds
  up the Neuse River, New Bern bound.
Those waters and lands are lovely to see,
  yes, Grandma shared her world with me.
She taught me the kind and gentle ways
  she told me of God and how to pray.
Grandma was blind, but her heart could see
  the right way to live was what she left me.
Though she has gone and will never return,
  from Grandma I'll never forget what I learned.

GRANDPA'S LAST VISIT

We never think of Granddaddy with
  sentimental thoughts in mind
A statuesque hard working man
  keeping everyone in line.
This picture I had of him, also
  with respect and fear,

With Grandma he watched and
    listened to each of my dreams and plans,
As I told her of wonderful gifts I
    would bring from foreign lands.
Being told to go to bed, and
    they thought I had,
But like all children hiding
    I listened to the good and bad
Grace, he said, it hurts listening to
    his dreams afar
Knowing he will chase them all and
    what the prices are.
You know traveling to me has been
    a way of life
I have not been as good a husband
    as you have been a wife,
We have mellowed with age
    and time has passed few pleasant days.
We'll never settle our differences
    that have spawned in life's ways.
Starting to leave he spoke softly
    to Grandma, which I didn't hear,
From my hiding place I saw his quivering
    lips, on his cheek a tear.
I wished I could have found the
    words to tell him that night,
That I would chase all my dreams
    but not get lost in their flight.
I am still looking for it Grandpa,
    as I pass through life's door,
I know somewhere I will find
    a love that can't be lowered.

Boy's Home

Covington, Virginia and Boy's Home were a long way from Petersburg. Now I was in the mountains and exposed to a new culture, that of the mountain people, commonly called hillbillies. It was easy to tell them from the flat-landers because when you went to their house they always entertained in the kitchen and the flat-landers would take you into the living room. It was that simple. Hillbillies are people of strong convictions, not nearly as hardheaded as they were given credit for by storytellers and song writers. Nor were they as dumb as some thought them to be. Well anyway, let me tell you about Boy's Home.

Owned by the Episcopal Church, the home brought in a variety of boys from around the country. Some were from broken homes and others were orphans. It didn't matter whether or not you were Episcopal, in fact a couple of the boys were Catholic. We did observe the Episcopal customs in church. Religion was not taught in our school, but on Sunday we did all troop down in the valley to the church. If the weather was bad, services were held in the dining hall.

There were six two-story cottages of an old English style situated in a crescent. They had a stucco siding with wood trim and were all painted different colors. Gordon cottage was blue, Watts cream color, Clayton brown and Langhorn where I stayed was yellow. They would each hold 20 boys plus a housemother. Richmond cottage was green and used only for administrative purposes. Norfolk was white and was used as a guest house. There were no fences or strict boundaries to keep the boys in, only established routines that kept everyone busy. On Saturdays we were free to do as we wanted, and usually we headed into town in various-sized groups. We were easily recognized, because we wore ties. It looked rather ridiculous, with kids in a variety of dress from bib overalls to knickers, each with that tie on. Neither hillbillies nor anyone else wore ties, but we became so accustomed to it that it didn't seem that big a deal. It didn't dawn on me until years later that the tie really was aimed at identifying us to the other folks. We just figured it was some old English custom.

To start out with, my chores consisted of gathering trash with the other boys and delivering it to a drop-off point at the heating plant. The heating plant fascinated me, the boilers and steam pumps. All things mechanical interested me a lot more than playing like most other eight-year-olds would want to do. Soon I was transferred down to the farm with new duties. I guess other boys had arrived to take over the trash chores.

Boy's Home was completely self-supporting with its own farm which included a dairy herd, hogs, and other animals. I don't remember who the farm manager was then, but my duties were laid out by a couple of older boys, Cecil Headrick and Richard Stone, both of whom had been at the school for a long time and were without parents. After three or four weeks at the farm, I pretty well knew where everything was, tools, equipment, and other gear. When the new farm manager arrived, things changed considerably. He was a man in his late forties with a wife named Dorothy and two daughters, Katherine about twenty and the other a couple years younger, named Elizabeth. He recognized that I was the smallest kid at the farm and said that my new job was to follow him around. This sounded odd, but I didn't mind. Things were disorganized and he aimed to straighten them out. He had some of the boys from the carpenter's shop build outdoor wall shelves to store the tools. He would draw me a picture of some tool he wanted, and send me off to find it. Pretty soon things began to get organized.

His name was Tucker. From the day he arrived until the day I left I never knew his first name, just Tucker. Through his first winter, Tucker leased new lands for the Boy's Home. That spring he planted these fields to the crops that would be needed to sustain the home for that year. On the land that belonged to the home he planted and then plowed down clovers and other legumes that would enrich the soil.

It was enough to make a farmer cry to see that knee deep clover disappear under the plow rather than to be made into hay.

On another part of the farm, a field that would not drain properly had turned into a bog. He had a bulldozer dig a five-foot-deep ditch to a natural drainage point. After the area had drained, we filled the ditch with boulders and covered it back up with soil. He called this a hidden drainage ditch, and it worked.

Tucker hired a man with some oxen to plow the field we had drained. We had to build a lean-to for the oxen and they were there for a week, but nothing happened. Tucker could see that I was becoming impatient to see these cows plow the bog. He said, "He's just giving the oxen time to get used to this area." Finally the man started to use the oxen to pull up the bushes that spotted the field. He used no whip or reins, he just talked to the oxen. I never saw anything like it before. Tucker left me to keep track of the plowing, and every day I gave him a progress report. Finally the field was plowed and the man and his oxen left. I never did know his name.

After Tucker's first season, the barns were full. In fact we had to build a new corn crib and silo to store everything. The barn was packed with hay, and we had harvested much more than we needed. "There," he said, "We have enough stored to withstand two years of crop failures."

Tucker also had a holding pond dug for the cow manure from the barn. He reconstructed the gutter system in the barn so that from the gutter the manure would flow to this pond. With an old Model A engine and a fire pump he had gotten from the city of Covington, we pumped water from the creek into the pond to dilute the manure. With a mule pulling a cable attached to a spring harrow, the pond was stirred from one side to the other then back again. In the spring the manure was pumped out into tanks and spread on the fields. Tucker didn't believe in commercial fertilizer, and through his farming methods he proved he didn't need it.

With Tucker's supervision, the boys provided all the labor to operate the farm and implement his ingenious farming methods. New ideas, however, sometimes met with resistance, and that happened one day as the boys were busy with the spring plowing. Mr.

Wishmore, the accountant for the Boy's Home, appeared and told Tucker he was going to have to cut back on the amount of land he was leasing, and that he was spending too much money.

Tucker didn't say anything at first, but after Mr. Wishmore offered some more advice that I couldn't hear, Tucker spoke up, "Do you know where your office is?"

"Of course I do," said Mr. Wishmore.

"Then best you go back to your office and take care of your business now, because I know what I'm doing down here," Tucker snapped.

Mr. Wishmore never showed up at the farm again, though I'm sure he complained to Ronald Rogers who was the overall director of Boy's Home. They left Tucker alone to manage the farm, and he was still there when I left. His methods were unconventional for that time, but it was obvious he knew what he was doing as the farm operation prospered.

About the only thing that I remember we purchased was eggs. Mrs. Tucker had a few of her own chickens, but we didn't raise any on the farm. Everything else was owned and provided for by the Boy's Home. It had its own hydroelectric plant to provide electricity to all of the home, plus some neighbors. A flume carried water from Potts Creek to an old 1920 generator that put out 2,300 volts. This place fascinated me, and at one time for a couple months I was able to help Mr. Rudersule, the maintenance supervisor. I would have preferred to stay there rather than work on the farm, but that was not to be.

The home also had its own water system. They collected mountain spring water in a large pond then pumped it up into a water tower to provide pressure and flow to the home three miles away. It also flowed to the heating plant where steam was produced to heat the buildings and run the cannery and laundry which was upstairs in that building. Mrs. Worth ran both the cannery and laundry, and the boys were detailed to provide the labor she needed.

My regular job on the farm was feeding the dairy cattle twice each day. From the cottages to the farm by the road was three miles, but if I came down the hill and across the creek it was about a mile and a half. The dairy barn was over a hundred feet long with stanchions to hold

80 cows, but at that time we had around forty-five. My other job as always was to keep Tucker's mind fresh as to where everything was. Guess I became his storekeeper, making sure the tools and equipment were properly stored.

Supervision at Boy's Home consisted of one housemother for each cottage. Two other supervisors, Mr. Copper and Dad Hollenback kept us in line. Of course we provided a lot of our own supervision. If one boy got out of line and caused a problem, the whole group was restricted until the guilty party confessed, then the restriction was lifted. Normally we knew who was at fault and he would get the third degree behind the barn until he confessed.

If there was any fighting between boys, it was usually in the six-to-eight-year-old range. Here again, we policed our own activities and shaped these boys up until their manners were right. Getting those boys used to how things were done around the home was like breaking in a new horse. If you throw the whole harness on him, he's going to kick. But, if you slowly put one piece at a time on, chances are he's not going to kick it off.

Those of us who were in elementary up to the sixth grade walked to the home school each day. Mr. Copper or Dad Hollenback walked with us in the morning and back with us again at night. It's not that we required the supervision, it's just that part of our path went along Route Sixty, and that was a busy highway. Guess they thought that maybe one of us boys might step into the path of a car and get killed. The boys in the seventh grade and up got to ride the yellow bus to town, but I left the school before I reached that grade.

We had two teachers, Mrs. Batson and Mrs. Bird. Mrs. Bird was reserved; she didn't give any quarter and she didn't ask for any, but through a little accident I got to discover her human side. My front tooth got busted while playing around in the bathroom. They had to send me to Covington several times to get it repaired, and one of those times Mrs. Bird volunteered to take me. She was a pretty good-lookin' lady and she drove this 1939 Buick. When I climbed in I noticed that the speedometer went all the way up to 120 mph. I said, "I'll bet it'll never go that fast." Now in those days it was unusual to see a lady drive over 40 mph, but she looked over at me with a grin and said, "Hold on to your hat and we'll find out." She surprised me when she pulled her dress up to work the pedals, and I could see well above her knees. That about blew this ten-year-old's mind, and I said to myself, "What have I got here." Now if she would have looked at me, I know I would have been embarrassed, but she had just unconsciously done it out of habit as the old Buick was a straight stick, not automatic.

We got beyond the S Curve and still climbing that mountain faster than I ever been in a car. When the road leveled out and we had a straight shot to Covington, the needle laid right over on the 120 mph mark. I said to myself, "This is a pretty good woman." It seemed that her shell of reserve was just there to maintain the respect of the other kids, but as a ten-year-old, I learned that there was a lot more to people than what you could see on the outside.

Mr. Copper was another person in a self-created shell. I don't know what his problem was but he must have had one. Always a poker face, he did his job very well and was fair, but not friendly. Dad Hollenbeck was the opposite. He was jovial and in his spare time served as scoutmaster, and he was a good one. In fact, I earned most of my scouting badges under him. You could only earn four badges every six months, or something like that, and I earned the maximum you could get. Dad had been a medic during World War I when they probably didn't have a lot to help the boys other than iodine and bandages. We respected him a lot.

Now one of my big dissatisfactions with life at Boy's Home was the fact that I really wanted to work in the boiler room and not on the farm. I spent a lot of my spare time hanging around there and pretty much learned what to do as far as the operation. I didn't know everything, of course, but Mr. Rudersule did take time to explain things and let me help.

It was about 4 a.m. on a cold morning around Thanksgiving time, when walking down to the farm I heard a different kind of noise coming out of that boiler room. Something just didn't sound right. Curiosity got the best of me, and I made a detour down to the boiler room. As I opened the door, the heat was tremendous. Steam was blowing out from a lot of places it shouldn't have been.

As I surveyed the gauges, a real problem was evident. The water gauges were empty and the steam pressure was over two hundred pounds per square inch (psi). This boiler was about ready to blow. The old man that was supposed to watch things was asleep. I tried to wake him, but he appeared drunk. He was nice and warm and not about to wake up and he was too heavy for me to push around. In an attempt to get rid of the heat I opened the fire box doors and raked the coals out on the concrete floor. I also opened the top drafts and closed the bottom drafts. The heat was enough to knock you down. I eased the water pump on a little at a time. I tried to open the relief valve, but it was stuck down and I couldn't get to the bottom blow down valve. The whole thing started rumbling now, so I grabbed the watchman by the arm and collar and dragged him outside. He kinda got up on his feet and started to go back in where it was warm, so I shoved him over the cinder pile.

The thing was really rumbling now, so I went back in to work on the safety valve. When the pull chain finally broke, I said, "Boy, I better get out of here." I figured that I'd done everything I could think of to relieve the pressure and there wasn't time to do anything else.

There was no time for the door. I ran up into the coal bin, and when she blew, the manhole cover over the coal bin blew clean off. I was shaking a little, but finally it was obvious the pressure was gone and steam was just spewing about, so I left by the outside entrance.

When she blew, I guess everybody heard it. The boiler itself didn't blow, just a tube, but it was a very loud noise. Dad Hollenback came running up and asked where the watchman was. I said that I had got him out the door, and he was over on the cinder pile.

"Was he drunk?" Dad asked.

"It looked like it to me, and it's more than likely if you can find him you should be able to smell it," I replied. It was still pretty dark outside.

A few minutes later here comes Mr. Rudersule to see what had happened. He was supervisor over all the plants. I liked him because he was a nice fellow and always patient. He wanted to know where the watchman was, and I said that Mr. Hollenback had gone to get him. He walked into the building to see how much damage was done.

He cut off the pump and said, "Well did he run out or what?" I didn't want to tell him the watchman was drunk and I dragged him out 'cause Mr. Rudersule was death on drinking. About that time, Dad Hollenback showed up with the watchman who had pretty well sobered up, and they all went off for awhile. The watchman wasn't with them when they came back. I guess they fired him as I never saw him again.

Mr. Rudersule said, "Well Ted, you've been snooping around here for almost a year, let's see if you can fire up that donkey boiler."

The donkey boiler was a little auxiliary boiler that sat next to the two big ones. They had to have steam to the cottages, and it didn't take long to get it fired up. Wood to start out with, then as the fire got goin', I gradually fed in the coal. In no time at all I had my steam pressure up around seventy pounds per square inch. Mr. Rudersule didn't leave, he just stayed around and watched, though he did go outdoors a couple times and inspected the safety check valves.

I said, "Mr. Rudersule, I'm going to have to go down to the farm."

"Don't worry about the farm, you stay here. I'll take care of Tucker."

Well now, I really thought I had it made. I didn't even go to school, just sat and tended that boiler all day. I began to daydream about learning all those mysteries of electricity. All I really wanted was to find out how an electric bulb put out light, the science of it, as well as the knowledge of mechanical power. What was happening now was just what I wanted out of life.

About the time that school got out, Mike Lee, one of the older boys, came over and said, "I guess I'm going to have to take over." I replied, "You gonna run the boiler?" "Yep, me and Leroy are going to take her in shifts." I was still feeling good about proving my abilities and thought it would probably be three eight-hour shifts, me gettin' one of them. Wrong, two twelve-hour shifts.

Mr. Rudersule said, "Ted, you've got to go back to Tucker at the farm, and I'll have to rely on Mike and Leroy."

That pissed me off. I thought I had made the big time, and now back to the farm. I was really let down because here under Mr. Rudersule I could have learned the things I wanted to learn.

After a couple days of depression, I finally said to hell with it and went up to the dining hall with a knapsack. I knew Sally McCoy the head cook and when she wasn't looking I got my knapsack filled with food. I then took off up in the mountains and stayed by myself for a couple of weeks.

Well, I don't know whether they sent out search parties or not, but they could never have found me in those mountains anyway, because I knew them like the back of my hand. Most of the time on weekends when the weather was good, instead of heading to town like most of the boys, I'd go to the mountains. Catching fish and feeding myself was no problem, and I found out that each time I learned something new about nature and myself.

I had learned a lot about outdoor survival from Dad Hollenback in my Boy Scout training. Occasionally I could snare a rabbit and that would provide several meals. The bread finally ran out, but if I could get some corn I knew how to grind that with rocks to make corn meal. One old saucepan was my only cooking utensil and an old canvas with a blanket inside kept me comfortable at night.

The Boy's Home was only about 15 miles from West Virginia and sometimes I'd be hiking over in that area, not far from a little place called Alleghany.

When I came back, I figured I'd get whipped. Mr. Rogers told me to come up to his house. He said, "There's no need of whippin' you, 'cause in your own mind you had a good reason to leave. I am, however, going to try to convince you that you were wrong." It all went in one ear and out the other, and the more I heard the madder I got. I just wanted to forget the whole thing.

When I showed up at the farm, Tucker said, "How'd you like the vacation?"

"Pretty good," I said.

Later I ran away a couple more times because it just seemed that they were holding me back, and that was wrong. They all agreed that 12 years was too young for the knowledge I was seeking. I'd just have to be patient. Tucker was extra patient with me. That's probably what kept me around there those last couple of years. He had a way with boys. He talked to us as if we were men. He always said, "If you have

something in your heart, say it. If you don't, keep your mouth shut."
That gave me some backbone, and I made it a policy to speak my mind
and take what consequences might follow.

One thing funny happened at the Boy's Home, and yet it wasn't
really funny. Another boy named Robert and I were supposed to get
the barn cleaned up for a new paint job. After milking, Tucker left us
there for a couple hours to make sure it was ready. Well, it was a hot
summer day and not too far from us was old Billy the bull with his
testicles hanging extra low. In my back pocket, I had a slingshot which
I had made the previous spring, and it was as perfect as any store-
bought one. I was also quite talented at hitting what I wanted to hit.

Robert looked at that old bull and said, "I'll bet you a nickel you
can't hit him in the balls."

I said, "Where's your nickel?"

"I'll have it by Saturday," he replied.

"I'm in the same boat, I'll have mine by Saturday too."

So a bet was struck, and I got that slingshot out of my back pocket
and out of another I got a round rock which I had found in the creek. I
pulled back and let go; I must have hit both testicles, because old Billy
quickly went up on his hind feet pawing the sky with his front legs.
When he came down it must have been jarring for he let out a beller,
and I realized that I had really hurt that bull. Old Billy came out of that
back pen heading for the lounging area and without any problem went
through some two-by-eight inch oak planks separating the pens.
Shortly thereafter we heard Tucker yell. This scared the hell out of me
for we didn't have any idea that old man was in the barn. Well, I threw
the slingshot up into the rafters, and both Robert and I ran to the next
pen. There in the hay rack was Tucker with the bull almost rubbing his
chest. He didn't dare move, and was hollering for his wife Dorothy to
bring the gun. I don't think that old bull meant to hurt Tucker, he just
wanted something to ease his pain. Dorothy arrived with the gun, and
Tucker jumped away from the bull, grabbed the gun, and shot old
Billy behind the ear. Poor Billy was dead with that one shot, but
Tucker moved around and shot him again. I felt bad about that old bull
because he had always been pretty good-natured with us kids. We
never did tell Tucker the truth. We didn't dare to. Tucker had a

butcher come from town, and old Billy was butchered out providing the home with a good supply of beef for quite awhile.

Late that summer I again created a little stir around the farm, and the same boy was with me that took part in the bull's demise! Tucker called me and Robert over and wanted us to take two mules and rake five acres of hay in a field a couple of miles away. Now it seemed funny to me that he would send two of us to rake that little bunch of hay when one of us could do it in two hours or so. I figured that he just wanted to get us out from underneath his feet and knew we probably would goof off a little and stretch the job out for most of the day.

"Now," he said, "Ted, you can ride old Jack up to the field, but don't ride him back or you'll have problems."

Hell, I knew that old mule. I'd been around him as much as Tucker. Robert climbed on Pat and I on Jack, and we rode up to the field. The rakes were already in the field, so we hitched up and went right to work. It wasn't long before we were about done, so we decided to take a break. We took the mules down to Potts Creek and staked them out close to the water where there was grass to eat, and we went off to visit the neighbors. Visiting the neighbors always meant lots of treats being offered such as apple pie, plum pudding, and I think sweet cherries were in season then. Anyway, we fared pretty good. When our stomachs were full, we stopped visiting and came back and finished the hay. On the way back down the road to the farm, Robert was riding Pat and I was leading Jack.

"I don't see anything wrong with this mule," I said.

"I don't either, just climb up on there," was Robert's reply.

We rode on and everything went well, past the school and on down the road until the stone gateway came into view, and Jack spotted it. It was a warm day, and Jack knew that inside of that cool barn was where he wanted to be. He took off like a streak of lightning. I didn't know that mule could go so fast as he was really stretchin' out, probably 25 miles an hour. I was pullin' back for all I was worth, and my feet were pushing against the bottom side of the hamps. I wasn't a real strong fellow, but then I wasn't a weaklin' either. I couldn't stop him. All I could see coming up was that barn door opening with about a foot of clearance between Jack's back and the top of the door opening, and I knew I wasn't going to fit through. My feet were tangled in the harness too, so there was no getting off. Well, he cleaned me off his back like a coat of paint. Guess I was out for a couple hours. That scared Tucker to death. I woke up and heard the ambulance coming and got up. They told me to lay back down, but I just wanted to stand up and get my balance. The ambulance people looked me all over and had me roll my eyes around—guess they figured I'd make it. I had one thing in mind, and that was getting in the barn to even things with that mule. Tucker was busy talking to the ambulance drivers and his wife Dorothy was distracted doing something, so I slipped into the barn. There was this two-by-six that we used to clean the manger, and with a mighty swing, I caught Jack across the nose. His feet went out from under him and he hit the side of the stable.

Tucker heard the noise. "What you doin' in there?"

"Just feedin' the mule," I replied.

He knew I was lying because there wasn't any feed around there, but he didn't say anything until the next morning.

"Don't ever turn your back on old Jack or he'll kick your brains out."

"I know he will sir," and I walked away.

The school provided plenty of recreational activities. We had a fine gym, and there were always games to get involved in, like basketball and softball. We also did a little trapping in our spare time to make money. It was kind of a status symbol to have a few quarters in your pocket when you went to town on Saturday, and the muskrats and rabbits we caught by the creek provided some income. I think that the man who bought the pelts was always pretty generous with us. Even though our pile of pelts might be worth only $3.50, we usually left with a dollar apiece in our pockets. One thing that always caught our attention, though, was the bobcat pelts that he paid $15 apiece for. Now everyone knew that there were plenty of bobcats in the mountains around the school, and we figured that one of those pelts would save us a lot of time making money. We just had to figure how to catch us one. After asking around a little, we found out that bobcats love the herb catnip just as much as house cats do. Behind Clayton Cottage there was a large catnip bed, so from the cannery we got some gallon cans and filled them with catnip. We poked holes in the can lids, then sealed the holes over with wax. With such a perfect bait, we still had to figure a way to catch them.

There were three boys involved in our trapping operation. Although we were all pretty gutty fellows, Roy Waller from Norfolk was the most nervy and he said, "If you guys can lure a cat beneath a tree limb, I'll jump on him and cut his throat."

I could see the problem with that plan right out. "Roy, if you cut his throat and stab him real bad, you'll ruin his pelt," I said.

He thought about that for awhile and then said, "I know how I'll do it!"

"Besides, Roy, he'll scratch and bite you to pieces," I added.

"I ain't seen anything yet that can tear me to pieces," he boldly replied.

One night we slipped out with a can of catnip and headed for an area in the mountains where we knew the bobcats hung out. We scraped the wax off the holes of the catnip can and put it on a trail below a tree. Roy took up a position on a limb just above the can. He was armed with a small hunting knife that had a blade that wouldn't fold. It wasn't too long when out came a medium-sized cat to check out our catnip can. Roy came down out of that tree and on top of that cat's back, and while one of his arms forced the cat's front legs underneath him, the other brought the knife around and deep into the cat's throat. Roy was really quick, and the cat didn't have time to struggle out from underneath him until it was too late. We had ourselves a bobcat and Roy proved he could do the killing job with very little damage to the pelt.

We made plans to continue this venture. Now we knew that some people might consider this a dangerous activity and also we weren't interested in giving away our secret of success, so we kept our mouths shut as to how we were coming up with the bobcat hides. We still trapped a few muskrats and rabbits to ward off suspicion, but the buyer always was curious how we managed to kill those cats without messing up the hides. The first couple we skinned out and cut the head right off. He didn't like this even though he paid us the $15. "Next time bring them in whole boys. I'll do the skinnin'," he said.

The hides were prime around the holidays, so we concentrated our effort in the fall. This was late night work, so we had to slip out after bed check. There were two bed checks. One at 9 p.m. and another between 11:30 and 12 p.m. We'd slip out after the first one and put dummies in our beds so they wouldn't know we had left. Roy Waller and Fred Woodard both lived in Watts Cottage and I lived in Langhorn. As soon as they came on the first check I slipped out the upstairs window and onto the roof that covered the entrance door. From there I climbed down the latticework to the ground.

We didn't do it real often, but for two years we managed to slip out past Dad Hollenback or Mr. Copper and keep our operation secret. I don't know though, maybe they knew what was going on all the time. We averaged eight to ten cats each year, and Roy never got hurt doing it. He got some scratches from some of the cats trying to get away, but never because they were trying to fight him. A lot of them would get away after he stuck them, but they didn't make it far before we found them. I would have been scared to do what Roy did, but soon it was routine with him.

I can recall one other secret operation we had going at the Boy's Home. One of the three trappers was Fred Woodard, and with World War II taking place, his brother was in the Army. As kind of a souvenir, Fred's brother was mailin' him an M-1 rifle, one part at a time. Now one of Fred's jobs was distributing the mail to everyone when it came, so when he saw a package come for him, he could separate it out with no one being the wiser. It probably took a year and a half before we got all the parts, but we finally got it all assembled except for the firing pin which his brother didn't send. I forget now what kind of a story we concocted, but by describing the kind of part we needed, we got Mr. Rudersule to make us one. It did not fit perfectly and would hit the shell slightly off center, but it looked like it would work.

Fortunately his brother also sent some souvenir shell casings, so now we had to manufacture some shells. We could buy 22 caliber shells without any problem, so we could mold our own bullets and provide powder. We hammered out the firing pin indentation on the M-1 shells and in the end we had ourselves a real M-1 that worked. I was the first to bring down a deer with the rifle. It was a real long shot and was I proud. I took the deer over to Tucker at the farm.

"How far away was he when you shot him?"

"About a quarter mile I guess."

"Why'd you shoot him? You gonna eat him?"

Tucker's remarks made me feel ashamed inside. Hell, I hadn't thought much about it. I was just trying out our gun. He was trying to make me understand I needed a reason to kill that deer. I didn't go deer hunting again, but Fred did and took the deer over to Tucker. Tucker liked venison and never made any big deal over how we were such good shots. Of course we never did tell him they had been shot with an M-1. Like the bobcat operation, this M-1 thing was a dangerous project. It's a wonder we didn't blow our heads off with that homemade ammunition and toggled up gun, but we didn't. As proud of our accomplishments as we were, we were smart enough to keep our mouths shut. Word never got out, so we didn't get in trouble.

One thing life at Boy's Home taught us was to be able to take care of ourselves and our belongings. We didn't have a lot of clothes, but what we had was our responsibility to make do with and care for. On Mondays, Mrs. Fudge, our housemother, would lay on each bed some shirts, one pair of work pants, and one pair of casual pants, underwear, and socks. The casual pants were usually overalls, and we wore them for meals and town. They were to last all week, but the work pants were changed on Wednesday. Those of us who worked on the farm wore shoes year round, but those who didn't went barefoot in the summer. It was the years of World War II, and shoes, like many other things, were rationed and the school could get only so many pairs each year. We kept all our clothes, towels, and washcloths in an open locker, and our other valuables in a footlocker. Nobody stole anything because if they did, we found out who did it and served up our own punishment. The guilty party was forced through a gauntlet, and we whipped his ass good with switches.

We did have one rather sick incident take place in the dormitory where I stayed. It was the only incident of sexual harassment that I was aware of. Harold Ramsey was a pretty good-sized lad who always seemed to carry a chip on his shoulders. He came to the home with his twin brother Robert. Because of his size and age, Mrs. Fudge put him in charge of us boys. He always seemed to be bothering this little boy named Diamond. We suspected something was going on. Harold's bed was close to the Diamond boy's, and at night I could hear the movement of bodies. We let it slide, but it kept gnawing at my guts. One evening we were in taking a shower and I noticed some bruises on the Diamond boy's back.

"Where'd you get those bruises?" I asked.

"Harold hit me," and then he shut right up as if he had said something he shouldn't have.

About that time Harold stepped into the shower and being older, he had a lot bigger tool than the rest of us did. He was acting macho and kinda swinging his stuff to get attention.

As he walked toward us, I said, "Boy, you take your dick and put it where you want to, but don't put it around here."

Harold looked at me kinda funny, and the Diamond boy slipped out of the shower room. I followed the boy out. When Harold came out of the shower room, I was pretty much dressed and sitting on my locker contemplatin' how I was going to handle this situation. The Diamond boy was in front of his locker and hadn't put his underwear on yet. He was bent over workin' on drying his feet when Harold went by him. Harold kinda pushed himself against the boy's butt. At that moment all hell flew into me. Harold's locker was number nine in the corner, perfect. I grabbed him by the fleshy part of his neck and drove him into his locker with his head underneath the shelf so there was no way he could fight back.

"If you ever put your hands on that kid again, I'm gonna kill you!" His brother Robert was wide-eyed behind us, and I added a threat to him, "If you want to get in this, I'll stomp the shit out of you too!"

He offered no opposition. Harold's tongue was hanging out, and he was turning a little blue, so I let go. My finger and nail prints were evident on his neck.

"If you ever come up behind my back, you may take me, but you'll never do it the second time," I warned.

To Robert I said, "You better straighten your brother out."

I walked downstairs and there was Mrs. Kathie Fudge.

"Teddy, what's the trouble up there?" she asked.

"If Harold Ramsey ever steps out of line again, I'm going to stomp his ass!"

"You can't talk to me that way Teddy!" She said.

"I'm tellin' you what's going to happen," I replied.

I believe she was about to burst out laughing, and could hardly hold it in. She had some idea what was going on but couldn't catch Harold. Anyway, as far as I know, Harold never bothered the Diamond boy or anyone else again. Even though he was a head higher and twenty pounds heavier, he seemed smaller than me in everyone's eyes that day. Sometime later the Diamond boy came and thanked me. He said Harold had left him alone.

The Boy's Home was not a bad place, and we didn't really have much time to think about where we came from. Some had families and some didn't. During the years I was there, my mother visited me once, I went home twice and that seemed to be enough. We were always busy, with little idle time. If we weren't doin' chores or school-work, we were playing softball in the summer or basketball in the gymnasium in the winter. I did feel, however, that they were holding me back. I wanted to work in the power plant and learn new things, and they would not let me off the farm. I said to hell with it, and over the course of time took some more unauthorized vacations.

Melvin Pennicost, another boy at the home, knew I was unhappy. He said he was going to take off for his dad's place in Madison Heights, and invited me along. This trip lasted three weeks and took us beyond Lynchburg which was about 100 miles away. From Covington we went around Cliffton Forge and ended up spending one night at a farm outside of Iron Gate. We hit the place about chore time and traded some labor for a place to sleep and a meal. The farmer was happy for the help and didn't ask too many questions. People kinda minded their own business in those days.

The next day we hopped a ride on the school bus to Eagle Rock and from there on to Fin Castle and Cloverdale. We cut across to Bedford, then on to Lynchburg and Madison Heights. We didn't have any set timetable, just wandered through the mountains and along that route at a leisurely pace. The only problem was that when we got to his dad's place, his dad was intent on taking Melvin back to Boy's Home.

Melvin was irritated and didn't want to go.

When we returned we got our hands hit with a strap and restricted from going into town for a month. That was no big punishment for me. I'd rather be in the mountains than town anyway.

The next time I took off a boy named Moody went along. Melvin Pennicost had already left for good several months before. Moody and I spent a couple nights in the hills, then stayed overnight at that same farm outside of Iron Gate. The next day we caught a ride with a truck driver. He said he was going to make a brief stop in Roanoke, and then on to Lynchburg. I had made up my mind to go back home to Petersburg.

We trusted that truck driver, and took what he said at face value. He stopped in Roanoke all right, right in front of the police station where he turned us in. I told him he was gonna go to hell for lying to us.

The police called somebody in Covington or the Boy's Home, and later we were picked up and taken back.

Another year passed and I didn't take any more long vacations, but I did take off up in the hills for a couple days at a time, and I guess they finally gave up on me. They called my mother and told her that I was unruly and determined to do things my own way. I guess I just ticked them off, and they decided that they couldn't make me into a product they wanted, so they might as well get rid of me. Before the end of the school year in May of 1945, I returned from Covington to home.

BILLY'S LAST RUN

On Pott's Creek I walked with
   a friend of mine
Both of us doing nothing but
   passing away time.
Being a boy and full of
   mischief such as I,
A perfect fork in a hickory
   tree fell upon my eye.
Remembering an old tire
   tube left behind,
Thoughts of a slingshot
   begin to form in my mind.
Within the heart of any boy,
   at the age of eleven,
Fulfillment of a child's dream
   was just part of heaven.
With perfection the fork was
   seasoned and trimmed.
For the pocket a shoe tongue
   made a perfect bend.
Proudly it was shown and
   accurate was its aim,
To miss an object was
   one's self to blame.
Doing chores in the barn
   I spied Billy the bull,
Testicles hung low a perfect
   shot I knew I could.
Doubts in my friend's mind
   confronted me with a dare
A nickel bet was placed on
   the target standing there.
With a sharp shooter's aim
   I let the rock fly

A loud roar old Billy
   climbed to the sky.
Wild with torturous pain Billy
   jumped about
Tucker fearful, knew a crazy
   bull no doubt.
From Tucker came a cry of
   terror "go get the gun
That bull has made it's
   last wild run!"
Shocked back to reality as
   fear gripped my heart
I knew with my prized slingshot now I must part.
Four shots were heard throughout
   the countryside,
With no doubt I should be
   where old Billy now lies.

Back to Petersburg

At the age of 14, I was back in Petersburg. My life was certainly different from the structured institutionalized ways of the Boy's Home. When I returned, we had moved off of Washington Street and down to Grove Avenue. I got back together with my old buddy, Jack Moore. He had been busy raising a little hell here and there, but not enough to be sent to reform school. I also ran into some other old pals, Bubba Moore and Sonny Grubbs.

It was late spring and school was still in session. Although I didn't attend, I did get set up and registered for the fall. I didn't get to see my friends much during the day, but after school we'd get together over at Swanson's Drug Store for a Coke, and I got to meet some other kids. I'd never had much association with girls before, but we met Janey Skelton, her sister Agnes and Joyce Taylor. We all got to hangin' around together on a regular basis, playing volleyball and other games, and I began to more than like Joyce.

Joyce was built a little like a football player, no fat, but solid and strong. I found out how strong she was one day when we were all down to the river for a wiener roast. She gave me a little shove into the edge of the water, and not to be outdone, I gave her a bigger shove and she ended up in the center of an eddy from the river. This hurt her ego I guess, 'cause she came outa there and picked me up and threw me into the river.

This kinda busted up the party for awhile. I walked down the river bank a ways and tried to dry my clothes out some. I might just as well left them on for as much as they dried. Well, the wiener roast did go on, and I guess you could say that from then on Joyce and I started going together. Once in awhile we went to a movie, mostly just a walk and talk together. I learned from Joyce Taylor what true love is. We were young, but I cannot ever remember her or me using each other in a selfish way or in a disrespectful manner. You never forget the warmth in your heart and the completeness of that first true love.

While I was at the Boy's Home, my mother married a second time. The man's name was William Coral, nicknamed "Buck". This marriage didn't last any longer than the first as they were separated by the time I arrived home. I'm not sure what the problem was, whether he found favor in other women or just couldn't meet my mother's expectations. I didn't ask, just figured those things happen and it wasn't my business. The rest of the family didn't necessarily feel that way.

We were all sitting around my cousin Thelma's house one night. My other cousin Cecil and her husband Wallace were there plus cousin Bill had come to fix Melvin's car. Melvin was Thelma's husband. Well, they all were sitting around chewin' the fat and I was listening. There's always a black sheep in the family, and this evening they were busy running my mother down. It was Helen's second unsuccessful marriage, blah, blah, bullshit, on and on. I didn't say anything, but after awhile I had enough and stood up.

"I'm tired of hearing you all put my mother down. Cecil, you and Wallace shacked up for six months before you were married. Thelma, you and Melvin shacked up at our house on Washington Street before you were married, and Bill, I know you had your dick out of your britches before you and Francis got married. Now I will tell you right now, if you don't like it, we can step outside and I'll whip your ass all together or one at a time. It don't make any difference, 'cause I don't think there's a damn-good fight in either of ya."

About this time, Wallace stood up too, "Teddy, I'll tell you right now, if anyone of them tries to put their hands on ya, they're going to have to walk over my Czechoslovakian ass before they get to you." Well, that ended any potential confrontation and welded a solid friendship between me and Wallace.

A few nights later I was over at Cecil and Wallace's house. Cecil asked, "What got you so riled up the other night, Teddy?"

"I didn't figure there was any reason for the pot to call the kettle black, the things they did wasn't any better than what they said my mother did."

Wallace spoke up. "Teddy, I'm goin' to tell you something. I don't care what Cecil thinks about it. Robert Ward was your real daddy, not Stanley Aldridge."

It wasn't a real shock to find out who my real father was. Something never seemed to jibe anyway. I had never seen Stanley Aldridge, but I do remember seeing Robert Ward just once, that time he carried me down the road with the wormy candy. My response to Wallace's information was, "Well, doesn't make much difference, I'm here to stay, only way I'm goin' is if'n somebody kills me."

I could understand why my mother kept who my real father was a secret. In those days, the Thirties and Forties, there were a lot of old busybodies. They used social occasions to run other people down for such things. Hell, nowadays nobody cares. I learned some other interesting things about my name from Cecil and Wallace that night. My first name, Robert was after my real father. My middle name was Edward, after my step-grandfather, and my last name Aldridge, was given to me by Stanley Aldridge who was married to my mother before I was born. Guess he just got hooked. Ha! Everyone always called me Teddy as a nickname, and I was never sure where that came from or who gave it to me. Come to find out, after Mother and Stanley divorced, she had this boyfriend named Teddy Rogents. She was still very young and he was a government employee, a pilot for the Department of the Interior. He used to scout for timber operations in the Thirties. I don't know how long that lasted, but it must have been fairly significant as she gave me his name as a nickname.

Several years later, I looked up Stanley Aldridge. His mother worked at a local factory and he came down to visit. I introduced myself and said that I didn't have any axe to grind with him, just wanted to meet him.

I said, "Haven't I seen you in Washington?"

He said, "I don't run a gambling house anymore."

Obviously I had hit on something sensitive. I was positive I'd seen him there and also I guess he remembered me. There had been a little argument over card game rules in which I was involved. His wife, a nice lookin' lady, was standing there as we talked. He looked uncomfortable. "Yes, I was married to your mother Helen, we had differences, but it wouldn't do any good to go into them now."

I never talked to Mother about this. I think she knew that I knew, but that was as far as it went. I never did see Robert Ward, my real dad, after that one time. Too many years passed, and I guess if he would have wanted to see me, he could have.

THE LADY

It was in that first summer after returning home that I stumbled upon an experience that would have an influence on me for the rest of my life.

I got myself a part-time job at the Tank Car Service Station. It was located in central Petersburg on Washington Street. That was a main road where Route One and Highway 301 went through. The station was owned by a good guy named Alfred Joyner. He said I could work regular in the summer, but that once school had started, he stipulated that to hold the job, I could only work two days a week and that I must show him my report card to prove I was keeping up with my school work.

I used the bus service to get to and from work. It was a fair piece from where we lived and I had to transfer buses in order to get home. After the first bus, if I walked down to Tabb Street, I could catch another and use my transfer token. Otherwise, I would have had to transfer twice and that would cost another nickel. Down at Tabb Street there was always quite a bit of time to kill before the bus arrived, so I would usually go in the restaurant there and have a hot dog. My mother knew the lady who ran the place. Mable was her name, and she had two daughters, Polly and Mary.

It was usually Polly working when I came in, and this particular evening I sat drinking a Coke waiting for Polly to bring me my hot dog. Pretty soon in walked this lady. She wore a plain cotton dress, but was nice to look at and had what they called then, a well preserved body. I'd guess she was around 35 or so, and I hadn't seen her around there before. I was going on 15 and at this time frame in my life I vaguely knew what went on between a man and a woman. This was kind of interesting though. The lady kinda ran her eyes around the restaurant and then came over, she looked straight at me and said, "Would ya buy an old girl a beer?" I looked at her kinda funny, my mind of course was racing with all sorts of thoughts. Draft beer would probably be only ten cents, so I said, "OK." I threw a quarter on the table and she ordered a beer and sat down.

She was easy to talk to. Right off the bat she started talking about baseball, football and things I liked. I told her about things I had seen along the river. Well it wasn't long when over came Polly. "Your hot dog's all ready for you," and she motioned that it was in a booth on the other side of the restaurant. In other words, get your ass over there. I excused myself, picked up my Coke and went over to eat my hot dog.

As I was chompin' away on my hot dog, I could see Polly's mother Mable watching me. She was working on her ledger, tabulating the day's receipts. Pretty soon she motioned for me to come over. "You leave that woman alone."

"I wasn't bothering that woman to start with, she came over and sat with me," I replied.

"I saw who bought that beer!"

"Well maybe someday when I don't have any money she can buy me a Coke or even a beer when I'm older."

In all honesty I certainly hadn't been trying to make a play for the lady. In fact, I wasn't at all bothered by moving away to eat my hot dog because the whole situation made me feel uncomfortable. Anyway, I was hungry and I didn't feel like continuing the conversation, so I went back to my hot dog. It wasn't long though, when the girl went to the bathroom and returned straight to my booth. In her brief conversation with me I think she had pretty well determined as to where I was as a kid. "I'd like to hear more about your catching herrings down at the river, if maybe you could afford another beer." I laid down another quarter and as she settled into the third beer I could see that Mable was pretty upset. In her eyes, I could see a determined look that she wasn't going to let me and that girl get together. Still, in all honesty, I really didn't know what was going on. We sat and talked for awhile, until I happened to glance out the window and then at the clock. "Shit, I just missed the last bus home. I gotta go now, see you later." Now I'd have to walk home, and I knew Grandma would be worried. I stopped at the door and paid for my hot dog and was almost at the corner of Bollinbrook Street when the woman was right beside me again. How she got outta that restaurant that fast, I'll never know, because I didn't think she was behind me as I left.

"I'm sorry I talked to you so long and made you miss your bus. How far you gotta go?"

"Not too far, three or four miles I guess."

"I feel guilty you having to walk that far when it's really not necessary. I feel like I'd like to have you stay with me tonight. Can you call a friend and tell them you're staying in town?"

BANG! It hit me what was goin' on. If she's damn fool enough, so am I. "Yes, I can call somebody, but I better not go back in that restaurant to do it."

We walked up to Louis's Restaurant, a block away, and I called Jack. "Jack, I want you to cover for me. I want to stay in town tonight." Well of course Jack came back with a lot of bullshit, but I convinced him there was nothing going on, just an all-night card game or something like that.

We walked three blocks up where Sycamore Street met Franklin Street. The girl lived in an apartment over a stationery store on the SE side of Franklin. Once we were up in her room the general rituals of educating a kid as to what was goin' on took place. She knew I didn't know a lot and was real nice and cautious about it. She took the lead in the proceedings. She turned the lights off and drew the window curtain, but a lot of light still came in from the city street. We went through the whole nine yards, and she finally made bingo with me. From then on, nature kinda took its course. Like a hog goin' to slop, once you get a little, you want a lot more.

Next day, I got back on the phone with Jack Moore. "Jack, I got a good thing goin' here, and I want to stay in town for a couple weeks. Tell Grandma we're going to your brother's place on Swift Creek, any lie you can think of."

"OK, but you're going to owe me."

The girl and I came to an arrangement on sharing living expenses. She worked at a dime store right across the street, and turned out to be a good cook and a very neat housekeeper.

It was a real learning experience, and she seemed intent in teaching me not only the mechanics of sex, but of life and understanding women in general. She told me the importance of making sure any woman I was with was clean, and that I take care of myself too. She also explained how women can deceive men with their dress and conversation, all for their own self-indulgence. She even talked to me about gays and how you can spot them. As I had pretty much grown up without a mother or father around, I heard things from her that maybe I would not have normally heard from parents. Where parents would probably have been a little reluctant to talk about such things, she told me straight out without hesitation.

She tried oral sex with me and I wouldn't have anything to do with it. She smiled and said that it was all right I felt that way. She was patient and understanding in the whole process, but after a couple weeks, the whole thing came to an end one Saturday evening. Whether she got tired of me or the other way around, school was over. On Sunday evening I headed back home. As I walked in the house I tried to act as if nothing new happened. You couldn't fool Grandma though. A couple days later she said, "Teddy, you have changed."

"Ah, Grandma, you just missed me."

She knew something had happened, maybe she sensed exactly what had happened. She was nobody's fool.

It certainly was a unique experience for which I was grateful. To say whether it was good or bad, I'm not sure. It would have to be classified as both a sexual and learning affair. Some of the knowledge I gained actually became a burden, for I could see people being manipulated, and it bothered me. I will not mention this lady's name, for she might still be alive and out of total respect I would not want to embarrass her.

JAKE

That summer I spent a lot of my spare time down at the river. As the woods and mountains had been my retreat at Boy's Home, the river became that haven back in Petersburg. We boys had constructed a canvas-type boat to use on the river for fishing. It resembled a canoe in some respects, but was not in proportion and it tipped easily.

We didn't paddle it, just used a pole to move it around on the river where we wanted it. Most of the river was shallow except where it came from behind the dam and through the powerhouse. There the swiftness had dug a deep channel. The tricky part was to give the boat a quick push with the pole to get her across the channel where the deep, fast water was.

Well, this one nice spring day I was really feelin' on top of the world. The day before a war veteran friend of mine, Edward Landers, had given me an almost new pair of Army combat boots. Combat boots were the fad then, and they really felt good on my feet, and looked sharp too. I figured this was a good day to head down to the river and net some herring. They had started to run, and it was my aim to get a nice batch. I had the river all to myself too, except for the black man down yonder. I had seen him from a distance several times before, but he never paid much attention to me and I didn't bother him.

I climbed in the old boat and poled her out to the channel. I gave a good push on the pole to propel her across the deep part, but something went wrong and the boat went over and I went out. Well, I could swim pretty well, but those combat boots weren't helping me any. I couldn't do anything except flounder in the water. Down I would go and then back up again, and now my boots were getting filled with water. I figured I was just about done for. I went down again and everything kinda went blank. Next thing I know, I'm layin' on the shore and someone's beatin' on my back trying to get the water out of me. It certainly couldn't be classified as artificial respiration, but it revived me and I started coughing and exchanging the water inside me for air. I struggled around to see who was working on me. What I saw scared the hell out of me, worse than the fear of drowning. Now I thought, "I guess I lost and did drown, and the devil has got me."

Now I've been to scary movies, but this man's face was something else. He was black and his face was just all beat up lookin'. His upper lip was split almost up to his nose, and his nose was all squashed and twisted. He had a bad scar leading up to one eye, which wasn't opened as far as the other eye. Besides not having front teeth, his ears were cauliflower looking. It was a cool cloudy day and I was shakin'. He could see the fear in my eyes too, so he put his old coat around my shoulders. "You OK boy?" With this gesture, and the warmth in his voice, my fear dissolved. I looked around for my boat. We were by the embankment where the old trolley rails used to lead across the river into town. He spotted my boat and walked down the river bank and retrieved it from where it had caught on the shore.

It took awhile before I collected myself to carry on much conversation, but eventually I asked some questions, and he was willing to talk. He told me his name was Jake and he had been a prize fighter for some time. His only reward was a beat up face and probably a broken body too. Jake said he had some trouble with the law too, but didn't go into a lot of detail. He said he made his living on the river catching minnows and digging blood worms to sell for bait. Sometimes he worked as a common laborer in warehouses too. His clothes looked old and he didn't seem to have much, but I guess he didn't need too much to survive.

That summer Jake and I became good friends. He loved the river as I did, and he seemed to enjoy the companionship. He taught me how to cook fish on a rock, and another method where he rolled them in clay and put them in the fire coals to bake them. That worked fine because the clay would harden and dry so that when you removed it from the fish, the skin and scales came off with the clay. "When you are out and hungry, you don't always have pots and pans, so this way works just fine," he said.

Jake taught me a lot more than just cooking fish. He had answers to a lot of questions I had. His responses were straightforward and simple, the kind a young boy could relate to. "Jake, how's come the sky is so blue?"

"Well, I reckon the sun is so far away that it makes our sky look blue. I'm not sure, but I'll bet the farther you went up, that everything would be black out."

"Why do the birds sing all the time?"

"That's the way they communicate Teddy, just a different language than ours." I don't know how Jake gained his wisdom, I guess if he didn't learn it in life's school of hard knocks, it was knowledge passed up through his family.

One early evening not far from the river, but up towards town, I heard someone strumming a guitar and singing. I walked up in that direction and there was quite a few people hanging around listening. When I strolled up to investigate, there sat Jake playing and singing the blues. He'd been doin' a little drinking to loosen up I suppose, but he was singing and playing real good. Everyone there was real taken up with his songs. I listened for a long time and his songs were all different and moody.

One day at the river I said, "Jake, how come you never sing the same songs over?"

"Well Teddy, you sing the way you feel, and different days you have different blues. You'll hear a lot of blues about women, 'cause as men get older, they all have women blues. Some people even sing blues about rainy days, but that's not right."

That got my attention, "Why not sing blues about rainy days?"

"Cause the Lord sent the rain for the earth and to give man a day of rest from his work, no farmin', no gardenin'."

I reflected on this, "I thought Sunday was the day God gave us to rest and love him?"

"How many days of the week do you love your mamma?"

"Well, every day I guess."

"OK, then you should love the Lord every day. What's the big deal about Sunday?" asked Jake. Well, he had me there, and I guess I haven't refuted that philosophy to this day.

Now the coloreds lived on Cross Street, but not on Grove, that was the dividing line. Jake put on a lot of informal music sessions up on Cross. A little drink, and he was on his way for the evening. Young and old alike gathered round to hear him play and sing. He used a bottle to move up and down the strings, but I came up with something better for him. My cousin Bill and my cousin Cecil's husband Wallace played the guitar. They both said that something made out of silver gave the best sound. Ma had an odd knife in her silver set, so I broke the blade off and gave the handle to Jake. That made him real happy, as it was easy to carry around and I swear it made the music sound even better.

I spent a lot of time with Jake the rest of that summer and whenever

I had spare time after school. He was a good teacher and made a lasting impression on my life. Also, because I was a friend of Jake's I felt comfortable with the colored folks up on Cross Street and even used to make some extra money selling fish to them when I had a good catch.

THE MODEL T FORD

About three quarters of a mile down the road from the old trolley car barn was Mr. Saddlers. He had an old Model T Ford out back that I had noticed occasionally. It had sat there unused for quite awhile. It was long enough after the war that new cars were coming out and I guess Mr. Saddler just figured the old Ford was wore out. It looked a little rough, but wasn't beat up. One day me, Jack and Bubba Moore approached Mr. Saddler with the idea of taking the old Ford off his hands. He said, "What ya want her for?"

"Junk," I replied.

He thought for awhile, then said, "OK." Well we boys looked at that old car and then one another. What went through our minds was the fact that we now owned one whole automobile, and on top of that none of the tires were flat. We told Mr. Saddler that we were going to push her down to the old trolley car barn where we could fool with her in the shade, where it would be more comfortable. Even though it was a pretty hot day, we just wanted to get away so we could feel a little freer to talk about our acquisition. Down at the barn we marveled over this fine auto. It had twenty-inch wheels, the big ten-inch headlights, three pedals — brake, clutch, and one which would select two forward gears or the reverse band.

"Yep," I said, "I believe this thing will run."

The next step, of course, was to get some gas. We collected all the pop and beer bottles we had picked up and with that money and a borrowed gallon jug, we sent Sonny out for a gallon of gas. "Break that jug, and we'll whip your ass." When he arrived back, we poured it in the tank. The tank was under the hood in front of the windshield, but the cap was on the outside. The gas just gravity fed to the engine, as there was no fuel pump. From there, we pushed her down the street where there was some slant to get her started. On the first try it came to an abrupt stop because we let the gear pedal all the way out into reverse. The next time we had the pedal only part way down, which was in second. As we again started downhill, she began to belch smoke, but didn't start, though we thought it might have fired. On the next try, we came around the corner and were so involved and frustrated that we ran into the brick foundation of a barn.

Well, for the next two weeks, we bugged everybody in town to try and get help to get that car started. We couldn't find a crank to start it. Probably just as well, otherwise we could have had a broken arm when she kicked back against the crank. Finally, my Uncle William showed us how to set the spark on the magneto with the lever, and we got her goin'. We had a ball drivin' up and down the river road. Boy, were we big shots. Pretty soon though, that got old and we decided to take her into town.

It was around 5:00 p.m. and we had scavenged up three gallons of gas, so downtown we headed. Straight down the main drag on Sycamore and then on to Washington Street before Sgt. Slater pulled us over with his siren goin'. He looked at us and then at the old car. You could about read what was going through his mind. Just a bunch of kids having fun. I don't think he wanted to be too hard on us, just scare us a little. "Who owns this car?"

"We all do." He was starting to write a ticket when Lt. Parish came on the scene.

"What's goin' on here?"

Sgt. Slater replied, "It's not hard to see. These boys are driving this wreck in town."

Lt. Parish looked me square in the face. "Teddy, this had to be your idea. You get into that car and get it down to the river and never bring it in town again. Sgt. Slater, you make sure they do." Well, down Davis Street, and then Cox's Alley to the river we went. Sgt. Slater turned around when he saw we were headed in that direction. We were mad because they had run us off, but happy nothing else had happened. Probably the fact that Jack and I were members of the Police Boy's Club helped.

A couple weeks went by and we stayed out of trouble. I would always go down to the river in the mornings when Jake fished and gathered his bait. He always did this on the tide, not in the evening when it was out. I found other things to do at night anyway.

After awhile, we planned another escapade with the car. We would take it to Lakeview for a day. Lakeview was kind of a resort on the other side of Colonial Heights. We managed to come up with five gallons of gas and collected enough food to fill a large picnic basket. Down the road we went, hollerin' and raisin' hell all the way.

After a fine day at the lake, we decided it was time to hurry back home before dark. The lights didn't work on the old car. The shortest way was Route One, which was the main highway through Chesterfield County. It was a busy highway and we were relieved as we passed through Colonial Heights and by the fire and police station. "Whoops, here comes the county cop with his lights goin'."

"Who's got a driver's license? Where's this car's registration? There's no license plate on the back!"

I meekly replied, "Plate musta fallen off."

"You know where the police station is?"

"Nope."

"You fellows follow me right over there." He pointed to the police station right back behind us.

When we got inside the station, I could see that the desk sergeant was enjoying this. Bunch of kids out hell raisin', he was probably thinking. But, it was a problem us being on that busy road with the old car. Might get tangled up with one of those big trucks. We didn't know what they was up to; goin' to arrest us or what. Just then, Judge Snead came walking in. "What's happening here?" The officer that stopped us explained the situation. The judge walked past looking at us, then came back to me. "William Squires your uncle?"

"Yes," I said.

He turned back to the officer that caught us, "You escort these boys back across the Appomattox River into Petersburg and be damned glad you got rid of this problem." Judges had a lot of power then and the fact that my Uncle Squires was an old drinking buddy of this judge didn't hurt us any either.

The officer said, "OK, get in boys. Let's go." Back to Petersburg we went with him right behind. When we turned off US One into

Petersburg, he was gone.

We sure had fun with that old car, all that summer and part of the next year. There was only one other instance when we got into a little trouble with her. It was down by this river landing where Bubba's daddy liked to fish. We was comin' down the hill and tried to stop, no brakes and the reverse band was inoperative. The front wheels were in the sand so you couldn't turn them away. Into the water we plowed headin' right towards Bubba's daddy who was in his boat fishing. She came to a stop just inches from his boat, but not before he abandoned it for the water. Boy, was he mad. He hauled us up on the shore, shook us, cursed us and our car. I think we scared him. Now we were concerned about our car. Water was running over the hood. "I don't give a damn about that car!" he said.

Bubba did some quick thinkin' and said, "Pop, I'll bet your old Toura Plain couldn't pull her out." Good thinking, for Mr. Moore was real proud of his Toura Plain auto. It was a fine six cylinder in those days, and ever since he had it overhauled, it would go sixty-five or seventy on the highway.

"Well, I'll bet it could," and off he went to fetch it. He brought an old chain back with him and yanked our car right out. Now we had the problem of getting the water out of the engine, and we didn't have the special tool it took to remove the oil plug which was not very accessible. We did the next best thing—tipped her over and let the water run out the top of the engine.

As young boys, I guess we were a little self-centered. We didn't always think about how what we did affected others, but I had a pretty fair idea as to what we could get away with. Now we didn't always have enough money to buy gas, so occasionally we would snitch a gallon out of old man Rutason's lumber truck. It sat beside the old ice house, so at night we'd make a little trip up to siphon off some. This one night we were after two gallons. We liked glass jugs because we could see how much we had in them, and even though we were stealin' it, we didn't want to overfill the jug and waste the gas. Well, we had one jug full and had started on the other when the police went by. Usually once they went by we didn't see them again for a couple hours. This time after they went by, they stopped and started backing up. We capped the full jug and began to scatter. Our escape route was well planned. We fled down this peninsula bordered by the river on one side and the creek on the other. We had a board over the creek, and the first one across would wait until the last came, then pull the board away. We could hear them coming behind us. It had to be Sgt. Slater in the lead as he was a big man and made lots of noise. They had flashlights too, but we had one other gimmick to slow a pursuer down. We had a wire stretched across the path attached to a little tree that was roped down. We released the tree when we went by and as it sprang up the wire was held up about eighteen inches or so. We were well across the creek when they ran into the wire. They were cussin' a lot but the wire gave us time to be well on our way. Of course when they got to the creek they could see our tracks in the mud and the board pulled across and knew they had been had. Fortunately they didn't know who we were.

A couple days later we were at the station across from the ice house buying some gas. Mr. Rutason happened to be there. He said, "Boys, I've been wondering if that car runs as good on this gas as it does on that gas outta my truck?"

Without thinkin' I said, "About the same I guess."

We were talking about it later and came to the conclusion that he might have known all along we were stealing his gas. In fact, he might have been watchin' from his front porch right across the street laughing about the whole thing. Because we didn't take very much and always put his gas cap back on, maybe he didn't care that much. We also probably had the feelin' we had done something wrong and weren't as sly as we thought.

ED LANDERS—THE '34 CHEVY—THE FIGHT

Edward Preston Landers was the WWII veteran I told you about that gave me new boots before I fell into the river. He stayed at our home in 1946 and 1947. I first met Ed in the fire station at Fort Lee, where he was a fireman. Occasionally Chief Butler would have some extra funds to dispense to us kids if we shined up the fire trucks there, so that's how I happened to run into Edward Landers. We took a liking to one another and I told him about how good a cook my grandma was.

He said that southern food sure sounded good, so I invited him over for some meals. Even though Grandma was blind she still did the cooking and Ed was impressed.

One evening after supper I said to Ed, "If you like the food here, why don't you just stay with us." Well, Grandma and Helen both liked Ed so he moved in and arranged a ride back and forth to work with another fellow.

Ed didn't have much spare cash, because he had an allotment which sent most of his paycheck to his mother and two sisters over in Davis, West Virginia. He did manage to come up with $85 and with $35 I had saved up we purchased a 1934 Chevrolet. The main purpose of this auto was to provide Ed with transportation over to visit his mother and sisters, which he hadn't seen in over four years.

One weekend when Ed didn't have to work, he and I and his buddy Alan Emery all started for Davis, W.V. to see his mother and sisters. It was a Friday evening and both Ed and Alan were real tired so they let me drive.

The old Chevy had a freewheel button. According to the law you were supposed to keep it pulled out so that when you let off the accelerator the engine would help slow down the car. If it was pushed in, it was just like having the car in neutral and she'd really pick up speed coasting downhill. Well, we were going through some pretty hilly country so I'd let her freewheel going downhill and by the time I started up the next hill I had the button back out so the engine would help get us up the hill.

At about 2 a.m. this cop appeared out of nowhere and pulled me over. He walked up next to my door and asked, "Are you freewheeling? I had you going about 80 miles per hour." He looked in the back seat and saw Ed and Alan asleep. Guess he figured they were drunk, 'cause he just said, "I'm not going to ask for your license because you probably don't have one. I just want you to drive those boys up to the next town which is Elkins, and get them some coffee and food. I'll be there." With that he left.

When we got up to Elkins he was waiting for us. I guess he could see then that those boys weren't drunk, just tired. He probably figured that if they were awake and sober they would be driving instead of me.

At least he didn't give me a ticket or ask for my license, which was a good thing. I was too young for a license anyway. I had done a good job keeping the car on the right side of the road so he must have figured I was safe enough.

Sonny Grubbs was a friend of mine, and one day we sat talking in the front seat of the Chevy that Ed and I owned. Sonny had a handful of pellets he had taken out of a shotgun shell, and as he sat there he kept tossing a pellet or two at the oil gauge. I told him to stop doing that or he would bust the oil gauge. Well, he kept throwin' them and finally I said, "If you bust that oil gauge I'm goin' to stomp your ass." The next few pellets were thrown a little harder, and sure enough the oil glass cracked. I brought my left hand around and caught him in the back of the head, bashing it into the steering wheel. He piled out of the car and from somewhere picked up a short 2x4 board. When I came out he hit my ribs with a blow that made everything hurt. I was full of rage now, and kind of lost control. We were in a lot next to Mr. Moore's driveway, and the next thing I remember was Mr. Moore pouring cold water on us.

Sonny just laid there. He was hurt pretty bad. I guess I had rubbed his face in the cinders 'cause it was all bloody and his right eye had popped out. I was still pissed off, so I just left him there and walked over to his step-daddy's house. When Mr. Southhall came to the door I said, "I just whipped your boy's ass 'cause he broke the oil gauge in my car. If you want to do something about it let's get it taken care of right now." Mr. Southhall didn't have much to say. He probably needed some time to sort things out. I just walked off.

They got Sonny's face fixed up and his eyeball back in where it was supposed to be, but after that he stayed away from me.

For the last couple years, except for a few brushes with the law which I already mentioned, and those two weeks that first summer when I had gained my manhood, I had been a pretty good kid. I did well in school, went to church regular, worked part-time and still kept up with the Boy Scouts. In 1947 my outlook on life changed considerably. That was my last year in Petersburg. I had only worked two nights a week at the service station during the school year and was usually home by 9:00 p.m. I walked about three and a half blocks to get the last bus at the corner of Sycamore and Bank Street. This corner was right across from Faye's Pool Hall, and on a regular basis I could see some of the church elders in there drinkin' beer. I tried to let this go with the attitude that probably all God's people slip in their religion occasionally. I didn't cotton much to drinking myself, as I had seen what it did to some people.

It was on one evening in early April that the pool hall seemed extra rowdy. I observed one of the church deacons in there with the elders, and they were playin' grab ass with some old gals. I said to myself, "Wait a minute now, that's enough. They ain't goin' to tell me to do one thing and they do another. Everybody can ride the white horse or they can ride the black horse, it don't make any difference to me." After that incident, I didn't go to church anymore. I did go to Boy Scout meetings behind the church though, for I had been an active Scout starting in the Boy's Home and would soon qualify for Eagle Scout.

The first Sunday I didn't attend church Mother didn't say anything. After a couple weeks though she asked why I hadn't been going. In not too vulgar terms I told her what had happened. "In church those men act as if they had never sinned. Then, they go down there and play with a bunch of women who are not their wives, and even if they were their wives, they shouldn't do that in public." I added, "I'm not going along with that." She never forced me to go back, though it probably put her in an uncomfortable position. Active in church, she also was paid good money to look after the minister and choir's garments.

It was May and I had only a couple of merit badges left to qualify for Eagle Scout. At the awards ceremony they went down the list of honors and well past the names that began with A. I was surprised they hadn't mentioned mine. "Must be comin' at the end," I thought. But when it was over, I sat there dumbfounded. There must be some mistake. I asked the presenter where my awards were. "Young man, you quit church which proves you are not reverent to God. No way can you become an Eagle Scout."

"Well if you feel that way, just keep them." I walked out and never went back.

It made me feel alone though. Now I was some sort of outcast. I just didn't fit in as well as I used to. Not goin' to Scouts did give me extra time with my close friends, Jack, Bubba and Joyce.

I had my ups and downs at the junior high school in Petersburg. I didn't do well in English, but I did enjoy history, math, government and geography. Mr. Scott, the principal, had me assigned to room 200 where the problem students were concentrated. Mrs. MacBurton made kind of a deal with me. If I would stay in room 200 and improve in the areas I was weak in, they would also provide those subjects I would be receiving in the 9th grade. If things went well and I passed all the tests I could move right into the 10th grade.

Well, instead of going into the 9th grade at the junior high school I stayed in room 200 and at the junior high. Even though I played hooky a lot, I surprised everyone and successfully completed the course work which would allow me to go directly into the 10th grade. I never did go into the 10th grade though. I just decided that helping support the family and working full-time was more important than school, so the official end to my public education was the 8th grade.

My mother had been working in Hopewell at National Allied since Forty-Two, but held off moving over there since she thought I was better off with my friends and the school where I was. Now that I didn't plan to continue in school, she decided to move us to Hopewell. Guess I missed Petersburg some, but didn't miss having my ass set in school all day.

In Hopewell we lived above King Brothers Electric. There were two apartments above the businesses; Clarence King had one, and Helen, Grandma and I had the other. W.L. Broaddus owned the painted brick building and downstairs Souwers Hardware was in one side and King Electric in the other. A door between the two businesses was kept open for the customers' convenience.

The electrical business below us fascinated me. When I had spare time I would hang out down there and occasionally they would give me a little work stocking shelves or loading trucks. It wasn't really a job 'cause sometimes it only amounted to a couple dollars a week, but I enjoyed being in there.

I did get a real full-time job right around the corner from where we lived. It was a combination service station and sports store owned by Charley Aderholt.

Charley had plenty of money and spent most of his time either hunting or in the sports shop talking about hunting. I did a little bit of everything to start out with, putting the sports merchandise out front on display, cleaning, and I eventually got involved in changing and fixing tires. In those war years, there weren't many new tires available, but a lot of old ones to fix. More and more my day was spent removing the tires from their rims and patching the tubes and putting boots in the tire itself to cover the holes and worn spots.

Another fellow named Buck was in charge of retreading tires that had become bald, so we had the full operation going and the tire business was increasing rapidly. Dick Cheely, a man about ten years older than me, also worked there. He was a little lazy and was more than happy to let me struggle over fixin' tires all day. We didn't change tires on Saturday though, except for once when this colored fellow came in. He said he'd pay me real good to fix some, because he had some pulpwood trucks that needed to be working over the weekend. I did it after hours and he gave me ten dollars extra. Charley seen me workin' on them and said it was OK. After that, we got all the guy's business.

I think old Buck thought I was getting the raw end of the deal on all the tires while Dick Cheely was slippin' by. He must have said something to the boss, 'cause he came around one day and said from now on I was only to work on tires every other day and Dick Cheely would fix them on the other days. That worked fine for a week or so, and then Dick started not quite getting his tires done and they would be left for me on my day. On one Friday, Dick really sluffed off and come Monday there were a pile of extra tires.

Buck said, "I see old Dick's pulling the wool over your eyes again."

"Wrong, this time I'm not doin' his."

Charley came around, "That's quite a pile of tires you got there." I explained that they were Dick's from Friday. He marked all those and said to save them for Dick. On Tuesday Charley checked all the tires that Dick hadn't done and carried them over again, and at the same time got on his ass about it. On Thursday there still were tires left and

Charley asked if I would do them. On Friday I made my decision and talked with the boss.

"Mr. Aderholt, I think I'm causing a problem here and I'm going to get another job. If you got to force a man to do his job, I don't want to be around him, and I don't want to do his work either."

"Teddy, why don't you just take a day to cool off then come back."

"Well, sir, if I'm not here Monday, you'll know I'm not comin' back."

I had heard the wages were pretty good at Hercules Powder Company, so I stopped in to see about a job.

The man said, "You eighteen? You got to be eighteen to work here."

"Yes sir, I can prove it with my draft card, but I left it home."

"Well, if you can find your draft card, we'll talk about a job."

Hell, I didn't have no draft card 'cause I was sixteen, but I did aim to get one. I took care of that the next week. I went in and lied about my age, and sure enough, they registered me and gave me a card. That's all it took, and I was a full-time employee at Hercules Powder sewing up bags of cellulose for those big guns used in the war. I was makin' big bucks now, $93 a week.

I decided that with all the money I was making it was time to show a little gratitude and take the old gang out for a first-class meal. I caught the bus up to Petersburg, but the only old buddy I could locate was Jack Moore. Jack was truly impressed with my financial status and we headed down to the Mayflower, a Greek restaurant, and by far the fanciest one in town.

There were no waitresses in the Mayflower, just waiters in tuxedos. All the town big wigs ate here; ladies wore big hats with feathers. We didn't look great in our sports clothes, and we didn't have ties, but we looked acceptable. I felt confident that I could sit down and feel comfortable eating anyplace as they had taught us eating etiquette at the Boy's Home. I didn't give a lot of thought as to how Jack would fit in, we were hungry and ready for a good meal.

"What you usin' that little fork for?"

"That's proper etiquette, Jack. Start from the outside and work in. The small fork's for the salad." Jack changed forks. When the waiter came for our order, we both asked for the same thing, fried chicken. Boy were we hungry. There was nothin' better than Southern fried chicken. When the chicken arrived and the waiter left, we dug in. Jack picked up a nice big piece and started chompin' away. I had just started on my piece when out of the corner of my eye I could see the waiter watching critically. I knew we weren't supposed to eat chicken with our fingers, especially here, but I was hungry and didn't give it a second thought. The next thing I knew the waiter was standing beside Jack with this frown on his face.

"You fellas don't eat chicken with your fingers in this restaurant!"

Jack replied, "We bought this damn chicken and we're going to eat it however we damn please!" Jack was pretty street-wise, and he could see the fire in that waiter's eyes. By the time the waiter grabbed him, he had already slipped his hand under his plate and was ready. Up went the plate full of food into the waiter's face. Out of the woodwork came more waiters and I let my plate fly. My plate of food didn't hit anybody, only a twelve-foot-long-by-four-foot-wide mirror behind the commotion. Things were really getting out of hand now, but the main struggle was taking place around Jack who was doing a fine job of fighting the waiters off. The cook burst through the kitchen with a knife in hand, and I made a quick lurch to get through the front door. Before I got to it, the door burst open and there was Lt. Parish.

"What are you boys doing here?" The owner was there now sputtering in his foreign tongue and Lt. Parish said, "You shut up and talk to me in English! Get your hands off that boy!" Jack looked like a little rooster already to fight some more. "You boys get outta here and go down to Louie's and get yourself some hot dogs." Now Lt. Parish looked at the owner. "You had no business letting these boys in here. They didn't have ties on and probably don't know your rules anyway. They obviously haven't eaten much and they're not paying for one damn thing." We were well on our way out and down the street before he finished. We hadn't had more than a couple bites to eat, but we hadn't had to pay for anything either. Only the Lord knows how much damage was done, especially the cost of replacing that mirror.

When we rolled into Louie's place, he said, "What's all the commotion down at the Mayflower?"

We looked at each other, "We don't know." We ordered a couple hot dogs and kept the story to ourselves. It was a small town, and Lt. Parish knew my mother. Also, our hides were probably saved again because we were members of the Police Boy's Club. In later years, Jack joined the police force. When I last saw him in 1954, he was up for Sergeant.

Back at Hercules Powder, I worked in the bag room sewing the one hundred pound bags of cellulose for only a couple weeks. I was then put on the washtubs where the chemical impurities were washed out of the cellulose. It ended up looking like grains of rice. While I was doing that work, I watched the man working on the dryers and learned his job too. In not too long, I was running the dryers on the night shift. The dryers took some of the water out of the cellulose. I'd only been running the dryers for five days or so when the day foreman asked if I would continue into the day shift as that man hadn't shown up. I told him I would as I didn't have much else to do. When my night foreman came in, he said, "How come you're still here?"

"Nobody to relieve me." Boy, he went up in the air as I had worked twenty-four hours. He sent me home to rest.

While I was on the dryers, I watched the man that ran the autoclaves. He had been doing that job for twelve years, and one night I asked him what went on inside. He explained that autoclaves blended the elements that made up the cellulose and removed the rest of the water and gases with super-heated steam. Another by-product was some 200 proof alcohol which a government man was accountable for. He started explaining the procedures, and I said that what I was interested in knowing was the mechanics that went on inside the autoclaves.

"Hell, I don't know what goes on in there." It was then and there that I said to myself, if this man hasn't learned what's going on after twelve years, this is no place for me. I'm not going to fall in that groove and limit myself.

The next morning I went into the Personnel Office and talked to Mr. Yeager. "Sir, I'd like to transfer into electrical or mechanical and learn a trade."

"Well, I admire your ambition, but it will be three years before I could get you into a training program."

"Well sir, that's too long. How much notice do you want for my resignation, two weeks or a month?"

"Isn't this kind of a quick decision, Ted?"

"No sir, if I don't learn a trade, I'm not going anywhere. I don't have a high school education and I can't afford to go back to school as I need to provide the money to help my mother."

"OK, Ted, two week's notice will be all right."

At the end of the two weeks, I left.

THE CHANGE

In my early years still a lad
   I wasn't the best, not all bad.
I had grown up fifteen years old
   this world, I thought, need not be told.
I was really living, earning twenty a week
   looked up to by kids on the street.
A woman I met, of question no doubt,
   I know not her name nor today her whereabouts
She gently coaxed me into a brand new world,
   taught me of real love the ways of a girl.
Men's useless chase for women at night,
   though for affection only fools will fight.
Learned women's use of stumbling blocks and fall
   with patience, she taught me about them all.
Fourteen short days it took to make a man
   she left like we met, gently as a lamb.
Puritans will want to put me down,
   writing of an experience of which I am bound.
She opened doors that are closed to most men today,
   unashamed she showed me a woman and their ways.

IF SOCIETY HAD KNOWN

Being pulled from the cold waters
   I looked into a hideous face
I knew the devil had me,
   I'd lost life's race.
Faintly a worried voice, nervously asked
   if I was beginning to feel all right.
A pair of dark gentle eyes
   loosened all of my fright.
For warmth, this black man gave me his only coat,
   I warmed a wet chill as he uprighted my boat.
The time of birth for this man, Jake,
   the Lord only knows when,
As a child, poverty set him free
   as the cold blowing wind.
A prize fighter was his aim
   in his early day,
Split lips, scarred face, a damaged eye
   told the price he paid,
He told stories of joys and woes
   and life in the ring.
Yet, he told of happiness received when
   listening to nature sing,
I loved listening as he sang and played
   folk songs of his time,
Also to eat his cooking brought
   in on a fishing line.
Fish bait was his daily harvest
   from the river's bowels
With our work finished I listened
   to Negro wisdom for hours.
Our love for the river, its ways
   and never trying tide
Nature had bound a friendship which
   to this day has not died.

Those days of bliss, in which society
    wouldn't accept our love, I hope are gone,
I pray Jake goes to his heavenly home,
    where people said he didn't belong.
They called him a no account, said
    he was just all bad,
But nobody really knew of the love
    that Jake and I had.

FIRST LOVE

It was the summer of my return from Boy's Home that I had met Joyce
Taylor, and she had thrown me in the river. She was part of our gang
along with Janie and Agnes Skelton. Joyce and I had started out as
friends, then pals, and finally as much more than that — a first love for
each of us. For two years, we went together in junior high school and
formed our dreams of a future together. It was just a matter of getting a
little older to make our dreams a reality. Like any first love should be,
it was innocent, open, and unencumbered by worldly motives.

When I moved with my mother to Hopewell, I didn't get to see
Joyce as often. I had to take my turn at the night shifts at Hercules
Powder, so we only got together once or twice a month. Joyce kinda
got used to this schedule and our love remained just as strong. Joyce
did say that she had a friend to see and would be away for awhile. I
didn't sense anything wrong when I went to visit the next few times
even though Joyce wasn't home. Her mother or someone would be
there and say she hadn't returned yet.

One day I ran into Agnes Skelton and she said Mrs. Taylor wanted
to see me. She didn't say why. When I went to see Joyce's mother, she
tried to explain why Joyce did what she did and why Joyce didn't want
to be burden to me. She tried to elaborate on the details, and I was a
little confused but I finally realized Joyce was dead.

The funeral had already taken place when Mrs. Taylor had given
me the news. When Joyce developed or had found out about her heart
condition, I don't know. I didn't know when she died; nor did I ask.
All that mattered was that Joyce was gone.

Six or seven months later I was doing a survey for King Electric for some street lighting. It was on a Saturday and I was by Lee School when Agnes stopped me. She asked if I knew that Joyce had died. The hurt was just as powerful as when I first found out. You never get over the loss of a true love.

FIRST LOVE

A hurried trip to southeastern
    Virginia in somewhat of a race
I found myself on a familiar street
    with things out of place.
Strange how I heard the
    voices and laughter of my friends,
It was here between youthful play
    my first love I did win.
The warmth of Joyce on my shoulder
    as she roughly squeezed my arm,
That touch which told of her love
    a natural barrier from all harm.
Our friends knew not of our love
    the change was talked about.
Absence from evening play was
    never questioned with a doubt.
We had nothing, but it was
    enough for her and me
Guess our friends could not see
    love setting us free.
Bad health quickly came her way,
    a note told of a friend she went to see.
Her mother said, after the funeral,
    a burden she did not want to be.
Strange how I feel Joyce's
    warm hand at times.

New Career

After giving Hercules Powder two week's notice, I went over to King Electric and asked for a job. We still lived above the store, so I was familiar with the store and the two King brothers, Paul and Clarence. Paul said, "I don't have anything for you to do." He acted as if I had been foolish to quit such a good-paying job at Hercules. After a couple days of my persistence, he relented and gave me a job straightening things up and cutting glass. Paul was an excellent glass cutter, and he taught me how to cut and polish glass for coffee tables, which were the rage then. My wages were only seventy-five cents per day. I guess Paul figured that for 75 cents a day he'd soon get rid of me unless I was really dedicated. The way I looked at it was that now I had my foot in the door and I was going to learn a trade. I had heard that in some places you actually had to pay for an apprenticeship.

I did my job OK, but I also schooled myself on every electrical item they carried in that store. At night I would take the catalogs home and study them. Within the first six weeks I worked there, I could recognize by name most of the components of the electrical trade. I didn't know what they were for, but I could identify them.

I knew Archie Kendrick was a good electrician. I'd seen him in the store several times, but he was always too busy to talk to me. Archie had owned his own business, Hopewell Electric, but it had gone under. He just didn't have enough capital to keep it going when people didn't pay him on time. Now he ran two crews for King Electric, and the financial backing for both the store and the electrical operation came from W.L. Broaddus, a local businessman.

Archie came into the store one day and was talking to Paul. "I gotta have a helper, I can't do everything and can't afford to hire another crew."

"Well," Paul said, "Take Teddy and see if you can do something with him."

My timing was great. With the war winding down and the GIs returning home, a tremendous housing expansion was on the way. My start was nothing fancy though. With a brace and bit, I was the new hole driller. We only had one electric drill, and that went to the crew that had the most holes to drill that day. Quickly I learned the right place to drill for the new wiring, for a hole in the wrong place was a lot of wasted energy.

Business was starting to boom, but for a couple years it was really tight. Paul took very little income from the store. Even though Archie got a regular salary, it wasn't a lot. There was a constant struggle to keep ahead of the bills and make the crew payroll.

Archie took me under his wing and taught me as much as he had time to. After work I read every electrical manual and book I could find. Probably I studied more than I had in all my years at school. Archie showed me how to read plans and figure an estimate for a job. He would methodically figure the wiring measurement for each outlet, and it seemed to take forever to get the estimate. I suggested a faster way to do it all. "Why don't I count the outlets needed, you figure the square footage, and we'll come up with a standard figure for each outlet. If we come up short, we'll add more the next job." He went along with that idea, and we started basing our estimates on seven dollars per outlet and a dollar per amp service. It cost around $340 to wire a typical house.

Soon we had four crews working, sometimes wiring three houses per day. One day I said to Archie, "It's not fast enough."

He looked at me, "Who the hell do ya think you are?" "Hey, fella, I got a stake in this too. It's my job here," I said. "If I can't make you a dollar, I know I'm out the door. If you can't make it, your ass is goin' right out with me." Well, I don't think he wanted to hear this out of a sixteen-year-old kid, and he looked ready to fight. After awhile he cooled down, and it seemed to sink in that I was just interested in seeing the company succeed. Shucks, this was the only life I knew, and I figured it was better to grow with a small company than to be with a big one and just get told what to do all the time.

We were overworked and still couldn't keep up with all the new work coming in. More crews were needed, but Archie didn't have time to train them, and he didn't feel that he could afford to split his crews so they could train them. His men were certainly competent, but he doubted that they were company-oriented enough to care about training someone new. We were working 10 to 14 hours a day, six to seven days a week, and things were getting tense. It all came to a head on an afternoon at Fort Lee.

They had constructed some barracks for the lady soldiers (WACS), and were installing electrical wiring for some washer/dryer units and also some night lights. The lights were connected for three-way switches, and one of the wires between two switches was not working. Archie was trying to figure out how to make the switch work without tearing out the cable, which would have been a big job. I stood there watching him critically. He said, "I'll work this out." He knew that I didn't know how to hook it up.

Not knowing when to leave well enough alone, I said, "Archie, that's not right."

Archie was tired and had tried to be patient, "God damn it, I told you I knew what I was doin'," he said, and started to take a swing at me. I caught his arm and now we were both off balance and down the long flight of stairs we went right outside to the ground. He was on top of me trying to swing, and I was trying to deflect his arms away from my face. A laugh came from above. "You boys got an argument here?" It was the Colonel from the post.

I replied, "We're goin' settle this sooner or later."

"That's all right, you boys carry on," and he walked away. That stopped Archie. We really weren't mad at each other, just tired and frustrated.

"OK, you set your ass right there on the steps, and I'll hook up the light." I sat there waiting for him to blow the place up. Pretty soon he asked me to try the switch downstairs. It worked. We switched the lights off and on several times from each position. "See smart ass, if you'd just listen you'd know something. I can't beat anything into your damn head."

"You haven't told me anything yet." It looked like we were going to get into it again when he suggested we go down to the post exchange to get something to eat.

We were both half-starved. When we had finished eating, he pulled out a napkin and pencil and explained the three-way switch. That was the beginning of my electrical training, and as Archie put it, learning to control electrical current.

Even though we were damn busy, we always kept our eyes open for bigger and more profitable jobs. Having done a considerable amount of work at Fort Lee, we got wind of the availability of this big contract for shops where parachute manufacture and training were to take place. Each shop required about 1000 light fixtures. In those days, contracts were awarded in a rather loose fashion, not necessarily to the lowest bidder, but usually to someone they felt had experience and could handle the job. The trouble was that they wouldn't award us that big of a job unless we were bonded. Well, Paul got ahold of W.L. Broaddus about the bond. As I said before, W.L. had been Paul's financial backer for both the store and electrical business. In the store came W.L. and he walked past Paul, and was asking for Archie. Paul was an excellent salesman and businessman, but a piss poor estimator and W.L. knew that. Archie wasn't there right then and he looked at me, "Teddy, you think they can make any money on that Fort Lee shop contract?"

"Well, if they stay off of their dead asses they can."

We got the bond assurance from W.L. When it came time to sign the contract, W.L. said, "Teddy, you put your John Henry right after Archie's and then you can make sure they don't sit on their dead asses."

I said, "Why do you want me to sign that? I haven't got a pot to piss in."

"You sign it anyway, so if anything goes wrong I can come after your ass too."

The contract for the shops at Fort Lee was our biggest one ever. Because I had my name on the contract, I spent a little extra time going over the general blueprints and specifications for the job. In reviewing the specifications, where it called for certain kind of lights to be furnished, it didn't say who was to furnish them and there was nothing in the detail specifications either. That certainly was a slip up. I went and got another copy of the specifications, and sure enough that one read the same. Well, I jumped in the truck and went over to see Archie. "Hey, Archie, I know you're pretty busy, but when you planning on starting on those shops?"

His reply was, "Why don't you just take that job."

Showing the enthusiasm of an eager young businessman, I said, "OK, I'll just do that. You know that the lights need to be ordered for that project?"

"I know that needs to be done."

I proceeded, "Do you want me to handle this as I see fit?"

"Yep."

"OK, tell you what, you're going down to Fort Lee, would you pick up a copy of their specs for me?" I just wanted to make sure that their copy said the same as the other two, and when Paul returned I found out it did.

I got a crew busy tearing apart the first two buildings. I called Tom Webber, a sales representative for Tower and Benford, and told him I needed ten thousand light fixtures. He said, "Teddy, this is 1948, I don't know whether there are that many in the country."

I asked him the price and he said $11 a piece. "You mean we're buying ten thousand fixtures, and that's what you're charging? If we have to, we can get the specs changed and buy somewhere else. Round it off to $10 and we can do business." He agreed.

When the light fixtures were in our warehouse, I was on my way to Fort Lee's Purchasing and Contracts Office. Mr. Drake was the purchasing agent, and I said, "Mr. Drake, where are the light fixtures for those ten shops?"

He looked at me kinda funny, "Ted, the contractor is supposed to furnish those."

"That's not what the specifications say."

"Well, let's take a look," and he went to get a copy of them. "This is a misprint, let's look at the detail." I already knew that the detail didn't mention the fixtures. "Ted, it's just a misprint."

"Well, sir, if it's a misprint, that's what we based our bid on, you furnishing the fixtures."

"I'll have to see about this," was his reply.

"Mr. Drake, I'm too busy to hang around here. I'll see you in the morning."

Next morning Mr. Drake relented, "Ted, I guess we'll have to furnish the fixtures."

"Well, sir, we're going to need them real soon or my men will be held up on the job, and then you'll be responsible for their wages until the material arrives." He was wound up tighter than a two-dollar watch when I left.

My next move was to call the Tower and Benford salesman from whom I had bought the fixtures. I told him the Army wanted to purchase the same number fixtures we had bought, and they'd need them pretty quick. I gave him Mr. Drake's number. After he confirmed the Army's need, he called me back up and said he didn't think that there were any more fixtures like that which would be available in less than a month. I offered to sell them back to him for $13 a piece, plus what his normal shipping and handling would be, a dollar and fifty cents. For another fifty cents we'd deliver them to Fort Lee. A round $15 and he grabbed at it.

I was real proud of myself for using a little ingenuity to take advantage of a contract error and do some good for the company. Let's see. I saved the company $100,000 for getting the government to furnish the fixtures that we were supposed to supply, and on top of that another $5 apiece, $50,000 by buying up the fixtures ahead of time and reselling them. Needless to say, we now had plenty in our petty cash fund, and Paul was real elated at how well the company had done. "From now on," he said, "it will be your job to thoroughly go over every specification that comes through these doors."

"But I've only got an eighth grade education!"

"Doesn't matter, what you lack must make you extra sharp, so that's what you're going to do."

Neither Paul nor Archie knew all the details of this deal. They knew that the company had made good money on the project and that through careful reading of the contract I had made them even more. What they didn't know was that through some pretty shady deception on my part, we had fleeced the government. It was on my shoulders, but I figured the right thing was for this company to do well and for me to have a secure job. There were probably a lot worse things being done to the government in those times anyway.

Archie hit the roof when he found out I had spent a good chunk of company money for a fancy dictionary. "I make this company a lot of money and you bitch about this." He backed off when I explained to him that my English was not too good, and I had to know for sure what I was reading in the small print.

It was a lot of responsibility reading those contracts, and my lack of knowledge made me work even harder, going over each one with a fine tooth comb. I certainly made my way with King Electric, and I did find more errors and opportunities to save or make them extra money. I also developed kind of a cutthroat business attitude that anything I did was justified as long as it made the company money.

Along with reading contracts, I was still doing a lot of studying to get my electricians's license, which I didn't have yet. The license was issued after you had passed a test administered by city officials. The test was kind of a good old boy operation, but I wanted to make sure I got it. Also, another thing happened that changed my career direction a little.

We had a bank of transformers to change on a forty-foot service pole, and although I had worked on poles before with yard lights and service connections, I had never attempted a transformer change. There was a wooden cross arm on the service pole that the transformers hung on; one transformer on each side of the pole. I felt confident that I could do the job and had post maintenance shut off the power. Unhooking the old transformers was no big deal, and I managed to work them in from the arm to the center and lower them without too much trouble. The problem was that the new 5-KVA transformer weighed close to 325 pounds, where the old 3-KVAs were about 250 pounds. If I would have hoisted the new ones directly to their position on the arm, it wouldn't have been a problem. But fearing the weight would break the arm, I instead hoisted them up the center and tried to work them out in position. I fought those damn things all day long, but I knew I had to do the job. I'll tell you my ass was draggin' come the end of the day and I told myself there's got to be a better way to do this. I'm going to the power company, learn to become a lineman, and find out how to do this right.

It was more than this one instance that sparked my interest in linemen. As a kid I remember being fascinated by watching them work way up high on the poles, and I also can recall live power lines flashing together after storms so I figured it was both a challenging and dangerous job.

Becoming a lineman certainly was a challenge, but in this time frame another challenge was to present itself which would eventually become a more formidable one.

It was in 1949 that I met Evelyn Louise Miller. She was a waitress in a grill not too far from work and a young lass that caught my eye. I sensed it was more than just another conquest for this eighteen-year-old. We spent a lot of time visiting when I went in to get something to eat and eventually I found myself rolling in there on a regular basis around six or six-thirty each evening. I'd order a grilled cheese sandwich or hamburger, shoot the bull, and then walk her home. Eventually we started going out on some dates to the movies and got more serious. She had a rough life as I did. Her mother died when she was ten and she was raised by her brother and father.

As time went on, we figured we were in love and decided to get married. All my friends tried to talk me out of this idea, even W.L. Broaddus said, "Boy, you better know what you're doing. Marriage is a lifetime commitment." Ignoring their good judgment, I got married anyway. I rented a house in Hopewell and set up housekeeping.

In February of 1950 I went to work for Virginia Electrical Power Company and started training to become a lineman. Things at King Electric had slowed down anyway, and I passed my test and received my electrician's license from Chief Cutterhide who gave them out down at the firehall. Although I worked for the Power Company, I never really quit King Electric as I still worked there Saturdays and sometimes on Sunday.

At the power company I started out as a groundman and worked my way up to a level of experience that allowed me to obtain a first-class lineman rating in May of 1953. That year I left Virginia Electric and returned full time to King.

At Virginia Power Company I became associated with the union for the first time. Before I returned to King Electric, I spent considerable time trying to convince Paul that going union would allow his business to expand, with a larger, more stable pool of electricians to handle big contracts. Paul was not convinced. "I don't want some damn union to tell me how to run my business."

Talking to Archie one day, I said, "The only reason I went to the Power Company was to learn the lineman trade, but if Paul isn't going to budge on this union thing, I can go to work for Bowman's over in Petersburg for a lot more money." That threat must have pulled the punch, for in April Paul called me in. "Teddy, I've decided to go union."

"OK, what's my position going to be in this?" I inquired.

"I'll need you to be superintendent," he said.

Without hesitancy on my part, I started laying out our course of action. "Unions can be greedy Paul. Better get ahold of W.L. and make sure the backup money is there when we need it." Next I expounded on my business philosophy, "Paul, this is not the same sixteen-year-old kid that came through your doors a few years ago. Business is cutthroat and dog-eat-dog. If we can't beat the competition, we either buy him up or break him. Forget all those things your mother taught you down in North Carolina."

King Electric expanded with leaps and bounds in the years after my return. Paul told Archie and I straight out that he would handle the contracts and lining up the money, but we would have to manage the field work and not to bother him with the details. Work was plentiful; industrial, hospitals, and plenty of military housing projects. W.L. Broaddus who backed us and provided bonding for so long was not able to provide the scope of our needs now. John Irving now took over in that capacity, at least on the housing projects. John Irving had been successful as an engineer and then he joined his father who had a big plumbing business in Hopewell. He was a man born with the ability to make money, and he was not hesitant in sharing his ideas. One thing of particular that I learned from him was a philosophy on how to apply labor for maximum productivity and profit. His contention was that it was better to hold off on a project until a deadline forced the use of a maximum amount of electricians on overtime to complete it. He said that men working longer hours on time and a half or even double time with a deadline to meet had a lot more incentive to bust their butts. They knew that with the extra money that they were making in overtime, when the project was done, they could afford to sit for a lot of days without worrying.

Archie didn't believe in John Irving's philosophy. He was a penny-pincher and if the job required nine men, he would put eight on the job long before the deadline. I wanted to try it John's way, so I would wait until everyone was screaming to get the job done, then go in there with an oversize force, run long shifts, and in the end come out money ahead of Archie. The quality of the workmanship was probably not as good, but the job got done on time. The men then had plenty of days off to rest up, and with extra cash.

We also were trying to expand into the Richmond area. Another firm, Southside Electric, had been our major competition there, and I told Paul they were becoming a real thorn in my side. Eventually, King was able to buy Southside which provided a total pool now of approximately 200 union electricians. This gave both companies added flexibility in shifting our labor force between projects and allowed for more expansion.

We were now working on multi-million dollar contracts. We were hooked up with F. W. Dodge, a consulting firm, which would provide for a service fee listing of bids and their size available within certain regions. In addition, they would provide pretty accurate labor and material assessments for our bids.

We were in the big time now, and more and more, making money was the most important thing in life. The end justified the means. Some things were done above the table and some below, but the bottom line was we had become a very successful company. We tried to concentrate on commercial and government projects rather than residential, because they made more money for us. I felt I had been instrumental in the business's success.

When I joined King, they were having trouble making the payroll, but now Paul could easily walk into a bank and draw out a million dollars. It wasn't just my contribution. Paul, Archie and his brother Doug all made it come together. We had fun, lots of problems, and some heartbreak too.

My work more and more become one of travel from project to project. I became the coordinator between the union project foreman and the company. I might initiate the start of a job at Fort Jackson in South Carolina, then go to Fort Bragg in North Carolina for another, and maybe finish one up at Fort Lee in Virginia, and then on to Quantico. The pressure and stress of all this was wearing me down. Too much of this business I was carrying around in my head and not enough was getting on paper.

There was also plenty of family-related stress in my life in addition to work. After we got married and bought the house in Heathsville, my father-in-law moved in. What was bad about this was that he was an alcoholic. In three years, we had three kids, and my tolerance for his drinking was quickly coming to its limit. I could put up with it to a degree. Hey, if the old dude wanted to go out and get drunk fine, let him come back and visit when he got sober. I just didn't want him in the house with me and the kids when he was in that condition. Supporting him was not the problem, supporting his habit was. We had terrible arguments. I insulted him, called him names, and raised all sorts of hell, but never hit him. As I think back on it, I think I should have physically thrown his ass out the door.

Most of the mishaps in my married life happened because I allowed them to happen. Sounds funny, but it's the truth. I can understand a guy occasionally getting loaded, but every time he got $10 or $20, he was drunk. I didn't see why I had to live with it and support it. Of course, Evelyn sided with her father in all the fights, and our marriage was on the rocks already.

Finally I arranged to get her father a job with Al Sly over in Hopewell. I got him an apartment there, and he worked as a tinsmith cutting ducts for furnaces. He proved to be an excellent worker in that field and also as a carpenter and painter.

I was determined my kids were not going to be raised around a drunk. In our last big blowup before he went to Hopewell and the job, I told him and Evelyn that he could do whatever he wanted to, but not in my house. "You behave and not get drunk, you can stay here from now on. When you bring your whiskey in my house, you set a bad example for my kids and your ass is going out the door." Evelyn started jumping up and down about that and raising hell, and I said, "If that's the way you feel about it, you can go right along with him."

Another thing that certainly added to our family strife was that I was on the road a lot, sometimes for two or three weeks. Evelyn could not handle that and was always on my back. Between the family and the job stress, something had to give as I was getting real tired of it.

I approached Paul one day and said that I wanted to start and finish one job like Archie and everyone else, and that I was tired of traveling around. He seemed sympathetic and agreed to leave me on the next job until it was finished.

At Fort Lee we had several projects going, so I was assigned to work with Archie on the new John F. Kennedy Hospital being constructed there. We had the Kennedy Hospital project out of the ground when along came Paul who stated that he wanted me to move over to the Muffin Hall job, which was also at Fort Lee, and get that going. Muffin Hall was the new Central Administration Building and involved an up-to-date computer system. I explained to Paul that Archie had more experience than myself to handle such a project, and besides, he had already promised that I could see the hospital project straight through. I fully intended to hold him to that promise and stated that if he took me off of that job I was going to pack my bag and go home. Guess he didn't believe me, but I meant it.

I think it was on a Tuesday that Archie came over and said that he was taking over the hospital and I was to proceed to the Muffin Hall job. I said OK and got some cardboard boxes to pack up all my stuff. From there I didn't go anyplace except home.

It wasn't long before Paul came over asking for me to come back. I said that I realized he may have had good reasons to shift me over to the other project, but that if he couldn't keep his promise he shouldn't have made it. "I'm tired of running all over the country for you or anybody else. I got a family that needs me." Actually it was a sign of the times that fathers were away for long periods working for a living and mine wasn't any worse off than anyone else's. The fact was though, that I missed the family and wanted to be with them. I'd seen enough of this country and didn't want to see anymore of it. Paul said, "Does this make us enemies? What are you going to do now?" I had in the back of my mind going to work for Willie White, another contractor, and as I hesitated to answer Paul's question he came out with an offer. "Why don't you take over the hospital boiler and generator hookup as an independent. You know the price of labor. I'll pay you that plus all expenses." I agreed, for I knew that when he included expenses, in that respect the company was generous. When I was traveling all over the country expenses meant tires and auto repairs in addition to my hotels and meals. He knew though that I had established a reputation as a dedicated company man and could be relied on to do what I was supposed to do and be there on time.

I remember once I was busy down at Fort Hood in Texas and was supposed to be up at another job at Fort Bragg in a couple of days. I knew it would take too long to drive it, and rather than hopping on a bus and being late, I used my horse sense and wrangled a military flight. I asked the sergeant in charge of the flights if they had any flights going that way and that I had all the proper security clearances. He looked at my identification and said I could go but doubted if I could get on because the flights were awfully full. I asked him what kinda whiskey he and the boys liked and with a case promptly delivered, I was on my way to Fort Bragg.

Now that I had things straightened out with Paul, and more time to spend with the family, I was determined to make another change in our lifestyle. I moved the family out on a farm where the kids would have a good chance to grow up in a wholesome environment.

I located a nice 150 acre farm for $18,000. I had saved up a pretty good chunk of money, but still needed to borrow some more to swing the deal. When Paul's brother Clarence died, I found out to my surprise that he had been putting part of my pay into a bank account on a regular basis for a long time, and that I had $7500 dollars there. After some thought, Paul agreed to loan me the other $5000 I needed. The payments would be spread out so that if things went bad, I could still make my payments on unemployment money. This made good sense to me, so all was agreed.

Actually, the farm was 160 acres, but Samuel Spain, the owner, wanted to keep six acres with access to a big two-acre pond that was really well stocked with fish. In fact, my boy caught a record small mouth bass outta there. Samuel was a real nice fellow. When he moved off the farm, he left all the farm tools for my use. The trouble was, I didn't have enough money left over to actually start farming. I leased my tobacco allotment of two point three acres to a neighbor, Mr. Hardgrove, and worked out a deal with another fellow to jointly use the soybean allotment. Also, I let another man run some cattle on the fields just to graze the weeds down. What I wanted to do now was save up some money to get the farm going.

The house was an old one, but pretty big with a lot of possibilities. There was water inside, but no bathroom, just an outhouse. I began bringing plumbing scraps home from work so that by the next spring I could install a bathroom.

By the next spring, I didn't have enough money to put in the bathroom thanks to the father-in-law problem recurring. Although he had a good job, every time he got some money in his pocket he would blow it on booze. We would get a phone call and over to Hopewell I would have to go with $10 or $20, sometimes $50, to help pay the old man's rent because he was short. Finally, later that year the phone calls and his whimpering came so often that I had the phone disconnected. Unfortunately that was a short-term fix for a long-term problem.

I continued to do projects as an independent for King Electric and also went to work for K&M Plumbing, which did work all over Virginia. Willie White was an industrial contractor and ran the company. I had done some electrical work for him on a Contrail Can Company contract some time ago and made him a bunch of money. He wanted to hire me away from King at the time, but I turned him down. He was too much of a pusher, even more so than King.

Working for Willie turned out OK. He was a fun guy to work for and although he had a lot of business, the projects were of a smaller scale. Along with electrical work, I was doing plumbing. I felt I needed experience in this trade too. I had more or less learned plumbing by watching Willie's men on the job during the Contrail job. I stayed with Willie until 1961 when we moved to Florida.

After less than a year on the farm, Evelyn started complaining. We had another kid, and she missed the conveniences of the city. Finally, to make peace, I said to hell with it and told Samuel he could have the farm back. I put $250 down on a house in Blackstone and moved off the farm, losing a good chunk of money in the process.

In Blackstone, things settled down for awhile. Father-in-law moved back in with us, and then one day it dawned on me how convenient I'd made things for him. He was within easy walking distance of the liquor store, so he could go there and bring his whiskey back home. I didn't do myself one damned bit of good moving to Blackstone. Another big fight erupted and the marriage continued to slide downhill. "I didn't marry your family or your daddy, and I'm not going to put up with this shit." In plain English I said, "All you do is love your daddy and yourself, and I'm just your pawn to support your everyday livin'. Someday I'm gonna find somebody to love and raise these kids and I'm gonna leave your ass right where I found it." Little did I know then that I would hold true to that threat.

It was a hell of a blowup, but finally I said that we'd just leave the state. She'd been talking about Florida anyway, and that's where my mother now lived. Mother had married again, this time to Adolph Watko.

We left Father-in-law the Blackstone house, and I packed the whole family, five kids now, in a station wagon and trailer and we headed to Florida. The year was 1961. What we didn't have room for, we left. I didn't even call my mother and tell her we were coming.

In Jacksonville, Florida, we moved into an apartment which was owned by Olita Smith, the lady that sold my mother her house. She was a fine person and let us stay there rent-free until I could pay her back.

I went to work for Sam Phebie doing the electrical work for air conditioners all around Jacksonville. It was just the kind of job I wanted because it gave me an opportunity to learn my way around the city. Within two months, I could take you about any place in Duval County, including the surrounding communities, Mandrian, Live Oaks, and the rest. In addition to that job, I also worked part-time for Sam's brother Clarence. Clarence used to work for Sam but broke off and started his own business and had an arrangement to do maintenance and new construction for the Winn Dixie stores. He was trying to go union, but hadn't made it yet. I earned a good chunk of change with him, probably an extra $2000 or so. It didn't do any good though. I would bring $100 in the front door, and the old lady would take $125 out the back.

I knew I had a problem here and didn't think I was gonna have much luck teaching her responsibility. Women's liberation was getting a lotta attention then, and she just wasn't showing much interest in keeping the marriage vows. Hell, seemed like it wasn't even worth having a wife if I had to put up with that shit.

Sometimes, to keep the pressure off and keep her mouth shut, I'd take her over to Craig Field Armory and listen to country music. I didn't know how to dance, so Evelyn would dance with some other guys while I listened to the music. A neighbor from the trailer park, Beatrice Miller, and her husband were there. She continually badgered me to get out on the dance floor. I finally said, "OK, if you don't mind me stepping on your feet." I didn't do too bad, but Evelyn was really mad because I danced with the lady. It was all right for her to dance with other guys, but it wasn't acceptable for me to dance with our neighbor, even with her husband there. At the armory is where I met Mary. Later on she told me that she had noticed me several times, but I hadn't seen her before. Anyway, somehow she and the old lady got together and she ended up over at our table talking with us. While the old lady was out prancin' around on the dance floor, Mary and I had a nice visit. I could see the way she talked about kids she thought they were pretty special, and the fact was, this woman wasn't married. I remembered what I had told Evelyn about finding a good woman to take care of my kids, and I said to myself, "Here's the kinda woman I need, right here." These were my thoughts, but little did I realize how soon Mary Adams would be part of my life.

My grandma, Grace Thomas (left) and her sister Maggie, who lived with us.

Below: Grandma with one of the kids.

Ted, his mother Helen and daughter Effie

Sailor on right: Wallace Edwards who married my cousin Cecil. On left: my cousin Bill Roberts, Maggie's boy.

Mary Adams

I was born in Wytheville, Virginia. It is located 90 miles north of Bristol, Tennessee, and about 35 miles east of Bluefield, West Virginia, which was the closest big town. Wytheville was famous because George Wythe was one of the signers of the Declaration of Independence.

My mother's name was Leona Glady Phipps. She was full-blooded Indian; half Cherokee and half Crow. Dad's name was William Howard Adams and he was three-quarters Indian and one-quarter German. The Indians called half-breeds like me apples; red on the outside and white inside. With all of the Indian in me, and the fact I was brought up in the Blue Ridge Mountains, I guess I could be considered an Indian Hillbilly.

The Crow and Cherokee tribes were never very friendly towards one another so when my grandmother, a Cherokee, married William Franklin Phipps, a Crow, she was banished from the Cherokees. Her name was wiped off the slate as if she never existed. She and Grandpa lived on an Indian Reservation at Beckly, West Virginia. That's where my mother was born. I don't remember my mother's daddy; guess he was dead before I was born. I do remember my grandma though, and even though I was only about three or four, I remember following her through the mountains as she looked for herbs. Grandma was an Indian medicine lady. She was a little woman, probably didn't weigh more than 80 pounds, but she was spry. Her name was Sarah Elizabeth, but I called her Little Mama.

Grandma knew how to prepare herbs into medicines for about any ailment. Of course, on the trips into the mountains for herbs, I was more interested in playing than anything else. When Grandma would find a patch of something she was looking for, I loved to grub around and help her dig it up. Grandma had a coat like magicians have with lots of pockets both inside and out. In each pocket she had one or more small bags like they used to have tobacco in. There, she carried the herbs as she gathered them. I wished I had been older to pay more attention to what she was doin'. I know she gathered ginseng, different berries, witch hazel, wormweed, wild indian tobacco, and dock root, which you know as burdock. Fresh dock root cut into wheels and hung around a baby's neck would relieve teething pain when he chewed on them. When it was dried and made into a tea, it was good for relieving cold problems, sore throats and chest pains. Little Mama never said much when things were going right. When she needed to, she would say something, but she never raised her voice and showed any temper. She'd come and visit for awhile, and then be gone for several months. Where she went, I don't know, back to the reservation maybe or healin' other Indians in the mountains.

We lived in the mountains with my dad's folks. Grandma Adams was a half-breed, Cherokee and German, but she was dark complected with raven black hair that hung down to her fanny. Her eyes were yellow like a cats; she was a beautiful lady.

I called Grandpa Pa, and my dad Papa. Grandpa was Cherokee and a big man, probably at least 6'4". When I wasn't following Little Mama around the mountains for herbs, I was following Grandpa around the farm. Guess I was a little bit of a tomboy, 'cause I didn't care much for dresses. I did love to climb into a pair of my cousin's bib overalls and trail behind Grandpa, getting pretty grubby along the way.

One day Grandpa was clearing a new field for a corn patch. At the end of the field where the woods started, he turned around to me and said that I should always look where I was going and absorb what I saw. Right where he stood a tree limb stuck out with a pretty fair sized hornet's nest glued on. He grabbed the limb, bent it back, and turned her loose. Of course the first direction the limb flops is the direction the hornets come out. I hit the ground fast, and the hornets exited right above me. Grandpa didn't say anything, just walked off. I didn't say anything either, but later I found this old dead stump at the end of the field. It was about my size, and I put my arms around it with the intention of pulling it loose. After a little shaking, I could hear some buzzing and discovered a nest of yellow jackets underneath. I eased off of the stump and walked back to where Grandpa was and told him I couldn't get the stump out. He said, "I'll get it." While he finished grabbin' out the roots he was working on, I moved upwind of the stump to the side of the hill. Grandpa went over to the stump and squatted down. He wrapped his arms around it, pulled, and out came the stump and the yellow jackets. The bees were all over Grandpa and up his pant legs. Grandpa always wore long underwear, red wool ones in the winter and white cotton ones in the summer. He had quickly shed his overalls and was dancin' around in his white underwear trying to get rid of the bees. Afterwards, he didn't say a word to me about the incident nor I to him, but I'm sure he told Grandma about it. Guess he knew then that I was paying a whole lot of attention to what was goin' on.

I can still see Grandpa in his old grey felt hat. He wore it all the time except for meals when Grandma told him to take it off. It hung on a chair while he ate, but as soon as he was through it went right back on his head. I once asked Grandma if he wore it to bed at night when he slept. She said he didn't, just hung it on the bedpost.

One of Grandma's best friends was a black neighbor lady I called Aunt Anny. I guess if it hadn't been for Aunt Anny, I wouldn't be here now. Grandma said that when my daddy was born she didn't have any milk to nurse him, and if it hadn't been for Aunt Anny, he'd have died. Fortunately Aunt Anny had just had a baby a few months before, so she volunteered to nurse Daddy too. Grandma said that at feedin' time Aunt Anny would come down and she'd have her baby on one boob and Daddy on the other. Didn't seem to bother Daddy that he'd been raised that way. It must have been good for him 'cause he grew pretty fast and tall. Guess nobody held much prejudice in those days, just did what was necessary to get along.

These were years after The Depression, when we were living with Dad's folks. Nobody had much of anything, and yet we never lacked for the necessities. It was a good life. Grandpa farmed a little, hunted, trapped, and made moonshine. Papa worked for the Work Projects

Administration (WPA) and then the Civilian Conservation Corps (CCC). These were both created by President Roosevelt to provide jobs during the Depression. These jobs only paid seventy-five cents a day or so, but in those times that bought what $20 would today. He worked on roads, bridges, and whatever other projects the government could dig up to keep men busy.

As I grew older, I really liked to go fishing. Usually I'd go with my mother and a friend of hers, a black lady named Flower Bowen. The trouble was that the shortest way to the fishin' hole was through this pasture where a black bull was kept. Every time that bull saw us cuttin' across his pasture, he'd be after us, and Mama's friend Flower was really scared of him.

One day I was goin' fishing by myself and there was that bull grazin' at the far end of the field. I decided I was tired of bein' chased by that blasted bull, and I had an idea of how to fix him. There was one lone old hickory tree in the field where I was going to cross. I went over and stood about 20 feet from the tree and started shakin' myself to get old bull's attention. I did a good job stirrin' him up 'cause he stood down there snortin' and pawin' the ground gettin' mad as hell. Finally, he came charging in my direction. I remembered bein' told that bulls close their eyes just before they hit ya, but cows don't. I held my ground as long as I could, then scooted around on the other side of the tree. Guess the timing was about right and old bully had closed his eyes 'cause he hit the old hickory and knocked himself out. I thought I'd killed him, so I ran off. When I came back from fishing, I see he wasn't dead. He'd just got up, and he was pretty shaky and dizzy acting. I went over to see if I could aggravate him a little more, but he just turned his back to me and walked off. He never did bother anybody again. I didn't tell Grandpa what I did though, as he probably would have tanned my hide.

Things were going good until tragedy struck our family. Grandpa was shoein' the mule one day and when he bent down to pick up a shoein' tool, the mule kicked him in the head. Grandpa always warned me to never turn my back on a mule. He'd say, "A mule will wait 20 years just to get you in the right spot, then kick ya." The mule got him right in the temple, and he never did regain consciousness.

Grandpa was in his fifties when he died. That would make my dad about twenty-six or so. In those days when someone died, you didn't haul him out of the mountains to a funeral parlor. Instead, some member of the family bathed and dressed him, and he was laid out in a main room of the house. I don't know how the word got out, but a lot of kin and friends came to pay their respects and to sit with the family through the night. The dead person had to be buried pretty fast 'cause they weren't embalmed and would start to stink if they were left too long.

Grandpa was laid to rest in the family plot up on the mountain, and then life seemed to go on as it had before. Grandma was a strong woman, and she took over the farmin'. As busy as she was, I swear she had a set of those cat eyes in the back of her head too, 'cause I couldn't get away with anything.

When I was about five, Papa went to work in the coal mines. Mama told me that he didn't want to, but Grandma and the family needed some extra income and he felt he had to. It was about 1941 and the war was goin' strong. My uncles and cousins were headed to the service, but Papa was classified Four F and they wouldn't take him. I guess it was because he couldn't read or write. He couldn't even write his name at that time. He went to work in a mine in Greenbrier Holler, about 12 miles from Welch, West Virginia. After he got established, he moved us to Mount Bell Holler. Aunt Clara lived there and her husband worked in the mines. We lived about three miles from them, and then another two miles down the road was Aunt Rudy, my mother's younger sister. Her husband Earl had been drafted and fought in the Pacific. He was involved in the fight for a little island called Palaloo. He said the Japs had it nailed down tighter than the hinges of hell. It was in the Army's Timber Wolf Division that he fought. When he came back, he told about a lot of funny things that happened, but wouldn't talk about the rest of it. I heard he had real bad nightmares for a long time after the war had ended. Dad's younger brother-in-law, Wes, also lived around there and worked in the mines, so there was lots of family close by.

It was Christmas after Papa had started working in the mines that I wished for a doll. Mama said, "If you can wait just a little longer, you'll have a real doll to play with." We were staying with Grandma for awhile then. She started teaching me how to handle and bathe a baby by practicing with a rubber doll.

On the twenty-sixth of January, the doctor and his assistant arrived. I tried to watch through the keyhole to see what was goin' on. When he left, Grandma introduced me to my little sister. Was she ever tiny, red, and wrinkled. With her butt in my hand, her head wouldn't reach my elbow. Grandma let me give her first bath. I tried to lower her in the pan of water so carefully, but at the last minute she slipped in with a big splash. She was so tiny we carried her around on a pillow. At night Grandma put her and the pillow in a cardboard box by the stove.

None of the clothes that Grandma or Mama had made would fit her, so I took the clothes off my old baby doll and they fit fine. She was a very fragile baby health-wise. We all thought we were going to lose her a couple times. Any bug that was going around, she picked up. I spoiled her rotten, as did everyone else. She had so many close calls with sicknesses, we were all overly protective. Caring for her became a new responsibility for me, and she was the new centerpiece of the family.

While Papa was working in the mines, I got to see John L. Lewis. He was a Union organizer who really fought like hell to get better wages for the miners. What a big man he was, with bushy eyebrows. He got higher wages for the miners, a dollar fifty an hour, which was really good, but in some respects it ended up working against the miners. Now there was even more pressure on the miners to put out coal, and you could only dig out so much coal in eight hours.

It was in 1944 or '45 that they came in with this big screw drill called Moe. With this they could drill right through the layers of limestone, granite and slate, to the good coal. Coal would be in veins, first a layer of slate and then the hard coal and finally the good soft coal. Blue Beacon, Pocahontas, and the best, Red Ash. The coal tunnels would just follow the vein back into the mountain, sometimes eight or ten miles. They had these little five to ten car trains that would follow the rails back into the tunnel to haul out the coal.

The miners didn't wear any breathing protection, just bib overalls, a heavy blue shirt, and a hard hat with a carbide light on it. It was dangerous work. To begin with, breathin' that coal dust would eventually cause black lung, but also when they got in a pocket of methane gas, the carbide lights would set off a hell of an explosion killin' miners and trapping them underground. They also had what they called kettle rocks, which looked like a wash pot with dark rings around them. If they were jarred just right, they would come down unexpectedly and sometimes bring a good part of the mountain down with them.

One night Papa was headed to work, and I had this terrible feeling something bad was going to happen. I raised such a terrible fuss that he decided not to go in. That night a kettle rock came down and hit the train car he would have been riding in. It crushed three men to death. When Papa found out what had happened, it scared the crap out of him. It happened one other time that I had this feelin' that something bad was going to happen, and again he stayed home. That time the electric coal train set off a pocket of methane gas that buried 27 miners. It was in shaft Number Five, and it took them a long time to dig the men out, but only one man that was close to the explosion got killed.

Even though the miners made good money, a lot of times the paycheck was spent by the time it had arrived. The company would furnish scrip that could be spent like money in the company store. It was like chargin' stuff, and it was easy to get yourself in debt to the company. The company owned about everything, including the housing, which was rented to the miners at a minimum rate. They even had their own sawmill to cut timbers for the mine.

Another thing that sticks in my mind about the mines is the big ventilating fans they used. They would have these big air shafts to follow the mine back several miles in the mountain. The fans were huge and mounted to blow in the shafts. We kids could sit on a hill a long ways away and still feel the suction from those fans. Every so often we'd let loose a leaf or two and see how fast it got to the fan.

In 1947, with the war over, there was a lot of construction going on. Papa wanted to get out of the mines. He hadn't wanted to be in them in the first place, and as he said, he wasn't meant to be a damned gopher.

He started helpin' to build houses in Kingsport, Tennessee. We moved to Long Island, Tennessee, where Kodak had a big factory. Papa walked the fives miles each day to his construction job in Kingsport. I was about eight and my little sister about two then. We had a nice garden where we lived that spring, but towards the end of the year things went bad. It was shortly after Christmas and Papa had walked the five miles to work, but didn't make it home that evening. The old folks named Millhorn lived up on a hill about three miles from home and had a phone. They called Mother and told her Papa was in the hospital. Some man came and picked Ma up, and they dropped us off at the Millhorns. Ma told us afterwards that the man had stopped when he saw Papa sitting there beside the road. He asked if he was all right, and Papa said his right foot was all black, and he couldn't walk any farther. Papa had been walking back and forth with holes in his shoes, had gotten frostbite, and gangrene had set in. The man had taken him right to the emergency room, and they had rushed him in and amputated his right leg to about six inches below the knee. If they had waited longer, he might have died.

After Papa recovered he was sent to Walter Reed Hospital and taught how to use an artificial leg. Through some program the government furnished him the artificial leg, and then taught him a trade as an upholsterer. While he was gone, we managed to survive on vegetables we had preserved from the spring garden, but things were really short.

Before Papa came back, they told him that he should move to a warmer climate, otherwise he might lose the other leg. So, in 1949, he packed us all on a Greyhound bus, and we headed to Orlando, Florida. Papa's sister, Aunt Jenny, and her husband lived there. We stayed there for about three weeks with them, and then Papa got a job offer in Jacksonville. He started work there in an upholstery shop owned by a man named Jewell. The man also raised greyhound racing dogs. Papa worked there until 1952 when he took another job in a shop a little closer to where we lived.

There was a real problem in our family that I haven't talked about, and it had been goin' on as long as I could remember. Both Ma and Papa were real big drinkers, maybe alcoholics. They were not drinkin' all the time, but on weekends it was bad, and they had terrible fights. Most of the time Mama would get fights goin' when Papa would just want to sleep and rest. Eventually, the weekends were full of bitterness and yelling, and I had enough of it to last a lifetime. Another thing was gnawing at me, a good case of jealousy I guess. My sister had become the family favorite, and the partiality Ma and Papa showed her didn't seem at all fair. They said once that I had just been an accident when they were having fun, and I resented that. So, between the drinkin' and my feeling of isolation, I was lookin' for a way out.

At school lunch time, I would go over to White Castle to eat. For a quarter you could get two hamburgers, fries, and a small drink. That was better than what the school lunch could provide. I was thirteen going on fourteen with physical and mental maturity well beyond that. While at the White Castle one day, I met this nineteen-year-old Marine. He was stationed in South Carolina, but home on leave visiting his mother. I figured he was the best thing since corn flakes, and we dated while he was in Jacksonville. He was a silver tongued devil, just a slick talker who wanted to get in my britches. But I didn't let that happen. He was about through with his service hitch, and this looked like a good escape from my problems at home. So when he was discharged and came home, I married him. His mama went with us over to Valdosta, Georgia, to get married. I was underage and needed parental permission to get married, so his mother signed for me. The judge asked who she was, and I said my mother. So, we were married.

When my folks found out I had gotten married, they didn't seem to care one way or the other. I was expendable. As far as it being an escape for me, it was like jumping from the frying pan into the fire. I knew my husband didn't drink, and he didn't get in my britches until there was a wedding ring on my finger. I also knew I didn't love the man and that it was a great mistake getting married with those feelings.

When I was 15, my first baby was born. My husband treated me good and was generous and a good provider. By the time I was 27, I had five children. He was workin' at General Motors, and we lived in a small town outside of Atlanta. It didn't seem like we had a very loving marriage going, but he didn't drink and did a good job of sup-portin' the family, so I just busied myself takin' care of the kids, house, and his meals.

It was 1959, my husband and his buddies had this garage next door where they tinkered with old cars. Next to that was a small store from which I had just bought a fresh loaf of bread for supper. I stepped through the garage door planning to tell him what time supper would be ready, when I heard him tell his buddies, "Yeah, the only reason I keep her around here is to have a piece of ass when I can't find any someplace else." I was in the right place at the wrong time. I eased back out the doorway. They hadn't seen me.

I was hurt, confused, bitter, and who knows what else. Beyond the anger, things seemed to fit into place. I knew something big was lack-ing in our marriage, but I didn't know he had been running around on me. He was a good provider and not a drinker, but I felt betrayed.

I thought about my situation for several days and made up my mind that I was leaving. I had a friend who lived on the other side of the lake from us. He was a judge, so I went over to talk with him. I told him what my situation was and what I had heard my husband say. The judge said that it was pretty common knowledge that my husband was running around, so I guess I was just the last to find out. He asked me how much money I had, then said he'd loan me a hundred dollars. He advised me not to try to take the kids, assuring me he would make sure they were properly cared for. They would expect me to go south into Florida where my folks were, so I should go north. He would know where I was, and would keep me advised as to what was going on. Wishing me good luck, he gave me a contact for a possible job.

I loved those kids, but I was running. Where, I didn't know, but I couldn't take five kids. He had plenty of money to support them, and I wasn't sure how I'd support myself. For that reason the judge advised against trying to take the kids; there seemed little choice left.

The next day I left on a bus for Detroit, and from there I went to Windsor, Canada. In Windsor I located Jock and Babbet Deprue, a French couple whose names the judge had given me. They owned a little hole-in-the-wall restaurant and I went to work for them as a wait-ress. My wages were $30 a week, plus free room and board.

My little room was above the restaurant and had just a bed, chair and bathtub. Jock and Babbet had living quarters behind the restaurant. They were both excellent cooks. Babbet opened and cooked breakfast and Jock came in later and would cook the other two meals. They closed at 8 pm.

We were open six days a week so I was busy most of the time, and that was good. When I did have free time I would go around the corner to a little library and bury myself in a book.

I had regular telephone contact with the judge back home and he kept me advised on what was happening. He confirmed that my husband had been running around with the next door neighbor who was divorced with seven kids of her own. They had a warrant out for my arrest on desertion. My folks thought he had killed me and threw me in the lake. I had no contact with them either.

Within two months, I had earned enough to repay the judge's hundred dollars. He informed me that my husband had filed for divorce, and it had been granted with him having full custody of the children. At least now I was free and standing on my own two feet.

I had been with the Deprues for about a year when one day I was flipping through a newspaper and an ad in the job opportunity section caught my eye. A dairy farmer was advertising for a person to help milk his cows, and it didn't say male or female. Shucks, I knew how to milk cows. I applied for the job and surprisingly enough, was hired.

The dairy farm was located not too far north of Charlotte, Michigan. The farmer who hired me was in his forties and had just gone through a rough divorce. He was sour on women and, likewise, I wasn't looking for any male companionship, so it was only an employer-employee relationship. I had my own apartment, one half-beef each year, all the milk I wanted, plus $500 a month.

We milked about 70 Holstein cows and at milking time they stood in stanchions along both sides of a long alley. We would have to move the old Surge milkers from cow to cow. Later the farmer bought another farm and put in a milking parlor. This made things much easier, for the cows would just move through the same two pens and while they ate their grain we would have the milkers on them. They moved instead of us.

I worked real hard on the farm; seven days a week and long hours each day. Not only did I milk the cows, I also helped baling hay, filling silo and all the rest of the farm work. We were farming about 1200 acres and we needed some additional help so my employer hired a man in his mid-fifties. His name was Bill, and he was still there when I left.

Bill was a good worker and I can remember once when he gave me a good laugh. He was over in the same yard as this big bull we called Jerry. Well, Jerry started towards Bill in a threatening way and Bill decided it was time to get out of there. When Bill jumped over the fence he came right out of his boots and ended up in a pile of cow manure in his stocking feet. He did look comical standing there in that cow manure with his boots on the other side, and Jerry the bull looking on.

The farmer I worked for was a good person, but when things didn't go right he would go into a little tirade. He had a habit of throwing his narrow brimmed felt hat on the ground and then stomping on it as he unleashed a few choice words. Well, this one day we were cleaning out the combine to get ready for the clover seed harvest. This was not a job we looked forward to, and things were not going well. I knew the boss would be blowin' off steam soon and I was ready. All of a sudden he took off his hat and threw it on the ground, but before he could get to it, I was already stomping on it. He didn't say anything, just stood there looking surprised. Finally, he reached down and picked up his hat, blocked it back in shape, then climbed in his old El Camino and left. He was gone for quite awhile. The boss's best friend was the local John Deere tractor dealer, so I imagine he headed down there to tell him what had happened. I had a good laugh out of it anyway.

While I was at the farm I kept up correspondence with the French couple I had worked for in Canada. They were really nice people, and when the letters stopped coming from them I wondered what had happened. Finally someone sent me notice that they had both been killed in an auto accident.

I found out through the judge that my ex-husband had married the neighbor with the seven kids that he had been running around with. They had a real brood then, especially if they had any of their own. I decided it was time to make a change in my life too, so I left the farm in Michigan and headed to Florida.

It was in 1967, seven years after I left, that I returned to visit my parents. They couldn't believe it when they saw me. I guess they really thought I was dead. I explained to them what had happened, and that I had sought legal advice before taking action. I had no regrets or ill feelings. I had made a decision I was satisfied with. To this day I have had no contact with my children, four boys and a girl. I have hurt too much for too long and see no reason to hurt them or myself by attempting contact. I don't even have any ill will against my ex-husband anymore.

In Jacksonville I got myself an apartment and a job as a waitress in a little greasy spoon restaurant. One thing I especially remember about that restaurant was that six blind people came there on a regular basis to eat. They were the nicest people. A cab would drop them off out front and pick them up again when they were through eating. They told me they could tell which waitress I was by the sound of my footsteps.

I didn't know anyone around this area anymore, but I did start to get acquainted again down at the Craig Field Armory. Chuck Goddard was the manager of WJAX, a hillbilly radio station in Jacksonville and he played bass in the band at the Armory. I had gone to school with his kids so when I said hello he introduced me to the rest of the band. Chuck was divorced now, but he had a nice girl friend that played drums in the band. The guitar player was nicknamed Tiny. He stood 6'8" and weighed about 300 pounds.

They charged $1 a person for each Friday and Saturday dance. The band got that money plus the profits from the concession stand. As a favor I helped to run the stand for them. I didn't dance, so I could listen to the Country and 50s Rock and Roll music and serve out the food and drinks. The armory dance closed at eleven and then we'd all go over to the Veterans of Foreign Wars Club (VFW), and they would play there from 12 until 2 am.

That fall of '67 I met Ted. He came into the Armory with his wife and another man named Ralph Miller and his wife Bea. I don't know why, but I happened to take notice of Ted. While their wives were out dancing, Ted and Ralph sat at the table, Ted drinking coffee and Ralph guzzling beer. Ted looked like the loneliest man I had ever seen.

Ted's friend Ralph came over after some drinks and invited me over to the table for a drink when I could. I said I didn't drink anything except Coke. He said that was OK. Later I did go over and joined the table for awhile. I visited with the wives as well as the men. Ralph got up and danced with his wife and Evelyn danced with another man. Ted didn't know how to dance and neither did I so we talked for quite awhile.

Bea Miller was Ted's neighbor and she worked at a Supper Club called Trader Glicks. She said they had a waitress job opening, and wondered if I was interested. The owner was a little Jew called Clickstein, but for some reason was nicknamed Ducky. Well, he hired me and although the wages didn't amount to much the tips were great. I was earning about $150 a week, and that was real good in those days.

The next time I saw Ted and Evelyn at the Armory, Evelyn came over to talk and invited me over. I was friendly to her, but there was something there I didn't like. I also could sense something wrong between them, but I didn't know what and didn't figure it was any of my business.

Mary — age 13 — fishing in Trout River at end of Pearl Street in Jacksonville, Florida.

Mary's parents: William and Leona Adams

Ted with Bea and Ralph Miller who introduced him and Mary at the Craig Field Armory.

The Split Up

I'd been in Jacksonville for about two months working for Sam Phebie when I bought the house on Pellise Road. Evelyn was real happy. She said the house was just what she wanted, but within six months, she was back bitchin' again, said she wanted to be somewhere else.

It was on a Saturday, and I was just loading up the first load of the next move when Al Litky came up behind me. I had bought the house from him. "What's wrong Ted?"

"Well, there's nothing wrong with the house, Al. The woman is just dissatisfied, and I got another place over on Dorthia Road."

I paid him and he said, "Ted, I got lots of other places if you need to look again."

The new place was real nice, big old colonial house, five bedrooms, nice living room, big kitchen, and beautiful wood floors. Now, Father-in-law shows up from Virginia. I got mean and told him to get his ass out. Course, when I wasn't around, he was in visiting. It wasn't long before Evelyn was dissatisfied with this place. It was too hard for Daddy-in-law to get in from town, and there were no bars close around Riverdale.

Next I purchased a half acre in Clay County. It had a trailer on it and kept her happy for awhile, but it was not long before she wanted to move back into town. She was just plain unstable. Either the neighbors didn't treat her right or she'd find something else wrong. It was beginning to get rough on the kids. We had six by now, John 3, Effie 6, Stanley 8, Henry 12, Marsha 13, and Robert 14. Robert had the hardest time in school, but both he and Marsha were good students. Henry was not doing well in his studies.

I was gettin' hot to get away from this old lady and get someone to

look after these kids. I had about hit bottom. All the money I had
saved was gone along with my patience, and time was running out on
this marriage.

Mary and I had some more visits, and she said she'd take care of
the kids if I had some place for her to look after them. I didn't care
about this trailer we were living in, but I didn't want to lose the land,
so I came up with a plan to get things started in the right direction.

Evelyn and I headed to the Armory one night, and I knew Mary
would be there. I said to Evelyn, "Well, if we're going to move back
into town, we might as well sell the land and trailer." Later Evelyn
was telling Mary that she was moving back into town, and we were
going to sell that damned place. Mary said, "How much you want
for it?"

"Twenty-five dollars and you take over the payments," said
Evelyn.

"Here's twenty-five dollars," and Mary shoved the money across
the table. The only thing now, was to figure a way to get the kids
with Mary.

I moved the family up to a flat on Fourth Street, and I furnished it
with stuff from secondhand stores and what other people had put out
for the junkman. I had changed jobs awhile back and for five years
had worked in the Jacksonville shipyard.

I started out in the electrical shop working for a man named
Murphy, but that didn't last too long. Murphy was a big drinker, and
he made sure his fat cat friends got all the overtime while the rest of us
scraped by on basic time, which wasn't much. The union was weak
and wouldn't do anything about it, so one day I confronted him. He
wouldn't budge and accused me of being a troublemaker and said he
really didn't need me. Well, the feeling was mutual, so I collected my
tools and headed for the time machine to punch out for good. The
shop foreman, a man named Turner, told C.I. Stevens, the overall
shipyard superintendent, that I had quit. By the time I got to the time
clock to punch out, another supervisor called Pepper stood there
holding my time card, "Where ya going?"

"I'm gonna punch out and go home."

"Ted, you got a job here. I don't like Murphy either, he's a two-faced S.O.B."

In the shipyard they built new ships and also did extensive maintenance on others. Pepper's title was superintendent and he was in charge of overall dry dock maintenance at the shipyard. The dry dock was a large floating platform that raised a ship right out of the water when water was pumped under it. Six 500 KVA generators powered the water pumps. Pepper pointed to the generators. "You know how to them them on-line?"

"Sure," I replied. I had never seen this set-up before, but I had installed generators for King, and even though there was still a lot I didn't know about them, I was always lucky working with them.

"I need to have that engine started," I said.

"Go ahead and start it."

"Nope, I am not an expert on engines. We need the engineer." This was just what he wanted to hear, as I knew the proper procedure to get things done. He called the Chief Engineer, a man named Palmer, who started the engine. In no time I had the generator ready to go on-line to furnish the dock power. "Ted, that's your job from now on. I don't care if I see your face around here at all, except when the dry dock goes down and we're bringing a ship in. When that happens, I expect you to be here."

What a deal this turned out to be. My shipyard paycheck wasn't a big one, but the only time I had to be there was when the dry dock was to operate. This gave me all kinds of time to do my independent electrical work for individual tugboat owners like old man Coppledge, Marvin Lane, and Richard Jaquchs, among others.

Although I had no experience as a marine electrician to start out with, when it comes to basic horse sense, I'm pretty well-endowed. I proved that and kinda made my reputation when I first got the job at the yard. Andy Anderson, a foreman, asked if I'd take a look at the new oceanographic ship that they had spent three years building. It was the first of several that were to be produced. I was mostly interested in seeing the generators, but as we walked down through her main corridor, I looked at the wiring set up and could see a real problem. I called Andy over. "Andy, you're going to have real trouble when this old girl goes out to sea."

He looked over, "What do you mean?"

"Look at the way this wiring is laid out, these lines are all stretched tight and securely tied down. There's no slack anyplace so once this thing hits open water, she's going to stretch and flex then snap goes these wires."

Andy hesitated to absorb my observation, "Well, I'll be a S.O.B.!" That ship went back to the yard for two months, and they put some slack in the wiring. Word got around, and I was in demand for electrical work from the tug owners.

One of the more interesting personalities I met at the shipyard was old man Coppledge. Wayland Thomas Coppledge was a millionaire many times over. I'd heard a lot of stories about him, and most of them bad. He must have been a good businessman though to accumulate all the wealth, and maybe people just envied him.

We sometimes did maintenance on ships that didn't come into port. We would run a tug right out in open waters to save the extra time and expense of bringing them in. Pepper wanted me to be able to take a tug out in international waters, which then was 12 miles, and to do this I needed seaman papers. He said that old man Coppledge could issue the papers I needed to take to the Coast Guard for the identification card (ID). "Now, when you go up to see Coppledge, don't be nice to him or he'll throw you out. He thinks when people are nice to him they're trying to screw him out of something." I knew that Pepper loved to play jokes on people, and I could smell one in the making. Pepper didn't mind reprisals either. In fact, he seemed to have as much fun when you played a joke on him as when it was the other way around.

I walked into Coppledge's office like a gentleman, and stood in front of his desk and didn't say anything. A few minutes passed, and finally he looked up at me and snarled, "What the hell do you want?"

That kinda put me on my guard, but keeping my cool I said, "Mr. Coppledge, I understand that you can give a man the papers he needs to get his seaman papers, and that's what I came up here for."

"That's all you river rats want is someone to give ya something. Don't no one ever bring anything to me? Get the hell out of here. I don't have time to mess with rats like you." I felt now like knocking him on his ass, but I could see that even though he was sitting down, he was a big man and also in his seventies. I kept my tongue in my mouth and headed out. As I passed through the door, he hollered, "Come back in 10 days." "There's no way that I'm coming back here," I thought. "I'll go see Mr. Loviek. He can give me the papers I need, and he's a gentleman." Loviek was owner of the Jacksonville shipyard and the Piggly Wiggly markets there.

Alec Steward was Mr. Loviek's right-hand man. I asked about the papers I needed, and Alec said that Loviek was away and wouldn't be back for a couple months. "Can't you get me the papers?" I asked.

"Nope, I could sell you that ship there for $10, but I can't sign the old man's name."

Well, it might be awhile before I needed those seaman papers anyway, so I decided I'd wait until Mr. Loviek came back or find some other way to get them. I didn't say anything to Pepper, but after a couple days he cornered me and said, "You walked up there and acted like a gentleman, didn't ya?" "What did he say to you?"

Pepper continued, "No, I knew if you'd have gotten those papers you would have had them to me the next day. Now go back up there and demand those papers, and I'll guarantee you'll get them."

It was right at noon when I again went to Coppledge's office. I said to myself, "If he's eating lunch, I'll go right in and interrupt him." Without hesitation, I proceeded into the office, strode across toward his desk, slammed a chair down and said, "Hey, old man, I want my ID papers, and I don't want any shit out of you."

Without a blink he said, "I think this old bitch can get you some." This not-so-bad-looking secretary, who was thirty-five to forty, calmly got up and walked into the next office. I thought to myself, what a hell of way to meet a man. If he's a millionaire, you'd think he could be more dignified. He doesn't even show any respect for himself. Maybe all those bad stories about him were true. Pretty soon the secretary came back out and handed him some papers. He looked at them, then signed and sealed them in an envelope. "Don't you want to know something about me?" I asked.

"I know all I need to know about you right now. If those guys at the Coast Guard give you any trouble, you call me. I'd enjoy gettin' in their shit." That was it. I picked up my papers and left with a "See ya." Down at the Coast Guard Office, I got a slap on the back physical, they took my picture, and I walked out with my seaman papers. Back at the yard office, Pepper had me file the papers with Bonnie, the secretary, and I had a special pictured ID to carry with me.

My second get-together with Coppledge was in the middle of one night down at the dry dock. We were busy checking the sea valves on what we called a super tanker. We'd lower her to the water for four to six hours, whatever time the machinist wanted, and make sure the valves closed properly. The shipyard was always noisy, even in the middle of the night. There was air blowing whistles, one or both of the gantries moving, or the shuttle crane, plus sandblasting, but you were so used to it you could still hear someone call your name. I could hear someone calling, "Ted." I looked up toward the front gate and there was Coppledge waving his arm and yelling at me. "What's the matter, won't they let you in?" I shouted.

He shook his head, indicating they wouldn't. The guard had orders not to let him in. I don't know whether being a non-employee was the reason because of insurance liability or because Coppledge wasn't liked by a lot of people. "What do you want from me at this time of night?" I asked.

"I need your help. I got a tug down, and I gotta catch the tide and get her out but the Coast Guard won't let her go."

"Why not?" I asked.

"No generator for lights, auxiliary has blown up."

"Why can't you buy one? You ought to have six in stock."

Coppledge replied, "I've tried that, somebody keeps stealing them."

"I can't leave the yard unless Pepper says it's all right."

"OK, I'll call Pepper and get it OK'd," he said.

"You get ahold of Pepper and let him tell me it's OK over the phone."

"Well, you're a trusting old soul," replied Coppledge. The guard handed the phone through the window.

Pepper was on the other end of the line laughing. "Go help the old man, and I'll get Danny Ardale to come down and run the generators.

He's as good as anybody."

I told Coppledge that I was gonna get my tools. When I came back, I said, "This is gonna cost you one hundred dollars for the first hour."

"We'll talk about that later."

"No, we'll talk about it now before I get started," I said.

"That's fine. OK, I agree." He didn't ask anything about the second hour.

We hopped in his new Chrysler and drove down to Sisters Creek where I could see the Robert Lee waiting. That was one of his better tugs, but beside her was the Monitorial, one of his oldest. I climbed on board and asked Cookie if he could get either generator working. "Ted, I don't know, maybe one."

"How about the engines?"

"I can only promise maybe one." They were diesels, Cooper Bissmores, smallest I'd seen. I could see the armatures on one generator were shot so I hooked a jumper between the two. Cookie, who was really the cook, but also a handyman and the engineer, got one of the engines running. I told him to run it wide open, and I got the lights going. I had them bring Captain St. John down to inspect and he said, "I've been through this shit with the old man more than I care to remember. You swap over so I can see how the other generator works." I switched off the generator, the lights went off, then plugged in the other and the lights were back on. He didn't know it, but because I had them jumped both generators appeared to be working.

Captain St. John now demanded that the electric running lights be hooked up. "They don't need to be hooked up Captain, those kerosene lanterns are legal according to regulations. She's ready to go." I picked up my tools, stepped over on the Robert Lee, and was dropped off on shore. It was obvious the Captain and Coppledge would be back at each other's throats in due time.

Back on shore the old man looked at his watch. I had been at work only forty-five minutes, but he peeled off five twenties, and as he handed them to me, he said, "I like the way you do business. You and I are going to get along fine."

It had been a couple weeks since I heard from the old man, but one night he called over at the yard maintenance office and asked for me.

"Ted, I need you to do some work for me."

"You sure your pocketbook is big enough, old man?"

"Yep, it's big enough," he answered. Well, it didn't seem like too big a job, he just wanted some external lights installed on a barge, the Robert Lee, and another tug. The trouble was, to do this at night was difficult as the ship lights hit you in the face and didn't shine on your work. I went down to Coppledge's salvage yard and found a pretty good quarter mile light. I didn't see him or his car, but out of the darkness I heard, "What ya stealing?"

"A quarter mile light, what's it look like?"

"Is it any good?"

"Yep, I don't steal unless it's good." I mounted the light on the top of my pickup and parked facing the barge so it was easy to see what I was doing. This tickled the old man, especially knowing I wasn't really stealing from him.

When I finished the light job, I figured up a bill which amounted to approximately $60 labor and $25 material. Coppledge looked at my bill kinda funny and said, "That's the most ridiculous bill I've ever seen." He took a pen from his pocket and adjusted the figures, tripling the labor cost and enlarging the material costs even more. It ended up around $500 with almost $200 in my pocket for labor. "There," he said, "don't ever hand me a ridiculous bill like that again."

The next time I heard from Coppledge was when he called over to the yard shop. Pekchick, the Dockmaster, took the call and handed the phone over. "Ted, I need you to come over right now."

"What do you want old man?"

"I can't hold a conversation about it over the phone, come on over." I wasn't too busy so I told Bonny, the guy in the office, where I'd be.

When I reached his office, I asked, "What's so damned important?" He wouldn't say but did indicate we needed to drive down to Tallyarand Ave. I made him drive. "I don't want to drive your pile of junk." He bought brand new Chryslers, never changed the oil or anything, just drove them until they started to need work, then bought another new one.

On Tallyarand we pulled up in front of the Florida Asphalt Paving

Company. "What are we stoppin' here for?"

"I don't really want to do this, but I have to." I followed him through the front door into the reception area. Everybody in the office seemed pretty busy, but they all looked up when he started to pound on the narrow countertop by the receptionist. "Who's the bookkeeper in here?" he demanded.

A little lady stuck her head up, "I am."

"You stay here. The rest of you get your junk and get out. I own this company." One guy started to give him some lip, but that didn't last long. "I told you I own this company, get your shit together and get out." I felt really small standing there associated with the old man. These were all respectable, older-looking people; the bookkeeper, receptionist, a couple older men in their fifties with ties on, and a couple of younger secretaries. They all began to disperse. Pretty soon a big Lincoln drove in and into the office this guy came, "What's going on in here?"

"You know what's going on, give me the keys to that Lincoln!" I stood there with a what-the-hell's-happening look on my face. The old man really lit into this guy, "You knew a long time ago you couldn't pay me back or never intended to pay me back. Get your shit and get out of here!" With the Lincoln keys now in his hand, he turned towards the bookkeeper, "Get Barnett National Bank on the phone." When the bank answered, she handed him the phone. "I want to talk to the president." When the bank president or his representative answered, the old man took over, "This is Wayland Coppledge, you got any CPA's that know what they're doing down there? Well, get one down to Florida Asphalt right now, no ifs, ands, or buts about it." I wondered what I had gotten myself into, the Mafia?

In about twenty minutes, a Volkswagon rolled in and the bank CPA presented himself. "Boy, do you know your business?" asked Coppledge.

"Yes, sir."

"Well, we'll find out. I wanna know what this company is worth, as quick as you can find out. Stay here all night, but don't stop until you find that out." To the bookkeeper, he said, "You got any cash?"

"Yes, we have some."

"OK, Mr. CPA, if you need some cash for food, she'll fix you up." The old man grabbed a phone book, opened it, and underlined his name and number, "You find out, you call me." He walked out to the Lincoln, opened and closed each door pushing down the lock buttons and then kicked the car. "God damn f------Ford."

We climbed into the Chrysler and down the road we drove at his usual pace, never over 20 miles per hour. "Old man, I've heard a lot of tales about you, and I guess you are the old S.O.B. I've heard about."

"That man knew he couldn't pay me, probably never planned to when I first loaned him the money to buy that business. He just thought if he didn't say anything, he could put the screws to me. Ted, a deal's a deal, and friends and deals don't mix. Deal with your friends with your heart and your business with your mind." He grumbled on, "Another damned business I don't need."

I heard later that he sold Florida Asphalt for a nice profit. I wonder if he really knew how much money he had. I saw a list once that showed he owned 68 tugs. In Jacksonville, he owned a bunch of tugs in a company called Florida Towing; another called Whitestack Towing in Charleston, South Carolina; one in the Faulkin Islands; in Haiti and Madagascar off the coast of Africa; and probably more.

The old man had a son they called Doc. He had been a dentist in Atlantic Beach. Why he gave up his dentistry, I'm not sure, for he had a reputation as an excellent dentist with many prominent patients. He did go through a divorce, and the old man had put him in charge of Whitestack Towing. He had a reputation of being mean and hard to get along with, worse than his father. There was a Cuban worker at the yard, can't remember his name, but he had warned me about Doc and his manners.

One day I was putting some lights on a tug as the old man had asked me to when along came Doc. "Who told you to put those lights on?"

"Mr. Coppledge asked me to."

"My name is Doc Coppledge, and I don't want you to put those God damned lights on." I didn't say anything, but just kept at what I was doing. "Did you hear me? Don't put those lights on." There were sticks around the yard that looked like baseball bats. We used them for levers on the winches. I picked one up that was handy and said, "You S.O.B., lay off me or I'll knock your ass in the St. Johns River." He was a big man and wasn't about to be intimidated by me or the stick, so he came a little closer and kept badgering me. That was enough. To his surprise I came up with the stick and some fast moves he wasn't expecting and over into the river he went. Then the dumb ass swam between the tug and the dock to get back up. If the tug had ever shifted next to the dock, he would have been crushed. Well, he shook himself off and left, but it wasn't long when the old man arrived.

"What's the idea, you knockin' my boy in the river?"

"If you talk to me that way, I'll knock you in the river too, old man."

"Ha, ha, I wished I could have seen it. No good S.O.B., isn't he?"

I guess as a manager, Doc had been goofing up down at Whitestack Towing, so the old man gave him a couple weeks off. Doc was kind of a high liver, and thought he'd use his time off for a little vacation in Las Vegas. It was about three in the morning when the old man called. I was asleep on one of the tugs. I could tell by the tone of his voice it was serious, but I lit into him anyway. "What are you callin' me at three in the morning for? If you're lonely, get yourself a dog!"

"Ted, I just got a call from Las Vegas and Doc got himself in debt to the tune of a quarter million, and if he don't pay up, they're going to do him in. I don't know how he got that much credit."

"I do, he probably just used some of your credit cards to prove he was a high roller, and they let him go."

"What am I going to do?"

"Here's your chance to get rid of him if you want to."

There was a long hesitation on the other end. "Guess I'll have to wire him out the money," said Coppledge.

"You call Bank of America, I know they have a twenty-four hour line and the money will probably be there in an hour."

When Doc called, I guess the old man told him to get his ass back here as fast as his car would go. Before he got back, the old man and I had another conversation as he still wasn't sure what to do about Doc. I offered my two cents, "I'd send his ass back down to Whitestack to get that mess straightened out. He's been living high on the hog out at that country club on Philips Highway on your money. I'm sure he's got some stashed away, so I'd take away all his credit cards and not give him another nickel until he gets his act together." I'm really not sure whether the old man ever got him straightened out or not. He just didn't talk about him much after that.

Coppledge did me some favors more than once too. I remember once when Robert really cut his foot bad. Mary wasn't home, so I took him down to Baptist Hospital and left him as I had to go to work. Mary and I went down about twelve that night and she did not like the way they were caring for his foot. "Let's get him out of here." I had a hundred dollars in my pocket, figuring twenty-five would probably catch the bill as he hadn't been in that long. We stopped by the administration office. A man presented me the bill, six hundred dollars. "Have you lost your mind, give me that phone," and I dialed Coppledge.

"Put that no account S.O.B. on the phone," said Coppledge.

I don't know what Coppledge told the man, but looking a little pale, he hung up the phone and said, "No charge, you can take the boy home."

When we got home Mary inspected Robert's foot. "Look, they haven't even cleaned it up properly. If we'd have left him there, he might have lost it." The next day she had me gathering herbs to get the foot healed up. At work I stopped over to see Coppledge, "What do I owe you for that hospital thing?"

"Nothing, I enjoy chewin' somebody out when they're wrong. I've contributed a lot of money to that hospital, and they know that."

One other situation was comical, but then I felt sorry for old Coppledge too. Pepper called and said the old man was having problems with a barge over at the banana dock, and I was to take a generator over so they would have light to see what they were doing. When I arrived, I could see the heavily loaded barge was sitting low in the water, and the old man standing alongside. "Here's your generator," I said.

"Good, at least something is going right. Now they can see to f--- up again."

"What's the matter?"

"Barge's got a hole in the side, leaking oil in the river, Coast

Guard's after me." Everybody was guilty of some leakage into the river, and this time it was Coppledge's turn to get picked on.

"Full of oil, huh?"

"Yep." They had a 250 ton crane positioned over the barge with a cable attached.

"They're not going to try to lift that out of the water, are they? They couldn't do that with two cranes the way she is loaded. You better stop them." He agreed and went to get the foreman, but it was too late. They had already taken the slack out of the cable and started to lift. Fortunately, the cable snapped, but in the process the boom flipped over backwards and left a huge hole in the deck. Coppledge walked back over to me, "I didn't make it."

"Any damn fool could see that. You give me fifty dollars and I'll take care of things."

"OK, what do ya want to do?"

"Have someone get the Robert Lee over there and tow another barge alongside so we can pump into it."

"We already tried that."

"Fifty dollars, old man, fifty dollars and you give me full authority."

"OK, OK, OK, here's the foreman." Coppledge told the foreman to follow my instructions.

When I told the foreman what to do, he said, "Ted, we already tried that and the Coast Guard said no."

"You just go ahead and do it anyway and send the Coast Guard to me." While they were getting the other barge around to set up the pumping operation, I nosed around to see who was representing the Coast Guard that day. It was that cocky young Lieutenant who had a reputation of one trying to get ahead. Wasn't long before he could see what was happening and was on the foreman's ass. The foreman pointed to me and over he came. "Who gave permission to pump water into that barge?" he asked.

"I did."

"Who the hell are you?"

"You're going to find out if you really want to get shitty about this, fella."

"I have full authority on this river!" he said.

"Like shit you do, you only have a choice. Either we pump some water in that barge to find the hole and lose about eight to ten barrels of oil in the river or we don't and lose maybe four thousand or more. The choice is yours, what are you going to do, Lieutenant? I'm not telling you what I'm going to do. The monkey is on your back. What'll it be, eight or four thousand barrels dumped?"

"I'll take the eight," he said in a humbler tone. The foreman knew what I was going to do, and he wanted to do it before but nobody would stand up to this guy. It wasn't long before they located the hole in the barge. They put a mattress of foam over the hole and held it in place with another tug while they began pumping the oil into the other barge. Hell, it wasn't thirty minutes of pumping, and it had already came up eighteen inches. I went back to the old man. He reached into his pocket. "Here's your fifty. Come over here, I want to show you something. See that guy down there in that pin stripe suit?"

"Yep."

"I pay that S.O.B. forty thousand dollars a year to f--- up like this."

I said, "Old man, I don't want to hear your problems, I got enough of my own, I don't need you crying on my shoulder."

"I want you to come to work for me."

"There is no way I'd come to work for you. That just wouldn't work."

I was putting in a lot of hours at the yard and should have been well on my way to becoming a millionaire, except Evelyn was spending it as fast as I brought it in. The arguing and fighting got worse, and it seemed that there was no peace at home. Evelyn was always complaining that Marsha, the oldest, wasn't helping enough. I found out that Marsha was doing most of the work, plus she got herself and the rest of the kids off to school while Evelyn slept in.

One night I came home beat and sat down to a spaghetti supper. "Who made this supper?" I asked as I helped myself to the spaghetti.

Marsha said, "I made the spaghetti." I picked up the dish with the sauce.

"I made the sauce," said Evelyn. I stuck the serving spoon into the sauce. It was layered. Cold sauce on the top and an inch of grease underneath. In a fit of rage, I threw the dish straight through the window. "Come on kids, we're going out and you're going to get a good supper."

"I want to go too," said Evelyn.

"No way, you put that shit together, you stay here and eat it."

After the spaghetti incident, I didn't spend nights at home anymore. Marvin Lane had just had his first tug built, so I slept on that while the second was being built. I went home most every day for a few hours to see the kids, sometimes at night, and other times I'd just slip in after work at four or five in the morning. I'd sit there until the kids woke up for school. Mary had the trailer and that property now, but I just didn't know how I was going to get the kids under her care.

One night something told me to go over to the house. Once there, Evelyn and I had our usual fight, and then a city police car drove in.

The officer came to the door and I opened it up for him. "You Ted Aldridge?"

"Yep."

"I got a warrant for your arrest."

"OK, just let me get a pack of cigarettes and I'll be right with you."

The officer was by himself and seemed real congenial. As we rode along in the squad car he said, "Seems kinda funny I find a man charged with desertion and non-support living with his family."

"There's a whole lot of shit that goes on in this county that you're not aware of, and this is a good example of one of them." He could tell I was pissed. I said to myself, "What am I goin' to jail for, something I haven't done, no justice in that." I knew as soon as I got there I could give old man Coppledge a call, and he'd have me out of there fast.

We arrived at the station house. "Guess I'm allowed one phone call."

"Would you give me fifteen minutes before you make your call?" asked the officer.

"Hey, fella I haven't done one damn thing to you, and you're asking me to wait a minute to get out of the jail that you haven't put me in yet, that I don't deserve to be in if you put me in."

"I know you think it's unfair buddy, but just give me fifteen minutes."

"OK, you got fifteen minutes, and then I want to make my phone call."

He went into the office, and I could see he was on the phone. When he came back, he said, "What I'm gonna tell ya, you're not gonna want to hear. I know you can make a phone call to Marvin Lane or old man Coppledge, and they'll have you out of here in ten minutes. What I want you to do instead is to get processed in and make your call at one a.m. or better yet around one-thirty. It'll help you a hundred percent." It was cold outside, and I knew that if I went out to the tug from here, it would take awhile to warm it up. I was too pissed off to sleep anyway, so I agreed to stay. They fingerprinted and checked me in, then led me back to a cell. The fingerprinting was no big deal, but I didn't like it in there with all the riffraff.

They didn't search me when they brought me in, and I happened to have this file in my pocket that I used to file points on electrical control boxes. I bent it into kind of a horseshoe shape and started fiddling with the cell lock. It was an old lock, and in short order it popped open. I just opened the cell door, walked out, and relocked it. A couple of my cell-mates looked at me as if to say, "What the hell's goin' on here?" I walked out to the front and to the desk Sergeant I said, "Put me in another cell."

His eyes got kinda big, and he said, "What are ya talkin' about? How'd you get outta there?"

"I just slipped through the bars." It didn't look like he believed that.

"What kinda cell would you like?"

"One I don't have to share with stinky assed people." He led me back to another cell, and I sat there until one-thirty when he came back to get me so I could make my phone call.

A few minutes after the call, the bondsman came in. "You Ted Aldridge? Sign right here and you'll be free to go."

On the way out the door the desk Sergeant asked one more time, "How'd you get outta that cell?"

"Just slipped through the bars," I replied.

It was about two a.m. now, so I walked over to Milligens Restaurant and got a hamburg and a cup of coffee. From there I had to walk back to Fourth Street to get my car and finally rolled into the shipyard about six a.m. I talked to the foreman and timekeeper and told them that I had to be in court at nine a.m. and hopefully would not be back in jail.

At the courthouse they were hearing some other cases. I could see Evelyn sitting over there with that Sergeant, and I could feel in my bones that things were not gonna go my way. In fact, near rage was building deep inside of me. During a short recess, a guy came through the crowd over to where I was. He shoved some papers at me, "You Aldridge?"

"Well, who the hell wants to know?"

"I'm an assistant district attorney, State of Florida, and I'm serving you with these papers."

"Well, whoop dee doo, you can shove them up your ass," and I pushed the papers back at him. "This is not my agreement in this divorce. I got my freedoms too." I knew that she was out to take everything I had. Dorothy Drake, the magistrate who was running the proceedings, was watching all this bullshit.

Finally my case came around and Mrs. Drake read the charges specified against me. Then she started directing questions at Evelyn. "Does your husband still reside at your house?"

"Yes, but he's never there."

"Who pays the light bill?"

"He does."

"Who pays for the groceries?"

"He does."

"Lady you have brought charges against your husband for desertion and non-support, and from what you have admitted here, these charges are false."

"Yes, but he's never home."

"These charges are false, and I'm going to throw this case out, dismissed!" Then she looked and pointed at me, "I want to see you after the court recesses at noon."

I said to myself, "OK, now the shit is coming. Old man Coppledge or somebody put me behind the eight ball trying to influence her with a dollar bill. Damn it, I'm not going to do it that way, I'm innocent."

When the morning cases were finished, I approached Mrs. Drake,

"You wanted to talk to me."

"I can't talk to you here, let's go to a restaurant and get something to eat."

After we ordered some food, Mrs. Drake said, "I want to know everything about your situation from A to Z." I kinda started out with a life history, what type of work I had done in Virginia and how Evelyn and I got together. On several things I told her she kinda nodded her head like she already knew the story, so I kinda stopped that and went to the Florida part of it and was telling her who I had worked for and what type of work I did. She said, "I already know where you've worked."

I looked a little puzzled at her, "What is it you want to know ma'am?"

"I want to know what you are going to do now."

"There is a lady named Mary Adams who has agreed to care for the children, and I'll pay her twenty-five plus a week."

"What do ya mean twenty-five dollars plus?"

"I mean that if it costs her more than twenty-five, say one hundred, I'll pay her that." I added, "Mary won't take care of the children though, until she talks to you."

Mrs. Drake took over the conversation now, "I'm going to give you some advice so this whole thing won't cost all your money. Go to the most expensive lawyer you can find, probably the best would be the attorney for the port authority. Get a written statement from him that he refuses to take your case, then go to the Friend of the Court's Office and tell them you need a lawyer right away. They are supposed to furnish one if necessary, but won't be able to do that for awhile. Get a statement from them too. "Now," she said, "Go pay your wife's lawyer seventy-five dollars to get his case started against you, and make sure he stipulates how you want the children to be taken care of."

"I know how I want the children cared for, the three youngest with me and the three oldest can choose," I said, "But why should I be paying her lawyer to start something against me?"

"You would have proof that you couldn't obtain a lawyer yourself, and somebody has to file some of the paperwork if a divorce is going to take place. Save yourself some money by letting her lawyer get things started, and then in court you can talk directly to the judge, not another lawyer." This lady was smart, and I guess I needed to trust her, though I certainly didn't have things all sorted out in my mind.

I did everything as Mrs. Drake told me to do, and the divorce went before Judge Robinson. It was a hearing in his chambers. He looked at the divorce papers and then at Evelyn. "It says here that some of the children may go with you."

"Yes, but I have no way of supporting them."

The judge continued in a way Evelyn hadn't expected. "Who's going to support that baby you're carrying?" Now I hadn't slept with her for a long time, and the judge already figured it wasn't mine. Mary had seen her at the Armory running around regularly. When she came in, the wedding ring came off and pretty soon, she'd be out the door with a sailor or somebody. I had no desire to catch some disease, so I left her alone.

Judge Robinson didn't waste a lot of time. He asked a few more questions, studied the papers once more, then said, "I'm going to grant this divorce today, but I'm not going to decide child custody for thirty days. Mr. Aldridge, you'll have to find a home for the children until I make a decision."

Things were looking better now. Mary had the trailer, had agreed to care for the kids and she had already had her visit with Dorothy Drake. Mrs. Drake had asked Mary straight out, "Are you sleeping with Ted Aldridge?" Mary said no, which was the truth. I was still sleeping on the tugs at the shipyard.

The divorce agreement required me to pay $30 a week child support to Evelyn. I guess, so she'd have money to feed them when they visited. After a few weeks, when Mary had all the children, this didn't seem right to me so I visited the Friend of the Court's Office to get some relief from this requirement. They dropped her thirty a week, so now I just needed to make sure Mary had enough. Things began to smooth out for awhile. The children were doing better in school, and for once they were having a stable home life. There were flare-ups though, when Evelyn came to see the kids. Once, when I happened to be there, she came over with her brother and tried to rip the wiring out of a station wagon I had given Mary to haul the kids around. I started to pick her up by the back of the neck, but released my grip remembering her pregnancy. I yelled at her brother, "Get her ass out of here and don't ever bring her over here again. You are welcome, but she is not."

"I didn't want to bring her over here in the first place," he said.

My mother asked me to stop over one day, said that Olita Smith needed an electrical box put in. As I said before, Olita had sold my mother her house and rented us an apartment when we first moved to Florida. I had done electrical work for Olita, but I couldn't imagine what was left to do. She said, "Ted, I don't need any work done, I just wanted to see how you and the kids are doing." She went on, "I had a long talk with Dorothy Drake about you awhile back. Told her I didn't like the way you were being treated or how you were treating yourself. Too easygoing, that's your problem. I knew sooner or later the shit was going to hit the fan, and you were going to end up with the wrong end of the stick."

Now I knew how Dorothy Drake seemed to know so much about my situation, and guessed that Olita had talked to Judge Robinson. Also, I remembered later that I had arranged for a free paint job for old Judge Robinson's boat awhile back. I had secured an air conditioner for one guy and later called in that favor to get the judge's boat painted. It was a big old yacht that the judge had, and as bad a shape as it was in, it would take more money to fix it up right than the judge would have. Martin Curry, the shipyard president, was an old friend of the judge's, and I had a good reputation with him too. So the pieces began to fall into place, and I could see that it was more than luck the way things happened in court.

Mary and I became closer in our relationship. Things just seemed to click when we were together. We started doing a lot of thinking and talking and finally decided to get married. Mary laughed, "Hell, I already got all your family, I might just as well take you too!" I won't say our get-together wasn't romantic, it was just not one of those gushy soap opera things. It was like that the first time I got married, and I could see how that ended up. The important thing was that things had settled down for the kids. When they were with Evelyn and I came over, there was always a blowup. After having been walked on for so long, I had reached my limit and wasn't about to put up with any more. The kids had been more or less taking care of themselves, and I wanted to turn everybody's life around including my own; and finally maybe it was going to happen. The only trouble was that Evelyn's destructive visits were often enough that I decided it was time to put some distance between us. I know it's supposed to be nice for kids to go back and forth to visit Mom and Dad, but in this situation it wasn't working for anyone's benefit. I lined up a job in Ohio, and planned for Mary and the kids to follow as soon as I could bring them.

If I had stayed in Florida, I would probably have been pretty well off today. Before I left Coppledge offered me a sweet deal, but I had to turn the old man down. It all started several months before I left, when for some reason, the old man and I were down looking at his tugs. One old tug that wasn't in use, the Dickey, stood out from the rest. It was obvious that it had been a long time since she had seen any paint or maintenance, and it was doubtful if she ever would. "It's a shame to let a vessel like that go to hell, rotting away 'cause you won't use your damn rusty dollar bills to fix her up. Shucks, you throw in a V-12 Caterpillar engine, put in a new generator, clean her up with a new kitchen, and she'd be something to be proud of." I loved to needle the old man, and never thought much more about it until a few weeks later when I noticed the Dickey was missing.

A couple months passed, and the old man asked me to come down to the docks and see something. That eighty-year-old man was like a kid with a new toy when he presented the Dickey to me. He had put in a new engine, generator, and several other major repairs. "What you think about that now?" he said with pride.

I walked around the deck, then stepped down inside and surveyed the improvements. "That's a damn shame to spend all the money, and will ya look at this galley, it's a disgrace. Would you want your eggs cooked on that stove? And the outside," I continued, "Do you call that a paint job? Looks like they slapped a little paint along the waterline."

Now he was wounded, "You're the God-damnedest man to please." It wasn't long before he had the Robert Lee towing her back to Bellinger. The next time the Dickey showed up she looked better than a new tug. The decks were clean enough to eat off of, and she had been completely repainted and rustproofed. The galley was all new. "Well, how the hell do you like her now?"

"She looks pretty damn decent, old man. What are you going to do with her now?"

"I'm going to sell her to you for ten thousand dollars."

In the shape the Dickey was now in, that was only a fraction of what she was worth. "Where am I going to get that kinda money?"

"You can earn it hauling oil from the oil depot at Owen, Illinois, to Stanford and back."

"Carrying your damn oil I suppose."

"Yep."

"I appreciate it, but I'm not reliable, old man."

He knew of my various family problems and didn't say much about it again.

VII

Moving North

With the decision made to leave Florida, I decided to return to line work and contacted the International Brotherhood of Electrical Workers (IBEW) Local Seventy-One in Columbus, Ohio. I received notice of an opening in the Cincinnati area with D & Z Electric, so on January twenty-seventh, I said goodbye to Mary and the kids and headed north.

D & Z, owned by Dave Zimmerman, was out of Blue Belle, Pennsylvania, but had been doing work in the Cincinnati area for twenty-five to thirty years. It turned out to be a good, comfortable job with line work up and down the Ohio River area. My plan was to get well-established, then bring Mary and the kids up in the spring.

I did have a little trouble at D & Z on my second day on the job. I was working with a man called Hoge. We were assigned a job that I figured was aimed at showing D & Z what I knew about line work. The job was no big deal, we were just changing out a thirty-eight thousand volt hi-line. We had a greenhorn grunt assigned to us, and he admitted he didn't know anything. "That's no problem son, you just do exactly what one of us tells you to do." I asked Hoge, "Do you want to talk to the boy or shall I?"

"You can."

We were using hot sticks to raise the wire. The sticks were insulated and held the hot line. Clamps around the power pole held the hot sticks as they were gradually raised into position on the pole. The boy was working the hand line to send clamps and the tools we needed up the pole. The utility poles were set in a little valley, and I could see that by pulling the line up from a little hill nearby we could save an hour's worth of work by not having to put another set of hot sticks on. I told the boy to set a frost bar on top of the hill. Hoge knew why I was doing that, I didn't have to explain.

The frost bar was just an eight foot long steel bar pointed on one end, with a chisel on the other. When jammed in the ground at an angle you could use it as an anchor to pull the line to.

The boy was back, and I'm up on the pole when along comes Assistant Superintendent Evans. I'm sure he had been watching us from a distance. Usually, when you set a frost bar to tag out a line, you pace off twice the distance from the pole. Well, he could see that frost bar way up on top of that hill, so he told the boy to get it and bring it back. Hoge and I were up on the pole at the time, and even though I could see what was happening by twisting in my belt, I let it go for the time being as I was busy. When I came down from the pole, I asked the boy, "Why'd you bring that frost bar down from the hill?"

"That man told me to," gesturing towards Evans.

"Well, you can take it back up to the hill now." He left again with the frost bar, and I looked at Evans, "And who the hell are you, fella?"

"My name's Evans, and I'm the Assistant Superintendent."

"That's the more reason you shouldn't be interfering with a line crew. I don't give a damn who you are, get your ass in that car and get the hell out of here."

Hoge walked up as Evans tore away in his car, "You know who that man is?"

"Doesn't matter, unless we are violating a safety rule he isn't supposed to bother us."

"Ted, you're going to get us fired."

"We'll see about that." When time came to do it, we pulled the line up from the hill, and sure enough it saved us using another set of hot sticks. I knew Evans was probably watching with a pair of field glasses from somewhere.

Pretty soon Ralph Queens drove up. He had Evans with him. "Hillbilly, you haven't been on the job forty-eight hours and already you got the Assistant Superintendent mad as hell at you."

"Well sir, if this man wasn't familiar with line work, I could excuse him, but here he is an assistant superintendent and he hasn't got enough damned sense not to interfere with a crew." I continued on, "He has no authority over what we're doing unless we violate a safety rule. I had that frost bar up there to save an hour of your time, and thanks to him, it cost an extra hour."

Queens looked at Evans, "Did you interfere with this crew?"

Evans meekly replied, "Yes, sir."

"You got three days off Evans, and today doesn't count."

When they left, Hoge looked at me, "I don't know who's asshole you browned, but damn it, you got the right one."

I knew Ralph Queens from back in the fall of 1953. He had been a lineman for Ohio Light and Power, and later took over his dad's business. I was working for King Electric and Ralph had bid on a job to install house service in two Ohio cities. There were about 800 units in Piketon and 400 in Waverly. He told me he needed the work to get his home paid for. His bid was $15, but I said we'd pay him twenty-five if he had them done by the first of December. The extra money over and above his bid paid for his house, and he never forgot the favor.

After the Evans incident, I had occasion to visit with him a little. "What'd you come up here for, Ted?" I told him about the divorce and that I was remarried and planning to make a fresh start up here. "Where's the kids?" Told him I was planning on bringing the family along as soon as I had a few week's work behind me. "You need some money, Ted?"

"I'm not going to take any money off your hip. Thanks anyway, Ralph, I'll get them up here when things settle down."

My regular pole buddy with D & Z was Lloyd Whittiker, who orginated from the mountain country of southwestern Tennessee. We saw eye-to-eye on most things, except I didn't stay in the barrooms as long as he did.

Most linemen were pretty regular drinkers. It was really just a form of cheap entertainment to combat loneliness and boredom. I was the exception. Beer made me sick and whiskey made me wild, so I just stayed away from all of it except for maybe an occasional mixed drink with supper.

As a lineman, my buddy Lloyd had one major problem, he was afraid of electricity. He had been a lineman for quite awhile with

Hinkle & McCoy, but his work had been on telephone lines. When that company laid-off, Lloyd applied for a position in open construction and line work. In the Cincinnati area, this was almost exclusively heavy industrial, so there was no telephone line work. I became Lloyd's teacher, trying to convert him into a regular lineman. This was dangerous business, because there was no way of knowing when Lloyd might forget he was handling high voltage and think he was back working on the telephone lines. Just leaving his rubber gloves off could prove fatal.

Lloyd and I did hit it off pretty good, both being hillbillies of sort and we both had a fair sense of humor. I still laugh when I remember the laundromat incident in Aurora, Indiana.

It was in the morning and having accumulated some dirty laundry, we both headed for the local laundromat. There was one lady there when we walked in. She looked up at us, but I didn't pay much attention to her. Unfortunately the soap powder machine was empty, so Lloyd left to find some soap, and I stayed with the laundry. By the time Lloyd returned, two or three other older ladies had come in. They already had clothes in the machines and sat over in the corner visiting. They were really giving Lloyd and me the once over. Probably just curious as to who we were and where we were from. Aurora was a small town, maybe 1500 people, and strangers kinda stood out. They were really staring at us now, and I could see Lloyd didn't like it. I said to Lloyd, "You think we should tell them who we are?" We decided we wouldn't, but instead have a little fun with them—carry on like a couple gays. I called him Darling and he called me Sugar. It went like this, "Darlin', you got your colors all mixed with the whites. That's not a good idea."

"OK, Sugar, would you help me sort them out?"

"Now don't fill that machine too full, Darling."

"How much soap should I use, Sugar?" We gave those old gals the full nine yards, and every so often we had to turn our backs to keep them from seeing us laughing. I could tell these gals were probably the town gossips. Our show only lasted three or four minutes, but when you're trying to entertain, it seemed like a long time. Anyway, we finally got the clothes in the machine. "Shall we sit down and read for awhile, Sugar?"

"Here, let me fix this chair for you, Darling." By this time, our lady friends were headed out the door without their laundry.

After awhile our clothes were completely washed and dried. The ladies still hadn't returned for theirs, which had been done for a long time. We were convinced that by now the whole town knew that there were a couple of gays at the laundromat.

The ladies in Aurora probably didn't have too much to gossip about anyway, no regular town drunks. There were a couple of girls that were pretty free with themselves and just as ugly as the habit they had. Lloyd said they must have been whipped with ugly sticks. "Well, Lloyd, they might think the same about us." We both agreed that there were also some real nice people in town, especially those at the restaurant. They had excellent food and put up special lunches for us to take to work. It didn't seem like they charged enough considering all we got.

On one Friday night Lloyd and I went out to eat, but the local restaurant happened to be closed. We headed down to Lawrenceburg to look for one. Linemen burn up a lot of calories, and as a matter of habit eat at the very best restaurants to keep their bodies in shape. We found a pretty good-looking place with a bar attached. Lloyd wanted to get a drink before we ate, so I said I'd join him and have a Tom Collins with my meal. The waitress gave us a good lookin' over, then took our drink orders. She came back with a drink for him, but not me. "I'll have to see your driver's license before I can serve you," she said. Now there's a couple things a hillbilly can't stand, and that's bein' lied to and when people beat around the bush and don't get to the point. You can steal from him, and he doesn't mind as much as this other bullshit. I looked at her, then at Lloyd, and I thought to myself what a hell of a come on. I may look young at thirty-four, but she knows I'm legal to drink.

I tried to be polite, "I don't have my driver's license, and I came here to eat, not put up with a lot of bullshit."

"I'll still have to see your ID before I can serve you."

"Well, I'll see you in hell before you see it, and I'm not going to get a meal either. Any idiot can see I'm over twenty one, and I'm not puttin' up with this horseshit. You can take this place and shove it up your ass."

Lloyd looked at me wide-eyed, and we got up and left. Outside Lloyd let go, "Are you crazy, that gal was tryin' to pick you up."

"I know her game. She just wanted to get my name and where I was from to start a conversation, plus I don't need pickin' up. If she'd come on more directly, I'd at least have had respect for her. That girl wasn't just lookin' for a good time, she was lookin' for one or more of three things; someone to support her, to roll him for his money, or she was pissed off because someone gave her a dose of clap and she wanted to return the favor to someone else. Just a sucker piece of ass." Lloyd just shook his head. I'm not sure I convinced him, but I was well-informed as to the variety of con artists around these parts.

Not all linemen were as conservative as I was. Most were pretty heavy drinkers, and the nature of the job and all the traveling gave the married man the freedom to live the single life if he wished to. Some took that path and some didn't. I remember a couple of boys, from some Local out of Missouri, who had rooms in Covington, Kentucky, but spent a lot of their evening's time over in Newport, Kentucky. Bobby Kennedy as Attorney General had made a big deal about cleaning up Newport, but that was just good advertisement for it was just as busy shortly after he left. Anyway, these two Missouri boys ran around together a lot and one day their two wives decided to make a surprise visit. They showed up at the only address they had in Covington. The old innkeeper didn't do those boys any favor. "Those fellas aren't here very much, just a couple nights a week," he said. "They're over in Newport the rest of the time." Those two girls didn't have any idea where to find their men, but went to Newport anyway. I guess they must have suspected devious behavior for they stuck their heads into the Pink Pussy Cat. Those boys had made one big mistake, they had left their cowboy hats and jackets hanging on a chair not too far from the door, and the wives recognized them. First they went through the toilets looking for them, but eventually they found the storeroom where the business was set up. There they both were in the saddle with just a makeshift partition separating the areas. No one ever saw those boys again. One broke into the line truck to get his tools. He left a note and a twenty dollar bill to repair the broken lock and hasp. The other boy just left without his tools.

Don VanWinkle was a groundsman (grunt) that worked for the company. He was a painter by trade, but had worked for D & Z for some time. As his title suggests, he did not climb poles, but supported the linemen from below. He was a real fine fella who had four kids, was good-natured, and really laid-back. He asked Lloyd and I to come over and help him one day, as the Little Miami River was going over its banks and he was afraid it was going to ruin a house he had in the area. Sure enough, the basement was full of water to within a few inches of the first floor. The freezer and the furniture downstairs were all under water. We closed the upstairs door and moved what stuff we could to protect it if the water got higher. Don didn't seem real concerned though, as he had his family living in another house in Cleeves.

Don did me two favors. He sold me an old 1957 Cadillac for $75, and he told me of a house that might be available for rent in Cleeves. Rental houses were scarce, and I had been looking for something so I could move Mary and the kids up. Charlie Shanks owned the rental house, and I remember he had a bunch of hound dogs. After Mary and the kids came up, he'd eat with us on weekends.

The old Cadillac looked a little rough, because a snowplow had taken a back fender off. After the second state policeman stopped me in as many days to warn me about it, I said, "I wish you guys could leave a poor hillbilly alone until I can get another fender." Word musta got around because they didn't stop me again, and I didn't get it fixed right away either.

I couldn't cover for Lloyd much longer. I'd been trying to convert him from being a telephone lineman, but he was still scared of electricity. He was a good worker though, and the foreman had been trying to give him work where he couldn't hurt himself. Lloyd finally left for a job around Eaton Rapids, Michigan. It wasn't two weeks before he was back. When I asked him what the problem was, he just said, "Those folks were asking me to do things I wasn't used to doin'. I'm not stayin' up there." Well, I knew that they had expected him to be a power lineman, and he wasn't one. He was a telephone lineman.

D & Z Electric contracted work from Cincinnati Light & Power, and we worked all over on their property. Shortly after Lloyd came back, I was transferred up to Ripley, Ohio, about fifty miles or so from Cincinnati. Most of our work at Ripley was considered maintenance type work, where we would be changing lines and putting in new poles. The foreman was Walt LaPointe, a good guy to work with. He had been a lineman for a long time and Ralph Queens, the Superintendent, finally forced him into becoming a foreman. Ralph said, "Boy, it's time to put your yo-yos away and start takin' on the responsibility to become a man. You got the ticket and experience, now you're a foreman." Walt was a real character and a lot of fun to work with. He was half French and half Jewish and was always sayin' that he regretted not having any Negro blood in him 'cause then he could have been rich, a lover, and free-hearted at the same time.

We were up at Ripley for two and a half months and then came back to Cincinnati. Walt had his own crew there, and I was transferred to another crew. That didn't last long though, because I had a serious run-in with Connelly, that crew's foreman.

Cincinnati Power had this old inspector named Victor who had been brought up under the old Twenty-three Phase Delta electrical system, rather than the Y system, which we now worked with. Victor hadn't changed with the times and kept himself updated with the new methods. What was worse was the fact that he was real picky and liked to dictate how the crews should operate. The problem erupted one day when we were laying out a five-angle line. If the angles are the same between your poles, it's easy to get the proper sag in the line if you just set out one angle and leave the other lines in the runnin' blocks. Well, Connelly, the foreman, said he wanted us to set each angle out then sag between each pole separately. Victor, the inspector, had told him that was the way it should be done and left. My previous experience with supervision taught me that if you let a foreman run over you with his authority when he was wrong, then that was a step backward, so I objected. Connelly said, "Are you tellin' me that you're refusing to do what I tell you to do?"

"Yes, I am, that's pole jockeying, and I'm not going to do it. You can call it insubordination or whatever. I suggest you call Evans or

Queens if you want to, I don't care." That was just up his fancy, as Queens was the Superintendent, so he called him.

When Ralph Queens arrived, he came over, "What the hell's the problem, hillbilly?"

"It's very simple. We got a five-angle set up, and I just want to sag it by setting out the odd angle. He wants me to set each one separate. Now that's unnecessary trips up and down and that's pole jockeying. When I came to work here, I told you I wasn't pole jockeying." He agreed and called Connelly over while I was still there. He spoke directly to Connelly, "You can easily sag that line by setting out one angle, so this man's within his rights for refusing to pole jockey for you." Connelly looked at him and then at me, and though he didn't want to eat crow he had to. Queens continued, "Now, Connelly, just for your sake, I'm going to take this hillbilly with me. It's obvious he doesn't want to work for you and you don't want him here either. This arrangement's not going to work. You get your junk, Ted, and I'll take you back to your car."

When I got in the car with Queens and we were on our way back to get my car, we started visiting about old times. Connelly didn't know it, but Ralph Queens and I had been associated 16 years ago. "Ted, I'll drop you off back at your car. You come on in tomorrow morning."

"OK, Daddy-O." He had picked up the handle Daddy Queens several years back. Anyway I would get paid for the day, but I was curious as to what would be in store for me tomorrow.

Next morning there outside of Queens' office, I ran into Walt LaPointe. Walt seemed lost in thought as he walked around kicking insulators and whatever else happened to be in front of him on the ground. Probably just like me, he was wondering why he was there. We ended up figuring Queens was going to put us in another crew, but that did not prove to be the case. Instead, he was making up two new crews and wanted each of us to be foreman of one. What actually happened was that Walt took over another crew, and I got the newly-formed one. Queens explained that he wanted us to take over the work up on Vine Street. Apparently they were having trouble there, and he wasn't satisfied with the work progress.

Vine Street goes up a hill and then weaves through town. It was kind of a third-class neighborhood but safe to walk through most times of night. Walt had a crew of twelve, and was working on one end of the line. I had nine men and was on the other end. The poles were already in, but this was touchy business because we were bringing this line over the top of hot lines. Work progressed pretty well, and eventually our two crews came together on opposite sides of the street. We both started to facilitate the crossover and bring the new line over the intersection under tension.

A few days before this, as our crews worked toward each other, Walt and I stood talking. I asked him if he had found out who had his crew before and why they had left. He said from what he could tell, the crew had lost respect for the original foreman, and the crew's effectiveness came to Queen's attention when various line problems surfaced. In the old days, say fifty-eight and before, the foreman commanded a lot of respect. Seemed like things lately had been changing and that the foreman was viewed as an obstacle to get around. New and younger men were coming in and there seemed to be less interest in work and more in money, faster cars, older wine, and younger women so to speak. Some of the foremen, to get along, had allowed themselves to be just one of the boys on the crew. When this happened, there was a lack of leadership, and the crew's performance left a lot to be desired. At the same time, the crew lost respect for the foreman. After a few days, like an old drill sergeant, Walt became an asshole, but at the same time pretty well whipped his crew into shape.

On Walt's crew was a man called Rude. We called him Old Man Rude. He was an awfully good lineman, but didn't want the responsibility of becoming a foreman. Rude was a good lead man and especially good working by himself up in the bucket truck. On this particular day as we set things up to cross the intersection, we did not have a bucket truck. The trucks with the insulated stick and bucket were in short supply in those days. They were just starting to be used a lot and production was behind demand, so you didn't always have one available when you needed it. We decided to go ahead and bring the line across without the truck. The line now was up and had electricity going through it. Temporarily, we killed the power for three spans on my side and hooked into Walt's pole where Old Man Rude was. We took up the slack, and then put the jumpers across. At the same time, Walt put a set of saddles on his side. A saddle was a number-two copper wire with a big U shape attached to the line. The purpose of the saddle was to be able to hook your hot line clamp into it and be able to isolate the line if necessary. The hookup was complete, the switch was closed, and the whole line was hot. Old Man Rude was told the line was hot. He was doing some secondary work, something to do with the neutral wire. It was dinner time and the crews were waiting below to go to lunch. For some reason, Old Man Rude started reaching up for that damn saddle. The saddle was kinda cockeyed, and maybe he was gonna straighten it or something. Walt LaPointe hollered at him, I yelled, other men on the crew tried to warn him. He did not hear us probably because of the noon hour traffic. Rude had taken his high-voltage gloves off, and, ready to come down for lunch, he just reached up and touched the saddle. He was killed instantly. Sterling, one of the truck drivers, automatically called for an ambulance and also a bucket truck. The company crews were spread all over the city, but they had a bucket truck there within fifteen minutes to get him off the pole. With all the confusion and everything I saw, I had to get the crew busy. I said, "Let's clean this shit up before we have another accident." Things got moving, tasks were assigned, but I didn't see Walt. I wondered where the hell he was. After the ambulance had taken Rude away, things settled down and everything was pretty secure. I told the men, "You guys can do whatever the hell you want to for awhile. I just gotta go someplace for a few minutes." There was a bar there and I stepped in and sat down. By now everyone knew what had happened outside. I ordered a coca-cola and the girl poured it into a glass in front of me. Pretty soon in came Walt. I don't know where he had been and wouldn't have considered asking him anyway. He didn't see me. He had a faraway look on his face. Ordering a whiskey, he sat there, and I decided after a few minutes this was not the time to talk to him. I left the bar and got ahold of Fairweather, a fellow lineman, and told him we'd leave him the pickup and to stay with Walt while I took the two crews back to the home office. I asked the men if anybody wanted to work the next day. Nobody wanted to. That being a

Thursday, I told them to take the rest of the week off.

When I went into the office, Queens was there, and I said, "You can fire me if you want, but nobody wanted to work tomorrow so I gave them the rest of the week off."

He said, "That's OK, that's good."

Evans, the Assistant Superintendent, sat at a nearby desk, "But our units will be down."

I countered, "Do you want to go out and kill somebody else just to get the units up?" Evans didn't like me nor I him.

**********   .

I was ready to leave D & Z and move on for a couple of reasons. Connelly and I had another run-in, and Mary and I had not established roots to stay here permanently. I called Buck Wooddell in the Union Office to see what was available. He said that there was a Cleveland-based contractor that would have work for at least five years. Buck asked about the family, and being August he suggested that this might be the best time to change jobs so there wouldn't be a school disruption.

Not too far from Springfield, Ohio, in a little town called Treemont, I joined Hubert Electric. They had a contract to put parking lot lighting in at a big assembly plant and the associated rail loading area. The trouble was that the materials to do the job had not arrived yet. The foreman, Ray Bowman, was a little guy, maybe 110 pounds at the most. Ray was a high-tower lineman and because of his classification he was foreman, but admitted this kind of work was new to him. He asked for our help, and we all agreed to make things work. It went along two or three weeks, and other than a few poles, we still didn't have our material. Don Hubert, the owner's son, just wanted us to look busy each day. Well, that was frustrating as hell because you can only look busy for so long. He really couldn't afford to turn the men loose because it took too long assembling the crew in the first place. Finally, one day old man Hubert came around and started chewin' on the boy. "Boy, haven't you learned one damn thing?"

"We don't have any material, so I can't work them."

"Well, damn it, send them to the bar until the material arrives!"

"But Dad, they can't afford life in a bar."

"Then pay them for it."

From then on, for several more weeks until the material arrived, we would show up for work for an hour, then go to the bar and play pool until three, then go back to work for a half hour, then home. Don Hubert gave the bar owner $20 a day for the use of the pool table, and the men seemed content. Don did give us fair warning, "You boys are on the gravy train now, but I expect to see nothin' but assholes and elbows when this material arrives." When everything finally came, we had the job finished in three weeks, though we had been there twelve.

Don asked me if I would go to Cleveland and work on a big project. They had the contract for city lighting. I said I didn't want to work in Cleveland, and he said he wanted me to do cable splicing and maybe some occasional rigging. He also reminded me that splicing paid a lot more and suggested I try it for a few days. I agreed to help with the splicing, but wanted to look around the city a little before I committed to the rest.

We pulled up to this manhole down by the waterfront where we would be splicing. I had done this a few times before. With the guards around the hole, I sent down the methane sampler, and it checked negative. The hole was dry, and I set the blower in for a little while. Once we got down there it was chilly, and I mentioned this to Don. He threw down a bag with jackets and out popped this forty-five caliber pistol. "What's this?"

"No nigger's going to catch me down in this hole!"

I replied with a passive, "OK." It was 1969 and all hell had broken loose in Detroit the year before. Cleveland only had a few small racial incidents, and yet people were still edgy. If things ever got cranked up here, it might take 10 years to settle down. It didn't seem like a great place to raise a family, plus, there was just too much traffic congestion in town for me.

It took us six hours to do the splicing at this site and Don said it would be another day before we would start again, though the pay would be continuous. I got to thinking that night and called Buck

Wooddell the next day. I said I wanted something outside of Cleveland. I let Don know I was leaving that afternoon and headed for another project at a substation near Aberdeen, Ohio.

At Aberdeen I was just a lineman, installing the steel structure and switches in a switch yard. Another crew from the Operators and Engineers Union (O&E) was also working there, and they got it in their heads that they were going to take the line truck we were using. The truck actually belonged to Ohio Electric, but we needed it. I called Buck to see what to do. Buck said, "Hold your ground."

"But Buck, there are fifty of those guys and seven of us."

"Hold your ground. I'll look into it."

Next day nothing happened, and again the O&E boys came over demanding the truck. "You're not getting this truck. You know the union rules as well as I do," I said. I took the truck keys and stated, "I'm not going to argue or fight you boys over it." I stood there casually with my hands in my pockets trying to see a stick or something to fight with in case they rushed me.

They left, but before evening came that same day, they all again came over and one said, "We're takin' that truck in the morning!"

"You better think twice about that," I said. I had been trying to get hold of Buck all afternoon, but he hadn't been in his office. I tried to get him that evening at quitting time, still no answer. Next morning I did get ahold of Ray Bowman who was a regular lineman that happened to be in the office. "A lot of good you boys are doing for us in the Union office. I'm in the middle of a hornet's nest."

"Just a minute, Buck's just coming in," he said.

Buck came to the phone huffin' and puffin', "We got it all settled."

"What the hell you breathin' so hard for?" I asked. I knew the O&E Union office was only a couple doors down from Buck's.

"We settled it the old-fashioned way, out behind the barn. You got your truck." Ray later told me that Buck looked liked he had run into a Mack truck. His clothes were all torn up and he was banged up too. Buck probably weighed 225 pounds or so, and the O&E business administrator (BA) was probably as big.

The O&E boys at Aberdeen hadn't gotten the word yet, and here they all come after the truck. I told Larry Demar, "Tell the boys to either go home or get a bat or cant hook." The cant hooks were a rounded steel bar with a sharp point attached to the end of a wood pole. They were used to move the heavy power poles and would look intimidating to these boys. "They ain't taking the damn truck," I said.

"Ted, we can't whip 'em all," said Larry.

"No, but maybe a few of them." I thought it would end up just Larry and me because he was fool enough to hang with me, but instead all seven stayed.

They saw us armed with the cant hooks, and even though the odds were seven to twenty or more, they backed off. Of course Larry had to open his big mouth. "I don't think there's a fighter in the whole damn bunch." I was thinking, "Thanks, Larry, that's all I need."

Another man from O&E came up to the group. "I don't know whether you got it from your BA or not, but they settled this up at the Union Hall."

Larry's response was, "Yeah, I suppose they probably settled all right, just when I thought I'd get a chance to rip somebody's ass."

"Larry, you're just asking for it now," I said. Larry was Indian, and all he could think about was fighting.

From Aberdeen we went over to Russellville where we had a real serious incident that got everybody's attention. The General Foreman, named Jimmy, was supposed to cut the power to the line. An old buddy of his showed up, and they got to visiting. Well, he tagged the switches as being cut off and told us he'd cut the power, but he never really opened the switches. Jim Callicoat had this funny feeling about the situation when he saw Jimmy come back with this big grin on his face talking to his buddy.

We were sitting in this black jack pole, and Jim had everyone put on their high-voltage gloves, as these poles were excellent conductors of electricity. These poles were pine and loaded with creosote to preserve them. They also were extra strong and were used on corners and other areas where automobiles might accidentally hit them. As we lowered the pole into the hole, the top touched the power line and boy did the smoke role out. Obviously the power had not been cut, and Jim had saved our ass with his funny feeling and the high-voltage gloves. We left the pole at an angle in the hole and did not finish setting it. If you couldn't trust the supervisor, then that was no place to work. We went to the bar.

Jim Callicoat was a fine man, an excellent lineman with experience in all forms of electrical work from high towers to general distribution. He was proving his capability as an outstanding foreman as well, however, he had gone through a rather dark period in life before he had become a foreman.

I had climbed poles with Jim up in Cincinnati and also down at Ripley, and we were good friends. Jim had cultivated a bad habit though, as we all do from time-to-time. When the spool on the truck was taking up line, instead of positioning the line around the butterfly, which held the line on the spool, Jim would flip it over. This had historically proven to be a dangerous thing to do. If the line didn't catch on the spool and happened to form a loop or half hitch, it could catch a man's hand and dislodge his shoulder, arm, or remove a hand. I had warned Jim about this habit and told him if he didn't stop doing it his days would be numbered. Even though I had warned him a few times, I really had no deep-seated feeling that anything would happen.

I was working on a pole quite a way from the line truck, when I saw the ambulance coming. It didn't seem like it was a real critical situation as the driver wasn't racing and only occasionally turned his siren on for a couple seconds. The sound did seem to cut out when he got down by the line truck, so, sensing something was wrong there, a couple of us walked back. Nothing seemed wrong with the line truck. If it had hit a live wire, the tires would be smoking or burned flat. Several of the crew were standing around in the road next to the ambulance. Jim had a bloodstained shirt over his arm, and I instantly knew what had happened. "Have you found his hand?" I asked. Somebody said they hadn't so I suggested we make a thorough search.

Still with a sense of humor, Jim said, "It's the one with the ring on it." We scrounged all over there but couldn't find Jim's hand. The ambulance driver said that he could only wait around for another fifteen minutes or so, otherwise it would be too late anyway to save the hand, and also Jim might go into shock. We conducted another good search, but no hand. As the ambulance left with Jim, I really had guilty feelings. I should have insisted he quit flippin' the line, damn it.

The next day we found Jim's hand. We took the ring off, and Queens took it to the hospital.

We kinda lost track of Jim Callicoat for quite a period of time until Jim's wife called Buck Wooddell. She said Jim was all blue and down in the dumps and had been drinking up all their grocery money. Could Buck put him back to work drunk or sober? I really gained a lot of respect for the way Buck handled the situation, and it was a tough one.

Shortly after Buck had talked with Jim's wife, he called and got Jim on the phone. "You get your ass up here tomorrow morning. I got work lined up for you." Jim must have given Buck a little bullshit on the phone. "Callicoat, if you don't want me to come after you, be here at eight a.m. tomorrow morning."

Jim did show up the next morning, and I wasn't there, but another guy called Ray told me what happened. Jim looked pretty good; at least he'd shaved and taken a bath. With some pretty harsh words Buck told Jim to get his ass in the office. Ray said that Buck slammed the door real hard behind them, but it popped back open a foot. Buck's secretary was in there and didn't know what to do, but she stayed and told Ray what happened.

Before Buck ever reached the desk in his office, he turned around to face Jim. "Callicoat, who in the hell do you think you are? You lose four fingers and a damn thumb, then put yourself in a jug and expect everyone to show you pity. I'm not going to show you a god-damned bit of pity, you sorry S.O.B. You better get some sense in your head. I want you to come back tomorrow morning, and I don't want you to look like you came through a threshing machine. You are a disgrace as a human being. I'll have a job for you tomorrow. You better have your facilities together." Callicoat stomped out of the office. Buck had made him mad. Buck came out of the office with tears rollin' down his cheeks. To the secretary he said, "How could I treat a guy like that; another human being like that?"

I guess Buck's chewing out did the trick, because the next morning Callicoat showed up wide-awake and all spit-shined. Buck handed Jim a piece of paper, "Here's a referral slip and phone number for a foreman's job. I don't want to hear any more shit out of you. Get the hell out of here and keep yourself straight. If you don't, I'll stomp your ass every time you get outta line."

Jim made a great foreman and teacher too. However, he did get outta line about a month later. This crew was putting the basket on top of a high line tower with a crane. The basket is that portion with the arms that actually hold up the power lines. They come in different sizes, seven, nine, eleven, and fifteen ton. Sometimes they lower them on with a helicopter and use four men to catch it, but with a crane they just use two. Each man has a spud wrench made of a steel that bends. It comes to a long point, like a punch on one end, and on the other is like an end wrench. When they lower the basket, one man will pull the basket into position and put the spud wrench through the basket frame hole into the tower frame hole. The other man has only a few seconds to get his spud in, and if he misses, the first man must get his back out quickly or there could be a real dangerous situation develop several hundred feet in the air.

The second man on this crew was a young apprentice, and he missed getting his spud in. Jim, who was the general foreman, asked the crew foreman if it was all right to show the kid how to catch that tower. The foreman said it was all right with him if it was OK with the union steward. The steward said he didn't care as Jim was classified as an "A" Lineman, so up the tower pole Jim went and with one good hand and a hook for the other, Jim quickly spudded the basket in. Jim hadn't meant to embarrass the kid, but I guess he did and the kid complained to someone. Next morning here comes Buck, "Callicoat, you haven't been on the job 30 days and already you're in hot water." Jim started to say something, but Buck interrupted. "Forget it, I already know what happened. You're taking work away from the men." Buck continued, "You're in supervision now, you can't climb poles and towers and catch steel anymore. The fine's $500, and you'll have to take the rest of the day off." Jim didn't say anything, but it probably still made him feel good that he could still do the job even if he only had one hand.

From Russellville I went down by Springfield to install outside lights in a cattle feed lot. I was working for Hawkins Electric. The feed lots were located around South Carleston, and we had about 30 poles to set. They all went in without having to climb a one. We simply laid the poles down on the west side where the holes were to be and dug the holes from the east side. The transformers and switches were attached to the poles before we even set them. The four lines we had strung loosely between the poles. When the poles were all in, we tightened the wires and left things overnight to see how the sag changed. Larry Demar was just learning line work and didn't have much time in the hooks, so I let him climb the poles and tie in the lines. It was comical to watch Larry. He'd climb up ten or fifteen feet, slide down, see if anyone was watching, then start back up again. Took him about three days to get them all tied in. It took me about that long to make the meter hookup, and then we hung three transformers.

Larry was a good guy to work with and we were very compatible. Maybe 'cause we both had Indian blood, I don't know. I do remember Larry had the biggest feet I'd ever seen, size 14 or 15 boots. When he was up on a pole and you'd look up, all you could see was the huge soles of Larry's boots. Larry did like to fight though, and on this project it came to the surface again.

There were two hippies on the job that had come from some outfit in Alabama. They each wore a bandanna over their long hair with a feather sticking out. As far as accomplishing any work, they were about worthless. The most they'd do was carry a shovel back and forth, and sometimes misplace that. In those times, it was almost impossible to fire anyone unless you could make it stand up in court. It was the government's philosophy that if you kept everyone employed, the money would keep flowing through the cash registers. If you had somebody who wasn't productive, it was either the superintendent's fault for not providing work they could do, or the foreman's fault for not teaching them if they couldn't do it. It was never their fault so they should be kept employed.

One Monday morning when I came to work I could see Larry sitting on a pole with a faraway look in his eyes. I walked up to him, "What's the matter, you have a hard weekend?" Not a word, he just sat there staring out. The best thing I could do was leave him alone. I kinda watched him from a distance. All of a sudden he slapped his hands on his knees and got up, "I've had enough of those no account S.O.B.s." He walked over and grabbed each of the hippies by the back of the neck and started bangin' their heads together. Then, he pulled them up and dumped them on the ground. The bandannas and feathers came off and the long hair spread out. "You get your asses off this job. You've insulted my ancestors long enough." There was no resistance. Boy, did those fellas haul outta there.

About 10 a.m. the foreman came around, "I'd like to meet the fella that run off those two boys of mine." I couldn't see any sense of creating a scene here; the foreman was a pretty hefty fellow, but I figured Larry would kill him.

"He's not here right now, he's busy," I said.

About that time, Larry stepped from behind a pole, "I'm the guy that beat their asses, and I want to know what you're going to do about it."

The foreman's eyes widened, "I'm goin' to do nothin' about it except shake the hand of the man that got rid of them. I've been trying to run them S.O.B.s off ever since they started. I'd like to buy you a beer after work."

"What do you think, Ted? At least he was man enough to tell us what was on his mind," was Larry's response.

"Sure," I said, "we'll go down and have a cordial drink with him."

I had a coffee and Larry had a coke or beer, I don't remember, but we listened to the foreman sputter about not being able to get rid of people like the hippies who didn't do any work. "Those fellas haven't done 10 minutes' worth of work since they've been here. The government's got us by the balls, can't fire them unless we got an attorney who thinks we got a good case."

We started the feed lot lighting work in September and finished it before the month ended. Old man Hawkins came down to check on things because they hadn't expected us to finish until October. "You been pushin' things pretty hard, haven't ya? How'd ya get the poles up so fast with all that climbing?"

"Sir, we didn't do much climbing and didn't push very hard, but you know winter's coming soon."

"If you can put up a line that fast, we can use you on the internal wiring too." Inside wiring was done by journeyman wiremen. They were electricians whom we referred to as JWs. Mr. Hawkins worked it out with the JW Union so that we would have inside work to keep us employed. It kept us busy until around Christmas and then when the work ran out Larry left. Shortly afterwards, I went down to Russellville for awhile.

It was the early winter of 1970, and work in this area seemed to be petering out. Things hadn't worked out as I had expected. When I originally came up to Cincinnati, there was supposed to be electrical work on the new expressways that was to last several years, and that's why I brought Mary and the kids up to Mt. Sterling. We figured on settling permanently in the area.

The problem now was that the new expressway projects were getting out-of-control cost wise, especially on the East and West Coasts. I wasn't a big Nixon fan, but when he closed all the projects I don't think he did the right thing, even with cost overruns out of control. Now, I had to again travel around to find work.

Mary decided to stay in Mt. Sterling until something more permanent came up. She didn't want to move back down south, and I didn't want her to. We liked the Cincinnati area but really couldn't find what we wanted for a permanent home.

I heard that there might be some work available up in the Detroit area, so I called an old friend, Roy Simpson, who worked for Hinkles & McCoy. He had been a foreman but had since been promoted to superintendent. He said that yes, there would be plenty of work available because Hinkles & McCoy had a five-year contract with Detroit Edison. Roy said he would put a call in for me through Local Seventeen in Detroit.

I left Mary and the kids in Mt. Sterling and headed north. Once established at work, I started hunting around for a place to rent so I could move them up with me. I heard about a small place for rent in the little town of Linden. Linden was about an hour north of Detroit and a little west of Lapeer. That would be great because Mary loved to fish, and it would be nice for the kids. Unfortunately when I arrived, it had already been rented. I continued on up the road to Dryden and was just looking around when I noticed a vacant house out in the country. I couldn't find anyone around, even at the neighboring farmhouse.

Back at work I got to talking to one of the Canadian linemen and he started describing a house that was available up by Dryden. One of his buddies had lived there but had to return home for some reason. The more he talked about it the more it sounded like the vacant house I had looked at, and it turned out it was. The next time I went up in the middle of the week and talked to the owner. I agreed to rent the place, and he asked if I might be interested in buying. Said he had too much land and would sell 10 acres with the house. That sounded good to me, but I said I'd like to stay there for a couple months and have my wife see it before I committed myself.

In March we pulled the kids out of school and moved from Ohio to Michigan. Mary liked the place, and we agreed to buy it and pay our down payment in September. He said that the land would not be worked anymore and was ours to use.

Everything was going pretty good until one Saturday morning in the spring when I woke up to tractor noise. I looked out and our 10-acre field had been tilled and Dernberger, the next-door farmer, was out planting in it. I said to him, "Did that guy rent this field to you?"

"Yep, he said I could rent it for the next two years." That damn Lithuanian had lied to me. I called him up and said I wanted to pay the rent and talk to him.

When the owner arrived, I handed him the month's rent and then another month's rent. "I'm leavin'."

"What's the matter?"

"You lied to me, your word is not good." It was that simple. I had to get a place lined up to move Mary and the kids, but I knew I couldn't trust that damn Lithuanian. One good thing happened though. I had almost committed to buying 10 head of cattle and would have closed the deal the next day. At least I didn't have them to move too.

Not only would I have another home to look for, I soon found out that I would also have to be looking for another job. What happened, I'm not sure, but for some reason Edison backed out of their deal with Hinkles & McCoy. Old man Hinkles was really pissed. Edison had required twelve full line crews, four bucket trucks, and six utility trucks all for five years. The old man had pulled equipment and crews from Louisiana, Texas, and even Arizona to fulfill this obligation. We had only been going for six months. I got a letter from Roy Simpson later, and he said he figured that old man Hinkle got his contract money out of Detroit Edison, even though we didn't perform the work. Why Edison backed out I heard was just politics.

Next I arranged a call through the Grand Rapids Local to go to work for Hydaker & Wheatlake in Reed City. I had a month's rent paid in Dryden for Mary, so I headed to Reed City. I liked the area and later brought Mary and the kids up for a short stay at Rose Lake. Everybody had a good time, Mary fishing and the kids swimming. We still yearned for a place to permanently settle on.

Our break came when Roy Smith, a guy I worked with, told me about this place south of Big Rapids that might be available. He lived around there and knew the area pretty well. I went down and talked to the owner, a Mr. Higlee, about renting. He said he'd much rather sell it to me. It was vacant, and he wanted someone who would keep it up. I told him I'd like for my wife to see it, but before I left I had a rental agreement with an option to buy.

I hoped Mary would like the place. It was 15 acres at the end of a dead-end road surrounded on all sides by woods, a pretty setting indeed. The house was empty and needed a lot of work, but I was pretty handy fixing things up. There also was an old two-car garage, and not too far to the south was Quigley Creek. I knew the kids would like that.

When we all rolled in. Mary got out and gave the place a quick once over. She then came back, looked me in the eye, "I like it, let's buy it and stay." We had finally put down our roots for good. This would be our permanent home, exactly what we had been searching so long for.

A LINEMAN'S GRIEF

Unnoticed as he passed me in the bar
   wind-burned face pitted with scars
Whiskey he said as he pulled up a chair
   voice was low I noted a tremble there.
One swallow it was all down,
   motioned to the bartender another round.
Slowly this time he sipped his drink
   his eyes were set they did not blink,
The cigarette trembled in now pale lips
   he was falling apart bit by bit.
Holding his large hands as if a child
   curing his troubles will take awhile.
He was a broken-hearted lineman
   who witnessed the loss of our friend.
Grief I knew, but I couldn't help him,
   a thousand deaths he'll die before he will comprehend.

INNOCENT INNKEEPER

It was the year and spring of nineteen sixty-nine
    I had not been in Cincinnati but a short time.
I am one of those guys who chase dreams around,
    my job is to build power lines in your town.
We move around like gypsys and live day-by-day,
    most of us will share our lives in various ways.
Two boys experience a true article of life
    they were having a ball until each one saw his wife.
They looked at each other, as if stabbed in the back,
    both knowing they had carefully covered their tracks
From the girls they untangled their bodies, trying to stand tall
    both now knowing the elderly innkeeper was their downfall.
All of you who are foolish at heart, make your plans well
    let no one know, for they will innocently tell.
Keep this in mind as you go your foolish way,
    your wife can be the other party who wants to play.

In the International Brotherhood of Electrical Workers (IBEW), the local union official was the BA (business administrator). To hold this position, these men had to have been linemen previously. Most of them did a good job, but there were only a few who would do their job, plus the extra ten percent, and really stand out. R.L. "Buck" Wooddell was a special BA, a tough man, but the kind of person who would go the additional step and show the extra interest when dealing with his men. He inspired this poem.

SOMEONE

When life gets you down and
   things just don't fit
Someone takes time to show you
   the answers bit by bit.
At times knowing you are wrong and
   afraid of geting caught
With a special authority this someone is
   showing you it's all for naught.
When grief has come your way and
   your heart is heavy with pain.
Unexpected this someone lets you
   know he is a helping hand.
This someone you never quite understand
   of his many determined ways
His integrity and loyalty you respect,
   knowing he fights the devil each day.
You wonder how such a man
   could have a tender heart
Then you realize you are his brother
   voluntarily you become a part.
What each one does, bad or good,
   in this brotherhood is what counts.
This someone wants to show you its
   shame and rewards every ounce
Let your mind and heart be open
   towards this someone of today
Decisions for your welfare don't
   come casy for this type of BA.

Above: At the Jacksonville shipyard is Marvin Lane's tug Marlene that Ted helped build and wire.

Below: Ted and Lloyd Whittiker alias Darlin' and Sugar from the laundromat.

VIII

Putting Down Roots

I moved Mary and the kids to our new home and took some time off to get the place in liveable condition. Everybody was happy as was I to at last have a place we could call home. There had been too much moving since we left Florida, and it had been hard on everybody. Mary and I both knew, however, that although the family had settled down, my work would continue to keep me on the road. Even though I would become very lonely away from home, at least I would have the peace of mind to know that Mary and the kids were happy and someplace they wanted to be, and I would always have a permanent place to come back to.

Work for linemen was not as plentiful as it had been in previous years. When I came up from Detroit, I had heard that Hydaker & Wheatlake had a fair amount of general line work available. The first time I saw the operation I was not overly impressed. Looked like kind of an outpost, almost a little primitive compared to the equipment I had been used to working with. They didn't have a bucket truck or a hydraulic boom truck to set poles, just the bare necessities. In some respects it turned out to be a very enjoyable job because a man got the job done through using his own head, not because he had the latest equipment, which was a convenience.

Even though we were away from home most of the week, we were close enough to easily drive home for the weekends. We worked around Cheboygan, Gladwin, Clare, Baldwin, and on another project south of Cadillac. I ran a three-man crew and Garney Crawford ran the other crew. He was an excellent lineman, and besides being good friends, we thought alike and worked well together. Frank Wheatlake, the owner, was also a fine individual. He had started the company with very little but had been quite successful. He would have liked to be a lineman too, but he could never get himself coordinated on a pole. He was the type of boss that would let you do the job as you see fit as long as it was safe and you met your production goals.

The only guy I had trouble with was the general foreman, Charlie Rasmussen. The first time I irritated him was when I had a five-man crew and we were spread a little thin equipment-wise. We were working some hot stuff, and I needed a tension machine. I went directly to Frank for the machine, and he saw to it that we had it promptly. It irritated Charlie because I went over his head to get the equipment. From then on he had a chip on his shoulder for me.

My crew was well up on its production, so one Friday we left early for home. Most of the boys had 60 to 70 miles to go, and it helped them to leave early. Charlie showed up on Friday afternoon and found that we were gone.

Come Monday morning, Charlie rolled in to give me some grief about it. "Charlie, it's an unwritten rule. A General Foreman does not come around to inspect on Friday afternoon. These boys have a long ways to drive home to see their families. Besides, we were well ahead of schedule." That didn't satisfy Charlie, and the more a big deal he made about it the madder I got. After work I stopped in to see Frank. "You gotta get Charlie off of my back or I'm afraid you can take this job and shove it. Check our progress sheet."

As I said before, Frank was interested in production, "I'll take care of Charlie for you."

"Also," I added, "How's about delivering the crew's paychecks directly to me rather than Charlie?"

"No problem, Ted." Charlie did not come around and bother us again.

One day we were east of Alpena setting poles up around a little town called Atlantis. We ran out of dynamite, so I called Frank to see if he would bring some up to us. He said he would. We also told him to bring some butter but didn't tell him why. I knew that would make him curious. We told him where to find us, there where the first stream crosses the road from town.

We were setting poles through some swampy areas, and that's why we needed the dynamite. Once we had the pole upright and partially set, we'd drive a two-inch pipe down beside it. Down the pipe we would push a little dynamite which when detonated would open the ground underneath the pole and it would settle.

Even though we were out of dynamite, we had a dozen caps or so left and were doing a little fishing. By attaching the cap to a wooden float, we could get it out in the stream, and when a trout came by, we'd set her off and the stunned fish rolled up on his side. We had a few accumulated and a fire going to cook them up when Frank arrived. When he saw what we were up to, a big grin appeared on his face, "Boys, I sure envy you."

"Well, sit down, dinner will be ready shortly," I said. Frank got out his knife, got down on his knees, and helped clean a couple. That's the kind of guy he was, a manager that wasn't afraid to get his hands dirty or be one of the boys. The fish fried in butter were great, and we even had a couple extra to send home with him.

I worked for Hydaker & Wheatlake for about two and a half years. Work started to be more scarce, and the General Foreman started to become a problem again, so I decided to move on. My union card was now out of Local Eight Seventy-Six in Grand Rapids, so I contacted the union BA to find out where work was available. Of course, my first concern was to work as close to home as possible. They set me up with an outfit based in Flint called New Kirk. With them I worked around Roscommon in Lower Michigan until 1973, then another year in Michigan's Upper Peninsula with Rowen and Blair.

While in the Upper Peninsula, I got a little experience on oil static lines. I found out that if I was willing to travel out of state, I could make extra money and there was more work available. At least that was what I expected.

The first job was in Dothan, Alabama, putting oil static lines underground from a substation to the powerhouse. I had to get a little on-the-job schooling on this one, because I hadn't worked that much with this type of cable. The cables were used where really high voltage was needed. The three lines that went inside the cable had to be perfectly dry before they were pulled in. The cable was then sealed and oil was pumped in under pressure. It didn't take too long to get the hang of it, and I decided to stay with it for awhile because there were only five crews to do this type of work in the United States.

From Alabama we went to Florida, but a strike brought things to a halt there. I called the Union BA in Nashville as I heard there was a project there. He said he could use me, so I headed to Nashville. This was a low-voltage oil static line, thirty-eight thousand volts compared to two hundred and forty thousand volts on the one at Dothan. The line in Nashville was for the Grand Old Opera Theater.

I had called the Nashville BA on Friday and on the same day they went on strike there. When I arrived on Monday, the BA said, "I know who you are and why you're here 'cause I took your number. Trouble is, because of the strike I got too many men and not enough work, and I can't work ya. How's about I give you three day's pay and your travel expenses?" I said that was OK and I headed to Michigan and home.

In 1975 I again worked for New Kirk for awhile and then got a job in Midland, Michigan where they were constructing a nuclear power plant. That was inside work and paid several dollars more per hour than ordinary line work, but there were problems there. It was a merry-go-round, the most poorly engineered and mismanaged, wasteful operation I had ever seen. As an ordinary lineman and electrician I may not have always been able to comprehend the big picture, but I had worked on some big projects before with the Tennessee Valley Authority (TVA), so I did have something to compare this operation to. It didn't take a tree full of owls to figure out that something was amiss here.

For example, if you were going to put in a junction box, you'd mark your holes, then call in an engineer to approve it. He'd check the print, then call Ann Arbor for approval, and maybe six hours later, you'd have it in and the next shift would finish it up. Two or three days or maybe a week later you would find yourself back reinstalling the same box, because they'd decided to move it.

There were hundreds of engineers all with different ways of doing the job. When I checked around, this same inefficiency was going on with the pipe fitters also. I got ahold of the general foreman, a man named Duffy. I suggested to him that every foreman should take detailed notes as to how time was spent, and what was specifically installed by number, and the same when something was removed.

From the news we were getting, it looked like the Bechtel Company was trying to blame union labor for the tremendous cost overruns. They had bid the job for cost plus some percent, and the costs were getting out of sight. They were trying to blame the union for supplying unqualified laborers and the delay. We ended up with truckloads of paper detailing inefficient management and engineering. That junction box, for instance, that we installed on the first shift was finished on the second and then torn out on the third shift. For the little that was accomplished, the weekly operating cost was out of sight.

Another thing that looked fishy, Bechtel supposedly owned this machine shop in Kentucky from which we would receive truckloads of new tools, drills, lathes and presses. From what we could see, a lot of them were never used but ended up over by the Titabewasse River just to be buried. The boys hauling the stuff to the dump told me about it. They would try to take home as much as they could rather than leaving it to be buried.

A lot of money was wasted there to somebody's advantage. Consumers Power Company did not seem to have inspectors around to keep track of what was going on. Bechtel Company was mismanaging, misengineering, and trying to hang it on the union. It wasn't hard to see that the project wasn't going to survive. No wonder we're paying high electric bills today. From Midland I was called for a job down by Alma. Over a period of time I had developed a dislike for the BA out of the Grand Rapids Local, and this new assignment really pissed me off. I was almost 50 now and had been climbing poles long enough. The Alma job would be back on the poles while other linemen in their 30s and 40s would be left back at Midland working inside for more money. I tried to argue with the BA, "How about letting some of those young bucks climb the poles? I'll be 50 in a few months."

His curt reply was, "Sorry, you've got the experience needed, and you're being called."

"OK, if that's the way you want to operate, I'll make sure it's done your way."

At Alma right off the bat they tried to get me to do some three phase work by myself. It was an old rule that two linemen were required for that type of work. When I refused and contacted the Local BA, he said that they had changed the rules recently and that two men were not required. I said, "Bullshit," picked up my tools and left.

The Union fought hard for safe work rules, and any time you allowed these to be compromised, you threw away what the Union had worked hard to establish. Some locals obviously emphasized safety more than others. Local Seventy-One out of Columbus and Twelve Forty-Nine out of New York both had a reputation of providing first class linemen. In fact, if you did not obey Union established safety rules, you were fined by the Union, not just the foreman, but the workers too. That happened a few times and people were pretty careful to follow the rules after that. I always figured that safety should never be compromised and followed that principle even though it pissed off management at times. At least I'm still alive.

I had enough of Grand Rapids, so I moved my ticket back down to Local Seventy-One out of Columbus. From the Columbus Local, I worked in Scottsburg, Alabama, in '76 and '77; in Hammond, Indiana, until '79; Terre Haute, Indiana, through '81.

From 1969 until 1981, I was continually on the road. Wherever there was an opening for a Union lineman or, for that matter, an inside electrician, I was out chasing the job down. I made good money, but maintaining the family at home and me on the road left little in our pockets at the end of the year. For instance, in 1978 I made about $42,000, and yet at the end of the year we had only $1,100 saved up. Plus the Internal Revenue Service was continually giving me shit about my travel expenses. All this traveling after the good paying jobs and all this time away from home didn't seem worthwhile. Also there seemed to be less work available.

Finally, I said to hell with it. I took a layoff and collected unemployment for a year. I used that time to fix up the farm and enjoy being home with my family.

After the unemployment ran out, I checked with the Union and there was less and less call for linemen around the country. From then on, I just picked up odd jobs around locally. I did everything from picking sweet corn in the summer to doing small-scale electrical jobs.

I was just as happy, and it seemed that we were just as well off as with me traveling.

Mary had been just as busy as I had all these years. Besides raising kids, she had worked as a receptionist and assistant for a local doctor. When he left, she cooked at the Big D Restaurant close to the expressway south of Morley. Her down-home cooking was a real hit with the truckers, but it caused problems with her legs standing so much and the doctor said she ought to quit that.

Mary always had a big garden from which she canned lots of vegetables for the winter. She raised chickens, ducks, rabbits and for awhile we had a milk cow and sold milk. Mary also spent time out around the countryside gathering herbs for home remedies, just like her Indian grandmother had. Probably the achievement Mary was most proud of was in the middle '70s she went back to school and got her high school diploma.

Times were sometimes pretty tough, especially with another recession going on. Scraping up money for taxes was difficult for a few years, and we got behind. Mary helped out a neighboring sheep farmer in the spring when his sheep were having lambs, and that money helped. A couple of times I went to work for a man wiring a paint shop in Union City, Michigan. I'd be away from home for several months to try and earn enough money to catch up on expenses, but we always seemed just a little behind.

I'm not sure, but I think down at Union City I did some damage to my lungs too. There was a lot of open chemicals to breathe and coupled with the fact that I had always been a smoker left my lungs in bad shape. My hacking cough got worse, and the cold weather really bothered me to work. It seemed with any exertion I was huffin' and puffin'. When I checked with the doctor, he said I had some emphysema and should quit smoking. I had been a little scared though 'cause I thought I might have cancer.

Because of my lungs, for a period of time we were able to qualify for welfare. Guess this should have bothered me, but it didn't. I'd been a tax-paying member of the work force since I was 15.

It's nice to now have time to pursue some other dreams which I have been carrying with me for years.

I've always wanted to write short stories; maybe even a book. My poems tell of my experiences and real people, but I'd like my stories to stir the imagination of young people and maybe cause them to think more. I'd like to write something about the prejudice that exists. My grandmother told me that there was no difference between people whether their skin was black, red, white or yellow or because they spoke a different language. I think it's just plain ignorance on the part of parents for not telling their children the truth.

THE DOOR

In Jacksonville, Florida, on Swift Street is a door,
    through its portals I have walked many times before,
It was through this door, that lived my beautiful wife.
    Inside this door I begin to live my life.
She has stuck with me, through thick and thin,
    her wondrous love has held me up time and time again.
The temptation put before me, I have never fell,
    through my travels her love has kept me well.
We both have problems from day to day,
    right now I am job hopping to make my pay.
She makes her turn each day of the week,
    both are working for fifteen acres to keep.
I watch people where my work carries me.
    most people don't show me any love, that I can see.
The birth of a love is as wonderful as a child,
    the death of either one, it sets you back awhile.
I have seen so many do their loved ones wrong
    their selfish hearts ask what happens when it's gone.
My Mary will never have to worry about me
    our marriage has set us both free!
Life will die for us, this I know,
    our love we have in our children it will grow.
True love in any life can never be lower
    and to think it all started behind this door.

THAT'S A LINEMAN

A pole jockey he is
   sometimes called;
He works on poles both
   short and tall;
He rants and he raves
   about playing squirrel,
But he wouldn't change jobs
   for the world.
He works in the wind, the cold,
   and the snow;
Where a line's being built
   that's where he will go.
He will climb in his hooks
   or work from a bucket,
But when he gets mad
   he tells them to chuck it.
He will work a line hot,
   or he will work it dead.
How do I know so much
   about the things I have said?
I am married to a lineman—
   his name is Ted.

Published in IBEW
Mary E. Aldridge, Author
Wife of Ted Aldridge
Local 876
Grand Rapids, Michigan

PARTING WORDS

Ted likes to visit and he seems to have endless energy to do that. Unfortunately the coughing and hacking gets more frequent and it's time to excuse ourselves and give his throat a rest. Both Ted and Mary seem a little disappointed that we are leaving, but it's getting late.

After backing down the driveway, we start up towards Four Mile Road, and the return to Morley. With a glance back we have the feeling that the little cottage is more than just another house along the road.

Before we get back to Morley, I'll answer a few questions you probably have about all this. First, how did I happen to meet Ted and Mary? My farm lies east of Morley on Jefferson Road, and years ago I used to raise a lot of sweet corn. For awhile, Ted and Mary's sons Robert and John worked for me picking the corn. They were two of the best workers I had. Rain or shine they were out in the field each morning, and never complained or hesitated in their pace. I was curious as to how these boys had learned to become such good workers.

One season they asked if I could use some extra help, as their father was interested in working. When Ted started it was obvious to me how the boys had become such hard workers. They were just reflecting their dad's ways.

When I first met Ted, he was friendly, but in a distant sort of way. It was as if he was trying to size me up before he became too close. Ted helped out for a couple of harvest seasons and then in 1984 after the big fire we got to know each other even better.

My two big barns, most of my machinery and some of my sheep flock had been destroyed by the fire. One of the horses somehow got his head under the water tank heater and flipped it out on the straw bedding. A strong wind fanned the smoldering straw and before long the barn was ablaze.

Ted offered to help with the cleanup, and supervise building the replacement barn. He said he had experience in some areas of construction and I was more than happy to accept his offer. I felt that I could trust his judgement on the decisions that would have to be made. In the course of our conversations Ted also said something about writing poetry. I didn't give this much thought, probably because he just didn't fit my image of a poet. Ted appeared quite intelligent though, especially in the common sense department. He had told me that he hadn't finished high school, so I perceived that most of his learning came from life's school of hard knocks.

It was an evening in April when Ted came over to discuss plans for the new barn. He was carrying a briefcase, and said, "I brought my poms." I sometimes did have a little trouble understanding his mixture of southern and hillbilly drawl. "You brought your what?" "I brought my poms." I finally got it. These were the poems he had talked about writing.

Ted popped open the case and there was a stack of papers with poems on them. Some were typed and some handwritten. The papers were a variety of colors and sizes. I wasn't particularly interested in poetry, but I knew I would have to read some, or Ted's feelings would be hurt. He handed me one poem and gave a brief description of what it was about. As I finished that he did the same with a few more. "Wow, these were good," I thought. I certainly had no expertise on poetry, but his verse told a clear story of some of his life experiences, and in a way they stirred my emotions. I asked if he'd ever tried to get them published. He said he had taken them up to Ferris State University, but a professor said they weren't in the right format and wasn't that impressed.

I didn't know Ted's wife Mary very well, but one year I had to be away from home a lot during lambing season and she offered to help. She did a great job with the sheep and even had meals ready for the kids when they came home from school. From that time on, I had her help each year when the lambs came.

Over the years I became close friends with both Ted and Mary. Though Ted hadn't finished high school he kept current on world affairs and always had an intelligent opinion on everything from politics, religion, education to economics. I still remembered some of Ted's poetry that I had read years before, and one day I asked him if I could see the poems again. As I read through them they seemed even more special now.

Each of Ted's poems was about something that had taken place in his life. I suggested that the poems would be much more meaningful if people knew the story behind each poem and that they certainly would be a nice gift to pass on to his family. Ted agreed, and over the course of a year we spent many evenings recording the details of both his and Mary's life.

Now you know something about my friends Ted and Mary Aldridge. Before you go though, I'd like you to take one more trip with me. I'm sure you will find it a rewarding experience and one you will remember. Let's slip back a few years in time and retrace Ted's footsteps across this country. From a lonely hotel room in Alabama, to the shores of Lake Superior in Michigan and the top of a river bluff in Ohio. More than admiring the scenery we'll attempt to stand beside him and share his experiences and his feelings.

If you're not into poetry, forget it's poetry and imagine it as the true lyrics to a song about a man's life. Here we go, with Poems and Memories, the rest of the story.

International Brotherhood of Electrical Workers

Pension Member

This is to Certify that

ROBERT E. ALDRIDGE

has been a loyal and faithful member of our Brotherhood
for more than twenty years, and according to Article
XII of our Constitution, has been admitted to pension.

Jack I. Moore   *J. J. Barry*

MEMBER'S SIGNATURE

International Brotherhood of Electrical Workers

Local Union No. **71**

Proudly presents to

Robert E. Aldridge

this testimonial and pin in honor of your
years of service in our Brotherhood

Presented this ___ of June 19 93

Don Taylor
Wally Siebles

MEMBER'S SIGNATURE

103507   OFFICIAL   RECEIPT

SERIES 1-1968
**MEMBER'S
RECEIPT**

FORM 1 L   **INTERNATIONAL BROTHERHOOD OF ELECTRICAL WORKERS (AFL-CIO-CLC)** 36

I. O. PORTION		LOCAL UNION PORTION				PAID	
AMOUNT	CODE	AMOUNT	CODE	AMOUNT	CODE	DATE	TOTAL
12.80	9	4.00	10			33.21	
		16.41	4			3-27-69	

JAN	FEB	MAR	APR	MAY	JUN	JUL	AUG	SEP	OCT	NOV	DEC	L.U. NO.	TYPE MEMB.		CARD NO.
			X									71	A / X	BA	P-378527

RECEIVED OF

Robert E. Aldridge

Lineman
R. L. Wooddell
CLASSIFICATION

WHEN CODES ARE USED SEE BACK OF RECEIPT FOR EXPLANATION OF PAYMENTS   FINANCIAL SECRETARY

IX

Poems and Memories

In the spring of 1969 something happened in Ripley, Ohio that sparked a change in my life, though I didn't recognize it at the time. I was east of Moscow, Ohio, observing a high line right-of-way D & Z had carved through a forest area. From where I stood I could see where the cutout area ran from the valley up the mountain. To provide a spot for a tower, they had just carved off the top of the ridge. When this was done, springs were exposed and draining together they formed a stream of muddy water headin' down to the Ohio River below. I said to myself, "Now this was once a pretty mountain, and now its natural beauty is gone." A feeling of guilt went through my bones for I had been a partner in this destruction, and when we were doing it, it didn't mean anything to me. Now I could see what was happening right in front of my eyes, erosion, pollution, and altering of our ecology. A poem about this started to form in my mind and I made some mental notes regarding my feelings.

Even though this incident in Ripley originally stirred my thoughts about poetry, it wasn't until many years later that I actually sat down and wrote a poem.

It happened outside of Roscommon, Michigan, in 1972. A young lineman had reached up to grab two lines he thought were dead, but in reality only one was. It bothered me that this young man, only twenty-three, with a wife and unborn child, should be gone and might not be remembered. I tried to write a short story about it, but that didn't work. I remembered Ripley and decided instead that I'd try a poem. It was the first one I actually wrote down. From then on I started writing more of them. Different things would trigger memories, and I could put myself back in time and actually be there again with all my senses and bring forth each event in a poem. I don't know really why I did this, I just felt compelled to bring these real things out of my heart and put them on paper. I didn't particularly even want to show them to anyone as I felt they weren't very good. I told myself, "Dumb-assed hillbilly, you have no business writing poems anyway." I did remember one thing that I heard when I was a kid. Eddie Crosby told Caggey Stills that whenever you write a song from the heart, you will always have a hit. I didn't try to write any poem except about something that actually happened.

Once traveling up by Traverse City, Michigan, I drove by a place that said BILL THOMAS'S RESTAURANT in big red letters. I went in and ate; the food and service were excellent. That night I wrote a poem about my grandfather, William Thomas, whom they called Bill. I even started writing poems about the things I witnessed everyday. One chilly Sunday I stood on the shore of Lake Superior and took notes which resulted in the poem INVITATION. Another time after Mary and I had finished eating in a restaurant, she drove while I jotted down things about a lady we had met in the restaurant which began A CERTAIN KIND OF WOMAN.

Mary liked my poems and was supportive of this habit. I even got a typewriter for Christmas, and I used to carry it on the road so I could transfer my poems from napkins, old envelopes, or scraps of paper to a more readable form. The typewriter didn't last very long though. I was just coming out of the cabin in Palmer, and Red Wood, a fellow lineman, drove up to jawbone a little. It was the weekend and he didn't have anything to do, so I set the typewriter on the trunk of his car and came around front to visit. We probably visited for a half hour or so, and when he left I heard my typewriter hit the ground. I could have hollered at him, but he would have probably backed back over it and even offered to pay for it, but it wasn't his fault. I opened it up and no pieces fell out, but it didn't work either. I took it to a repair shop in Marquette, but the guy said I might better buy a new one as the frame was bent and unfixable.

Sometimes, I'd get inspiration in the middle of the night and I'd get up and make notes for a poem. Other times I would try to write and either couldn't get started or if I did for some reason I couldn't finish it. The way I feel right now, I'll probably be writing until the day I die. My only regret is that I let thirty years go by before I started — too busy chasing material gains. Maybe, of course, I just wasn't ready.

THE TRUTH

For years I traveled Mother Nature's trail
    I took her for granted not a bright tale.
I helped build power lines far and wide,
    with saws and dozers we carved out her side,
Cutting her trees and destroying her streams
    so men could fulfill their wishful dreams.
I didn't realize it then, but I do now,
    I was guilty of helping to tear her down.
Now I look into her fruitless valleys
    her winds cry out in a pitiful chatter,
I am ashamed of what I did to her
    I had the advantage I did not hear a word.
Yesterday's brains built wondrous machines
    no thought of the damages they would bring,
I will not pass this blame to another time
    it happened in my generation the guilt is also mine.

This is the first poem that I actually wrote down, and it was about a young man that failed to listen.

Paul had gotten behind in his pole climbing training, and Cal Russell had assigned him to me for a couple months to catch up with it. We were left alone during this period of training; there were no interruptions. Some say I'm a good teacher, and some say I'm not, but I taught him everything I could. I had him do his training on a dead line, and every morning I would tell him that I had grounded out the line and then wait for him to start up the pole. When he got part way up, I'd say "No, no, if you take anybody's word for that line bein' grounded out, you're a damned fool. You go back and make sure it's grounded properly, don't trust anybody." He'd grumble to himself, come down the pole, and walk back a span to check the grounding. That happened enough times that I knew I pissed him off, but that's OK because linemen work better pissed off. Next I hounded him about his equipment to inspect it good at the beginning of each day and especially before he went up a pole and not to take anything for granted. Also I made him work the dead line with rubber gloves just to get used to working with them on. Well, after two months, Paul was doing good work and I had built up confidence in him.

We were working in the Roscommon area and Mary had come up for the weekend so we stayed in Houghton Lake. On Sunday night I just couldn't sleep. I'd doze off for a little while then wake right back up again. This was very unusual for me 'cause once I go to bed, normally I don't stir until morning. Something was gnawin' at me to keep me awake, and it was still there at breakfast time. Something was wrong.

Before dispersing for work, we all gathered around the line truck. "Paul you're going to work with someone else today," I said. "I'm gonna tell you right now this is why I've had you train with rubber gloves and sleeves. Today is the real thing. You'll be workin' with hot lines. Don't take any chances, check your gloves."

Now there were testers and other ways you could check and see if the lines were hot. If the humidity was high, you could hold a pair of pliers in your rubber gloves just a little way from a line, and as the line charged the pliers you could hear a fuzzy sound. That worked on high voltage lines, but on lower volt lines, you couldn't tell. The sure way to be safe, of course, was ground the line and use rubber gloves.

I still had this bad feelin' in my guts. You try to be extra-cautious, but really you just want to get rid of this feelin'. By 10 a.m. I was at the point of being overly cautious, and that in itself can become dangerous.

A pickup truck came speeding down the road, and a guy pulled up with his head stuck out the window, "There's some guy hung up on a pole down there."

"Where's he at?" He pointed out the direction, and I knew then where they were because I knew the line they were working on. Lewis was my bucket truck driver, so I lowered the bucket and down the road we headed. A car was partially blocking the pole, and we had to back in from an odd angle. As Lewis was lowering the bucket feet, I was in the bucket raising it up. We weren't the right distance away, so Lewis rolled the truck back a little more. I raised the bucket up where the other lineman held Paul. With his rubber gloves on, the other lineman had pulled Paul off the lines. I could see Paul was dead. We hooked the hand line to his belt. I asked the other lineman if he wanted to ride the bucket down or climb down. He said he thought he could make it down, which was better. That would keep his mind occupied for awhile. I followed down with the bucket, lowering Paul at the same time.

Paul had not worn his rubber gloves nor checked the line. The sad thing was that the other lineman did not know how to give artificial respiration on the pole. It can be done, but it was too late now.

BLIND FAITH

It was chilly this morning
  I didn't get much sleep
Something was bothering me very deep.
  Slowly I walked up to the crew
Guys I well understood and I knew;
  my pole buddy stood a smile on his face
Another lineman you'll work with in my place
  be careful and let him set the pace.
He was a big man in size
  but still a boy in my eyes
I took him under my wing
  to make him the man of his dream.
I taught him how to rig and climb
  to hardware, sag, and tie in a line
To know the dangers before they occurred
  to use his mind, take no man's word.
To use his strength balance his hide
  many days we worked side by side.
Just after ten, word was brought in,
  a lineman in trouble was it him?
With haste I hurried to the scene
  praying to GOD it was all a dream
One look told me without a doubt
  his life was over, just wiped out.
Upon the wires my eyes did glue
  by the handprints plainly there I knew
No longer would his laughter be heard,
  because of blind faith in another man's word.

THORTON McGEE

When I was working for King Electric in Hopewell, I heard someone talking about a guy without legs they'd seen out on the golf driving range hitting balls. I didn't think much about it until one day Waverly Pittman's car was broken down so I drove him home from work. Just before we got to Waverly's place, he pointed over towards another house. "That's where the guy without any legs lives. He plays golf and everything, name's McGee." In fact the guy happened to be out in the yard as we went by. I didn't think much about it until after I dropped Waverly off and started back in that direction. I took another glance at the guy as I went by, and the wheels of my memory started turnin'. I remembered that after Nellie had cut part of Thorton McGee's penis off, they had gone back together for awhile and later he had fallen under a railroad car and lost his leg. That guy in the yard sure did resemble Thorton, but this guy was minus two legs.

I had already passed the house, but I had a strong feeling that this man was Thorton McGee. I stopped, backed up, and drove in the man's driveway. Slowly I got out and took a closer look at the man's face. It was Thorton for sure, same ruddy complexion. I walked up to him, "You don't know me do ya?"

"No, can't say as I do."

"Well, my name's Ted Aldridge, and I was the kid over on Wesley Street that used to sit on the porch and sing ya songs when you came home from work." He remembered, and we started having a nice visit about old times. "Teddy, I'm leavin' this world one piece at a time." "Thorton, I remember you had lost one leg, but how'd you lose the other?" "I was sittin' on a car and fell asleep, slipped off onto the tracks. Really destroyed my artificial leg too, took three months before they could work on fixing that leg back up." We talked about that for awhile, but there was something else that was on my mind, and he knew it too. It's like you're havin' a great conversation about apples, but what you really want to talk about is oranges. "Teddy, I know what you're wondering about. I had just as good a time with what I had left as I did with the whole thing." He went on to explain that he and Nellie did not have any children, but that later after they divorced, he remarried and did have a couple.

I visited Thorton several times before my job took me away from Hopewell. He was a real family man. Even though he was without legs, he played basketball and even football with his kids. He had a little cart he pushed himself around on, and it was no big deal to his kids 'cause when he got the ball they were routinely knockin' him off his cart. It was absolutely amazing to me, for here was a man that had lost a good share of his penis, two legs, and was still jovial about the whole thing. No big deal to him, he took it all in stride and was ready to press on with life.

****

Sometimes an adopted mother can have more love in her heart than a natural mother. I learned this firsthand in the years before Boy's Home. I rarely saw my mother. When I got up for school, she had left an hour before. At night she came home after I did, and it was only an hour or so before she went to bed. I'm not putting her down because she worked ten hour days supportin' us, but it was like I didn't have a mother. My grandmother filled that role, and I called her mother and my mother Helen.

MOTHERHOOD

A mother is that woman that is held
  close to each one's heart.
When we were children, a cake was cut,
  it is she who took the smallest part.
Her clothes and shoes show the most
  of time and wear,
But it seemed the time for needs and gifts,
  they were always there.
For some reason her needs and desires
  never crossed our mind,
Remember an article that you didn't need
  was bought with her last dime.
As a teenager she is the excuse,
  used by us one and all
Especially when what we tried,
  the right pieces just failed to fall.
There are times when some of us will not
  look at her with love or pride
Because we know she can see
  all our sins of lust and lies.
When we are troubled and this world
  has us down and out
This is the beginning of us learning
  what Mother's love is all about.
A woman can bear into this world
  a child through life's sins,
But true motherhood is only in a
  woman's heart right where it begins.

CHRISTMAS AND GRANDMA

Songs on the radio tell me it's Christmas time.
   It carries me back to the boyhood of mine,
Of the days with Grandma, I cherish so well,
   she taught me of God's way and of Hell.
She told me of Jesus and His wonderful birth
   in words a child understood what it was worth,
She explained all of the songs that I heard,
   about shepherds and angels never left out a word,
Spoke of the devil, how he would lie.
   Times have certainly changed since Grandma died,
Now it's Santa Claus that commands that day.
   Toys for girls and boys seems to be the way.
Now, I am not talking down Santa Claus one bit,
   but we have certainly let the true Christmas slip.
So mothers and fathers, when you get up Christmas morn,
   please tell your children when and why Jesus was born.

THOSE HANDS

In my early childhood I had a pair
   of helping hands,
They were a constant companion as I
   grew up, to me a strange land.
Those hands helped me put my clothes,
   on nice and neat,
Yet, it was my eyes that helped those
   hands to cross a street.
Those hands would carry me when I
   got tired from a walk,
Yes, those hands had a language but
   they never talked.
Those hands comforted my childhood frustrations
   from day to day,
It was those same hands that showed
   me how to pray.
An understanding that a blind grandmother
   could only give,
It was her patient hands that showed
   the right way to live.
With wisdom of many wise men
   they gave me a start in life,
With those sensitive hands she prepared
   me to meet the world's strife.
Jesus Christ now has my heart,
   He's made me an heir to a heavenly home,
Though my journey has not ended
   upon this earth I continue to roam.
I cannot help at times I wish again
   I were a child,
To feel the love of Grandma's hands
   for just a little while.

GRANDPA THOMAS

Grandpa sailed into the unknown at the age of twelve,
　　what he had to do he learned well.
He was away from home most of the time,
　　I'll never forget the tool box he said was mine.
From cabin boy to captain quickly was his claim,
　　sailing the seas for life he did not have in mind,
A home and a wife was what he had in his heart,
　　he never really had one, that's the bad part.
Lonesome for love will make a man go wrong,
　　yes, I know Grandpa, in that you are not alone.
I have listened to family talks put you down,
　　I am older now and of your ways I well understand.
Like you, I have to travel to make my bread,
　　a night in Traverse City I was surprised at a sign I read:
Bill Thomas, it said in colored light of red wine,
　　as I ate supper my thoughts went back in time.
Grandpa, time is different, but it's still the same deal.
　　People are still chasing dreams, I'm right on its heels.
Yes, Grandpa I'll chase it till the day I die,
　　like you and all people on earth I'll never be satisfied.

At the Boy's Home, it was my job to have the calf feed out by five a.m. To get down at the barn by that time I had to at least be up by four thirty. Tucker had established for himself a little routine whereby he would come down to the barn and check on the boys to see how the milking was going. He had a strict rule that there would be no kids playin' around disturbing those milk cows. Sometimes he would sneak up in the hay mow and watch us from above.

We had this one calf that was about twelve to fifteen weeks old, and we had taken him out of the holding pen and put him into a larger pen where he would have more exercise room with the other calves. The trouble was that he was small enough to get up in the hay rack and then get his head caught in the slats of the hay rack so he couldn't get out.

This had been happening two or three times a week for a month, and Tucker was getting mad about it. Not only was it hard to get the calf's head out, but it was disturbing Tucker's normal routine.

Tucker talked to some other old farmer about this problem and figured he had found a way to remedy this pesky calf's habit. He told me the next time that I saw the calf stuck, not to go into the barn but come right up to his house and get him.

It was on a Sunday morning when I next saw the calf stuck, so I went to Tucker's house and told him. He took the Sunday paper, which was pretty thick with the funnies and all, and rolled it up lengthways like a baseball bat. He told me to be real quiet when we went into the pen. Shucks, that wasn't difficult as we were just walkin' through soft cow manure. I quietly went over by the gate, and Tucker moved up behind the unsuspecting calf and hit him right across the rump with that rolled up newspaper. Tucker expected that the blow would startle the calf enough that he would bolt forward breaking the wooden slat loose and he'd be out of the hay rack. It didn't work that way. The calf just fell down with his head still caught. This pissed off Tucker even more 'cause that calf was big enough that it was like pickin' up a sack of water. Tucker broke the slat loose to get the calf's head out then lifted him out and put him down expecting the calf to get up and run off. The calf didn't move, he just laid there. Tucker pulled the calf's leg up and got down to check for a heartbeat. There wasn't any. Tucker really had a set of lungs. When he hollered, you could hear him three miles away. He was scared and yelled for his wife Dorothy to call the veterinarian. Bein' Sunday morning Dorothy was just layin' in bed dreading to get up and around and didn't move fast enough for Tucker. He was on the phone hollering at the vet; you could hear him all the way through the closed house door.

The vet instructed Tucker to cut open the calf right away and take out the liver so he could look at it when he got there. Guess he thought some disease or something might show up in that organ. He also told Tucker not to mess up anything else inside the calf.

Dorothy went to the barn with us, and on the way Tucker was grumblin' about how could a newspaper hurt such a fine beef. I held the calf's leg out of the way while Tucker cut it open and removed the liver. Dorothy wrapped the liver in a towel and took it to the house. We covered the calf to keep it warm as the vet had instructed.

When the vet arrived, he wanted to see the liver right away, but couldn't find anything wrong with it. When he opened up the calf to look inside, he said, "What'd ya do to this calf?"

Tucker stood there like a twelve year old kid, "I didn't do nothin' to him."

"Don't tell me you didn't do anything to him. You scared the hell out of this calf; that's exactly what you done. What did ya do to him?"

"I didn't do anything to him except take that newspaper over there and hit him."

"Didn't make a sound, did ya? No, sir, you scared that calf to death, caused a rush of blood that blew the side of his heart out just like a hose poppin' out of the socket." Tucker just stood there remorsefully.

A DAY ON THE FARM

My memories wandered back when I was young
daydreaming of the other children who used to be my chums.
Upon the Allegheny Mountains, down in
her meadows we roamed,
We were happy, but had dreams of
things to come.
My fondest memories are of the large farm
I can still see Tucker standing by that barn.
I would love to go back to lands where I belonged
to listen to Tucker speak with wisdom and yarns.
I followed Tucker around doing what I could.
He would look and smile at me like he always would.
Not one tale did I hear about him that was bad
but it scared him half to death when he killed the calf.
Up in the hay racks there the calf stood,
with an old newspaper he hit him as hard as he could.
Call the vet he screamed! But there was no doubt
even at five miles, you could hear that Irishman shout.
The vet told Tucker, but he would not believe,
man how can a paper kill such a fine beef?
The way he was hit by an Irishman's fit
the ultimate surprise is why the calf fails to rise.

All the cows at Boy's Home were milked by hand. These were thoughts that went through my mind when I remembered how scared I was when I first learned to milk a cow. I knew also of other boys that were equally apprehensive of this encounter, and I knew how they felt. Later I could see how funny or foolish the situation was.

EMOTIONS

The night was dark,
  though the moon was high,
We were all alone
  just she and I.
Light red tinted her hair,
  her wide shapely hips were bare,
Those eyes, a soft deep brown,
  and glad we were not in a town.
Her breathing was very heavy,
  those large nipples looked fine,
With a moist shaking hand
  I felt down her warm spine.
Like a lady she politely moved
  her large legs apart.
I trembled with emotions
  and a fast beating heart.
Though I am finished and thoroughly
  satisfied, I often wonder how,
I lived through my first experience
  of milking a cow.

It always seemed to me that nature was put out there for me as an individual. I think that most people that enjoy the out-of-doors feel that way. We spent a lot of time in power line right-of-ways in Michigan's Upper Peninsula, and it was a beautiful countryside. You can learn a lot from nature when you are close to it and observe it. It also becomes a companion.

AN INVITATION

Mother Nature, I feel by the winds,
   you blow by me
You are sending a message, it's
   me you wish to see.
Your soft breezes are a promise
   of warmer days to come,
It is your way of inviting me
   to your beautiful home.
I know you are changing your dress
   to a delightful green
You are cleaning your house,
   with a childish gleam.
The winds are gracefully grooming
   your tangled hair
Dressing up for me, knowing I
   will surely be there.
Flower buds in your kingdom have
   now bountifully appeared,
Like emerald jewels or the
   sparkling eyes of a deer.
But you are keeping a soft
   snowy white gown on
Hiding from me a beauty each
   year that is born.
Like a woman, you are putting
   me to a test

Making sure it is your world
    I love the best.
With the forest and meadows
    you are teasing me,
Knowing the passion for your
    beauty I desire to see.
But like a woman, a weakness
    you always have
Wishing for a companion to
    be with you there.
And in this world of trials
    and deviations
I gratefully accept your
    generous invitation.

This was not a prayer. It was a poem I wrote to God. It was not powered with imagination, it was powered by guilt. Through all our failures, the bottom line is that God hasn't let us fall because He loves us.

A QUESTION?

Lord I write to You a poem,
    my first at this time.
You already know the reasons
    with writing of the first line.
It's true I've witnessed the sun rise,
    as it made no sounds;
Yet its quiet warmth released
    me of the night's cool bounds.
I am a part of your plan
    as seasons one at a time go by,
But Lord I'm still astounded at
    the real reason why.
Of Your love I have read, and

heard there's none to compare;
Though as a child it was Grandma's
　　because she was there.
When a boy it was what my eyes
　　and dreams could see,
As a young man the ways of
　　the world and what I wanted to be.
On the expressway of life, as I race
　　toward my social goal,
Lord, I didn't see Your narrow gate
　　or where to pay a toll.
Fate at times has a way which
　　with us we think love is a deal,
Yet with hard and passing time we
　　soon know in life what is real.
With the devil some say it's him
　　who is my best friend,
For of my ways it was I, not
　　the devil who wouldn't bend.
In my heart of this world's
　　sins, I have committed them all,
Now I know the answer Lord, why you have
　　not let a sinner like me fall.

Probably linemen are not held in very high esteem in most social circles. Even though they are good-natured and tender-hearted, they also have a tendency to be raunchy, loud, and not afraid to clearly express their opinions in public. They would even lie occasionally to mislead some lady. I don't think that was all their fault, the job brought that out in them.

On the job linemen were always quick to criticize each other in no uncertain terms. If a guy was makin' a mistake, he was told about it. "Get you ass up there and quit f-----'up." There has to be that criticism, this check and balance against carelessness. If you took these remarks personal, there was always a good chance you could get your ass whipped and next time you'd be a better listener.

When there was an ice storm and people were without electricity, the lineman was as welcome as the President would be. They forgot all his bad characteristics.

I remember we were sent to Boston for three days after a real bad storm. We were working in the old part where they had cobblestone streets. Down some of the alleys there was no room for a pole, so they just put it beside a building with an eight foot arm sticking out holding the wires. Sometimes the transformers were mounted right to the buildings.

We were trying to find the transformer to get the lights on in this one area when a heavy-set Irish woman stuck her head out the window, "When you gonna cut my electricity on?"

"As soon as we can find the transformer."

"It's down the alley." We looked down the alley but couldn't see anything. Again she yelled. "It's down the alley."

"Maybe she knows what she's talkin' about," I said. We looked further in the alley and there it was. The door was blown off, so with our telescoptic hot sticks we knocked the ice off, reset it, and put a new door on.

It was a cold damp day, with a little sheet of ice still forming. When we came out of the alley, the Irish lady was at the window again. "You want some hot coffee and something to eat, come on up." You could see everything in her apartment was electric. She had the coffee goin' and was cookin' some eggs. One of the guys suggested that maybe some of the other linemen could use some coffee. "Go tell 'em to get up here." She ran out of bread and somebody went out and got three loaves. Before we were through, I'd say she had fifteen guys in there. She wouldn't take any money and we didn't push it, as we didn't want to insult her.

If it hadn't been for the ice storms though, we'd probably still be looked at as riffraff.

A LINEMAN

This man whose work is on the high
   towers through the land,
Some think of him as a drifter
   or a tramp.
An angel to the woman who
   shares his love
Knowing he is a Lucifer
   not a saint from above.
Yet he is different with a second look
   not as bad as been booked
He shakes the devil's hands each
   time when reaching to tie in a hot line,
He is wanted in the bars at night
   for truly he enjoys life,
So happy telling of joys and woes
   of adventures on the power poles.
Those that put him down for his
   favorite sin,
They all change their minds where
   damaging storms have been,
With open arms they are the first
   to welcome him in.
For eyes can see a lineman is
   a special breed of man,
He is the possessor of a talent to
   do this work he has to face.
With the lights on, homes are warm,
   bars are open, everything is in place.

Traveling the roads of this country to earn my pay, I experienced many lonely moments. It was comforting to know we had a permanent home in Michigan, but I missed Mary and the kids. In some obscure hotel room my mind would always drift back to those I loved.

ROSES FOR MARY

People send flowers to their wives and mothers,
    to loved ones, sisters and even brothers.
Some send flowers to remove suspicion and doubt,
    diverting attention so others won't find out.
I send flowers to my lover and enchanting wife
    whose presence is a beautiful article of life.
Flowers will say more than I could ever do,
    I am sending these roses because I want to.
These roses are the first flowers I ever sent,
    thanking my Mary for a true love that's never bent.
These roses I know in time will all die
    but I will still see the love in Mary's eye.
We age in our body and also in our way,
    eyes are our reflection telling it all each day.
Her love is my life in this world so dreary,
    now you know why I send roses to my Mary.

SO NATURAL

It's so natural to see the sun during the day
   take a fresh drink of water to chase a thirst away,
So natural when tired to take a moment and rest,
   a time so natural to reminisce of ones you love the best.
Nothing is more natural than to sit down when resting one's feet
   it's natural to turn off a dripping faucet so it won't leak.
As natural breath of air, which we all do need,
   just like the natural love of my Mary, that's life to me.
As natural as our children when babies wet the bed,
   she always has the answers to the problems in my head.
In summer it's natural for the next season to be fall,
   at times when in need, she naturally appears as if I had called.
Some are conscious or ashamed when in an unnatural position,
   my Mary is so much a part of me, it's her heart I hear when
      I listen.
When life's tides ebb, if she goes first to our heavenly home,
   my time will be short because my heart with her has also flown.

ANNIVERSARY TIME

Events are marked by
  certain days in a year,
New Years, Easter, or Christmas when
  beautiful carols you can hear.
The anniversary of our marriage
  is an everyday event,
An eternal love with its
  trials has never bent.
It seems my wife has always
  been a living part of me,
Sweet memories of our love are
  numerous as waves on the sea.
If I should forget this
  world's measure of time,
Remember Mary, you have and
  always will be mine.

After Christmas, in the early part of January, Mary and I had the bills spread out on the table figurin' how we were going to get everything paid. Young John was apparently listening to us; we were complaining about the price of things. In fact, some of the things we were bitchin' about might have been something we bought him. I know kids felt liner boots were expensive and seems like they went through them as fast as we bought them. We knew John was there, but we just took it for granted that he wasn't listening to us. Pretty soon John came up to my wife and gave her all he had, which was fifteen cents, to help us pay the bills. Well, we felt very small for letting the kids hear our money problems. The more I got to thinking about it, I was glad that it happened 'cause John had learned the importance of sharing.

FIFTEEN CENTS

Fifteen cents not much worth
   in this busy world to hold,
Precious stones have their price
   also pearls when it's right.
People have problems the world around
   they are solved in various ways,
Some with treasures, others with time,
   my eight year old boy solved mine.
When the wolf was at our door
   money it demanded before it would go
He came with such humble pride
   stood by his mother, looked into her eyes,
In his heart he had heard a call
   and with it he was giving it all.
A sense of sharing some never learn,
   parting with all his treasure he had earned.
Fifteen cents not much to hold
   but to us it's worth the world's gold
He offered it to help see us through
   so proud of what he could do.

I was working on an eight hundred foot RCA radio tower with the iron workers. We were in the process of what's called shakin' the tower down. What that amounts to is starting from the bottom and working up, tightening all the bolts and putting bolts in where they needed to be. This day we were working on the last span between seven and eight hundred feet.

Now eight hundred feet up on a tower sounds awfully high, but really anything over four hundred feet seems about the same. You just kinda get used to bein' at certain heights then work your way up. You had to stay in limbo to work. If you felt a tightening from the inside out, it was time to stop and have a cigarette or something until the feelin' left. It was no place to be overly cautious; you have to be able to move naturally.

Well I had no desire to spend any extra time on the ground this morning, that's where the hard work was. The easy work was up on the tower. This new guy arrived that I was supposed to work with, and I just said, "Hi, let's get started." I figured we'd visit once we got workin' above.

I sat down in the bosun's chair, and he sat on my lap with his legs hanging out the other direction. I had my arms around the two cables that held the chair and he had one hand on a cable and the other on my shoulder. We were at about five hundred feet when I felt his grip on my shoulder tighten significantly. I looked up to see what the hell was goin' on, and his eyes were as big as a hoot owl's. I thought to myself, "Holy shit." Grabbing the signal cable, I pulled twice. This rang a bell at the top and bottom; two bells meant we wanted to go down. The sensation of going down wasn't bad, kinda like a car goin' over a dip in the road at high speed. This fella was really grabbin' into my shoulder now, and I realized the danger we were both in if the guy really went berserk. At the bottom he didn't want to let go. They had to bend his thumbs back to get him to turn loose. When I got up, I could see he had pissed all over me. I was embarrassed and mad at the same time. Lloyd Brown hauled the guy outta there fast. He probably noticed my state and wanted to avoid me poundin' on the guy. Of course by now it was a big laugh among the other guys, me gettin' pissed on.

They took some money out of petty cash and bought me some clean pants, but Lloyd said the day was screwed up enough, might as well quit and go to the bar. "Lloyd, what's the guy's name?"

He said, "I'm not gonna tell ya."

A CINCINNATI EVENT

Been in Cincinnati's bars and dives just long enough
    to get my head feeling like a box of snuff (hot & dry).
On the job Monday morning feeling like a hound
    an eight hundred foot tower, I was to shake it down.
Being the last man, a strange partner I drew,
    come to find out he was new to the crew
Stepping into the boatswain chair I motioned to him,
    he climbed into my lap, we rose into the wind.
Halfway up my head began to clear
    thinking of Cincinnati's women so dear.
The guy sitting so tense in my warm lap,
    my mind dreams as the wind caught my cap.
As we approach the top I looked at his face,
    all my dreams flew to outer space.
For I saw, all frozen in his eyes, fear
    how I was to calm him wasn't too clear.
My talk told him we would not be harmed,
    like a child he held firmly to my arm.
I knew a wrong move would be our last,
    with things to do tonight I didn't want to crash.
Two rings on the bell meant to go down,
    I was never so happy to be on the ground.
A wetness I felt as he was being removed
    my dreams washed away, my mind he almost blew.

I was staying in this family-owned hotel in Roscommon, Michigan, when I met the oldest boy, Mark Matthew Miles. He had five brothers and two sisters, all younger than he was. The kids all had responsibilities to keep the hotel going, and he cleaned rooms. I could tell that the kids had been looking through my things when they cleaned the room, 'cause my papers were occasionally out of order. My suspicions were confirmed one day when Mark said, "You write poetry don't you?"

"Yes I do."

"You should write one about me."

"Why?"

"I just always wanted somebody to write something about me."

"I'll write one about you, but I won't tell you when."

Later on I did write the poem and mailed it to him.

A PROMISE

Today Mark Matthew Miles
    you crossed my mind
I am keeping a promise, though we
    didn't agree on the time.
Through your blue eyes you witness a world
    no one will ever see
In your mind it is up to you
    in becoming what you wish to be.
Your after school work puts you
    in this world a good position
To learn about the difference in people,
    if you only listen.
Your travels could carry you where the coins
    in your collection have been,
Wherever you travel never
    lose a chance to make a friend.
At the age of twelve, questions you will have
    in life's climb,
Answers will come at a fast pace
    yet for you it's forever in time.
When you reach manhood you will remember
    these younger years
Especially brothers and sisters,
    treat their love with care.
Your dad and mother will be wiser
    as you grow older
Ways in your life of reason will become
    less bold.
Things I have told you have probably
    passed your ears before
In reading this poem twice, think once,
    as you leave home through the door.

On my way to Chattanooga, Tennessee, I was on I-75 passing through Dayton, Ohio. It was rush hour, around 4:30 p.m. I guess, and in this industrial area people were heading home from work. The road made a split up ahead and there was someone standing on the three-foot median. As I got closer, I could see the person looked like a young hippie. Glancing in the rearview mirror, the traffic didn't look too bad, just a few cars behind. I decided it'd be worth it to pick this young kid up even if it did inconvenience the few cars behind me when I stopped. At least I might save him from getting run over.

When I stopped, the hippie threw his backpack in the back of the truck and climbed in. We'd been headin' down the road a bit, and nothing much had been said so I offered my rider a cigarette. He kinda signaled with his hand no thanks. This hippie sure had fair skin. "Where ya goin'?"

"Tampa."

"That's a long way from home, huh?"

"Yep."

We were pretty well past the Xenia exit, and I was a little worried about the person I'd picked up. Sure looked like a young kid and acted as if he was trying to hide something. Didn't really look like the typical hippie, and not taking me up on the free cigarette kinda confirmed that. I wondered what I had on my hands.

We just crossed the river at Cincinnati and were in Kentucky when I mentioned that I was ready to stop and eat supper. I pulled off the expressway to one of those overpass truck restaurants. We went in, sat down, and when my companion took his hat off I was surprised to see he was a she. "Well, I'll be damned." I thought. She seemed reluctant to order. "I'll treat for supper," I said. "I would appreciate it if you didn't order a T-bone though, but a small steak would be OK." She kinda laughed and then decided on a hamburger steak dinner.

I had to be in Chattanooga by ten the next morning, so we didn't spend much time visitin' in the restaurant. She did seem more willing to talk once we were on our way. She'd been raised in Detroit, and had hitchhiked from Tampa to attend her brother's funeral; he'd been shot. I asked if he had been into drugs, and she said no, that he'd been a victim caught in the crossfire between gangs.

I never was too big on funerals, never figured it made much difference if that person was gone. Musta been important to her though to come all that way. She started talkin' a little about her childhood and all the things her mother had told her. Her father wasn't mentioned, but the things her mother had instructed her about were reminiscent of things my grandmother had taught me. She said her mother had told her how important it was to keep her shoes neat because people look at you from head to toe and will have more respect if you look clean and neat. Most mothers are used to tellin' kids what to do, but hers, like my grandmother, told us if we did something, what good things would happen. The conversation brought back to me the innocence of youth and things I had been told but forgotten. From the short conversation with this 19 to 20 year old girl, my attitude on life changed. As time went on and I thought about it more, it had even more of an effect on me.

I found out she worked in a factory that made candles in Tampa. She was a little hesitant to talk a lot about it, but I told her it sounded like a sweatshop to me. She asked what that was, and I explained. They were required to produce a quota she admitted, and if their wax was not all used up at the end of the day they were charged for the reheating of it the next day. For two years she'd worked there, and would actually like to have her own shop. I said, "Well, there are two ways to save up the money you need to go into business. The Greek way and the Jew way. The Greek will spend what he needs to live on then save the rest. The Jew will put one tenth of his earnings in the bank, will live on one tenth, and pay his bills with the rest." She laughed again.

After I dropped her off, I was concerned about her. As I drove along, I thought to myself, "Hell, probably $200 would be all she'd need to get her own candle business. I could afford that, but I didn't have an address to send it." I wondered how she'd get along and if she'd make it.

CONFUSED

In my travels through life I have
    fought for where I am
Taking on all comers and daring any
    to put me down.
But in a meekness last night I
    talked with the Lord
Something I have not done since
    I was Grandma's boy.
Inside I have a fear of how Annie's
    welfare may be
It's the pains of not knowing what
    is really hurting me.
Something has turned inside out
    somewhere in my mind
I pray to God this confusion I will
    understand in a short time.

THANK YOU ANNIE MARIE

THANKS—
For the beauty I saw in
  your gray eyes;
THANKS—
For the gentleness in your
  manners, it will never die,
THANKS—
For your virtue though it
  put me to shame;
THANKS—
For your morality, for it
  I am a better man.
THANKS—
For your wonderful mind and
  purity of your heart;
THANKS—
For the moments in your life
  where I was a part.
THANKS—
For the warmth of your
  presence, it is a world's wealth;
THANKS—
Annie the most for just
  being yourself.

This poem was about Wilma Lee Black. She was a waitress in a restaurant down south, probably 16 or 17 years old. She couldn't wait to get out on her own and see the world. Her hands were a little rough from washing dishes, and she realized she wasn't as pretty as other girls, but to hear her talk, she expected that once on her own, life would be a bed of roses. This poem was my response to her.

A MESSAGE

Wilma Lee, your dreams will
   carry you to places in body and mind.
Just don't look for true fantasy
   or clouds which are golden lined,
There is no pot of gold at the end
   of God's beautiful rainbow.
That knight of shining armor
   left the world a long time ago.
Traveled roads that led to nowhere,
   I have been down many times.
Searching for wishes and dreams
   has cost more than precious time.
Nature will continue to beautify
   this world for your brown eyes to see,
She will be as kind to you
   as she has so generous been to me.
Be proud of your hands and
   the hard work they have done,
For truly they are all you need
   to get life's race won.
The gift of God to this world
   is at times hard to hold.
But Wilma Lee, it is a treasure
   of wealth more precious than gold.

I was home from work for the weekend and my son John, who was about eight, gave me a Valentine Card he had made. As things usually were busy as hell when I got home, I put off opening it right away. In fact, when it came time to go back to work early Monday morning, I still hadn't opened it so I tossed it in the glove compartment of the truck. It was a pretty morning with quite a bit of snow on the ground. We'd even had some hail the night before. Up early doing chores and packing for the next week, I left before John was around.

At work when I got time, I opened John's card. It was obvious that he had put a lot of work into that card, and I wished I had taken time to open it before I left. When I did get home again, I told him how much I appreciated it. I wrote this poem several years later.

DAD'S LETTER

Today seemed beautiful as the snows came falling down
    the sun had not shined and cold was the ground
In place of flowers and green meadows it was snow and ice,
    yet today inside I felt very warm and nice.
I received a letter, it was trimmed in gold,
    I opened it up and here is what it told:
I love you daddy, it simply said
    in uneven words of the Valentine he made.
One look told me of the struggles he had,
    he carefully colored it just for his dad.
It was not as pretty as one you would buy
    with its fancy laces and velvet hide,
The verse not written by some noted poet's quill,
    whose words give your heart a false thrill.
Simple love of a son to his dad, so dear,
    though his age was only of six years.

It had been twenty-eight years since I had left Boy's Home, and I was anxious to see how it looked. Yep, there was the white house that Tucker lived in, the barns looked the same, even the old horse stable. The road north out of Covington that wound around and passed down in the valley to Boy's Home was where the teacher had showed me how fast her Buick would go. The Boy's Home bordered up to Lick Mountain, and Mr. Cole still owned the top of the mountain where he had an orchard that we had visited as boys. What had changed in twenty-eight years was that the lure of a good coal vein had slowly gutted out and scarred the beautiful valleys where I had roamed as a kid.

Many years later I was visitin' with an old friend, George Morley. He had been a truck driver for a small circus, and I asked if he ever passed through Covington or had seen the Boy's Home. He said he sure had, in fact, with a blown tire he was forced to spend a night at the Home. We talked about how everything was, and he told me that the road out of Covington had been straightened, and in the process the gutted hillsides had been repaired and weren't that noticeable. It certainly hadn't looked that way when I wrote this poem.

ASHAMED

I stood looking into her side,
  scornful she said to me, "No alibis.
Why do you come back to haunt me,
  you are no longer a boy for me to see?
In your youth, those secret walks, I have missed
  for in the evening it was you that I kissed.
I loved to listen to all those childish plans
  I would answer so you would understand.
One score and eight years are now gone.
  did you expect me to wait that long?
Your look tells me of how I have changed
  I am ashamed, but the destruction is not of my hand.
Gone are the days when we had love,
  lost are the gentle ways of your touch.
The human race has too much of a lust
  and now as a man you want me to trust?
Leave my scarred valleys and torn mountainside,
  go back to your cities and have your cry!"

Sometimes I've been right and glad that I stuck by my convictions, sometimes I have been tempted to do wrong, and other times I have done wrong. A lot of the righteous teachings of my grandmother have gotten me through it all, and I'm trying to pass this knowledge along, especially for those that right now feel they're at the bottom of life's barrel.

UNSETTLED

To the eyes of this world I lead
   a gambler's life, well-planned.
You know, the kind that wins
   with a loser's hand.
Yet most people will never know,
   unless they looked beyond my eyes,
For in them, they will see hard
   roads, yet others an easy ride.
Many times I figured what's the
   use, do whatever to win;
Tempted I have been, and would have
   were it not for a friend.
When you think life has no meaning,
   feeling you have lost all you had,
Just the right moment, when you
   can go good or bad,
This friend I just can't shake
   now I ask that He be with you,
To clear your mind and heart
   of doubts, and see you through.
Because every gambler always
   needs that ace in the hole,
Just like my friend Jesus, He
   is the ace that I hold.

We all have different talents. Mine was electrical, mechanical, and rigging. These talents weren't earned, they were God's gifts. You hear people braggin' about being able to do this and that, but they couldn't have done a damn thing if God hadn't allowed them to do it.

THE GIFTS

At birth my Heavenly Father
    gave me a mind
It was taught by His many creations
    in His measure of time.
I have not the wisdom to know
    His greatest creation of all
But He also gave me a gift to understand
    some creations by its call.
I pray these gifts will do the
    kindness this world needs,
To share and show love, not bad deeds,
    or what our eyes fail to see.
May they be gentle and warm
    as a child's touch
The work these hands do I hope
    pleases my Maker very much.

I was a little down when I wrote this. When we were growin' up, we didn't have television, but we listened to the radio and went to the movies. It seemed like in all those shows, the good guys always won. The old folks kinda reinforced that idea in our heads, in that if we did right when we were growin' up we would come out ahead. As you go through life, you have a chance to evaluate that philosophy, and it doesn't seem to always hold true. I saw those who would steal ten dollars and get along fine, while I was bustin' my ass earnin' that much trying to have shoes and clothes without holes. Who really was the winner, the one that did the right things to get along or the one that bent the rules a little and got along better?

After evaluating life for a lot of years, I believe when it's all tallied up, the guy that does right will be the winner. He may not have a pot to piss in or a window to throw it out of, but what he did or didn't do will be the payoff. The trouble is that a lot of people are comfortable with doin' things the way they have been, even if it's wrong.

THE PRETENDER

When a child I was a cowboy
   tall, rough and wise,
The protector of law and order,
   I jailed all the bad guys.
A captain of a great ship
   that sailed the high sea
Sinking the pirates, upholding justice
   for all the world to see.
As a fireman there was never a fire
   too big for me to put out,
I drove the fastest trains because
   I knew what it was about.
As a child I was the highest measure of a man
   and heeded each and every call,
Yes, in growing up in my mind
   I imitated them one and all.
As I grew older the world and I both changed
   right before everybody's eyes,
What hurt most in reality was how people
   used each other's lives.
Now, I'm no saint and many times
   I have shaken the devil's hand,
I'm as guilty as them all
   that ever walked this land.
Diligently I have tried to tell people
   of my mistakes and selfish wits,

In listening, guess they were ashamed
   of the way the shoe fits.
In the distant years I will approach
   what's known as the mellow age,
As we all know my pace will be
   at a slower gauge.
This world and I again will become different
   as this life is ending,
I will turn my eyes and as a child
   again become a pretender.

It was in the spring of the year and I was headed over to Saginaw to
work for a new outfit. In town I needed directions to find the place, so
I stopped and asked this guy who looked a little like a bum. I got to
talking with him some and got the impression he was hungry and
would like to ask for a meal but had too much pride to do so. I
suggested we go in for a cup of coffee, which he readily agreed to. We
sat there talking and I said, "It's about eleven, why don't we have a
meal, too." He didn't know what to say, but finally made it clear to
me he had no money. "I'll buy it. I've been down on my luck before
too." That wasn't a lie either, for I could recall having been broke
several times.

He opened up to me a little, but didn't go into detail. He just indi-
cated that a short time ago somebody had put the screws to him. I'd
guess he was a blue collar worker, thirty-five to forty years old. His
clothes looked like regular work clothes, not dirty, but well worn. I
started to talk about what a friend was, and he said, "Don't give me
any bullshit about that." As he talked, his eyes told me more than
what was coming out of his mouth. He was down, and someone
whom he would normally have trusted to help him out had turned his
back on him.

IN NEED OF A FRIEND

What's this thing you call a friend,
   where does it come from, where does it end?
What does it look like, how does it feel,
   what is its purpose and how does it deal?
This friend, what does he do, where does he go,
   what is he for, how much does he really know?
I've heard a friend, softly spoken with a shout,
   tell me something about him worth hearing about
These questions I've asked and you wonder why
   it's not that I think you are telling a lie,
But I tell you fellow, I learned in travels afar
   when down and out you alone will tow the bar.
Questions and criticism rapidly voiced to me.
   of this fellow I looked at I could plainly see
A hard road he had traveled there was no doubt,
   wearing of his expressions told he was down and out.
How was I to tell him what a friend was?
   Hardships I saw in him showed what life does.
To a lot of people life is just a selfish game,
   being a victim this man's heart had gone lame.
I was at a loss as he hungrily ate his meal
   everything I said couldn't change the way he did feel.
This was one of the times I could not smile.
   I hope the streets of Saginaw give him an easy mile.

Nancy Pollin is the kinda girl you meet in later life and wished that you had met before you were settled down and married. There are no love scenes here 'cause she was twenty years younger than I. I did feel very comfortable around Nancy. She was someone I could relate to and had the type of attitude and personality to cement a good friendship. She met my wife Mary and also my son John. I also met Nancy's mother, whom the poem TAKING GRANDMA'S PLACE is about.

THE GIRL IN THE WINDOW

Going about my job as a lineman
   I was preparing to climb a pole
I felt a pair of eyes staring into me
   its feeling would not loosen its hold.
I looked to see if it were the devil
   he has a way of being around,
Satisfied in my mind I was alone
   I climbed the pole leaving the ground.
At forty feet I looked below
   and saw a wonderful sight
From a window, a beautiful pair of blue
   eyes had watched my upward flight.
Her golden hair glistened as the sun
   reflected from its curls
She looked more like a doll
   in the window than a full grown girl.
Beauty has a way of fooling us all,
   I am no exception to this fact,
Yet, her face showed a devotion that would
   be the same when I turned my back.
As I watched her from my lofty
   perch upon the power pole
My wish was that this girl in the
   window could be mine to hold,
But for a half-breed this treasure
   is beyond my eyes to see,
What could such a beautiful living
   portrait see in the likes of me?
But despite it all, if we were one,
   and in God's eyes it were right,
The hardest of times would be
   easy with her to help in life's fight.

NATURE'S CURSE

Today the weather is hot, the
   kind that puts you in a bind
But not like the thoughts that
   are bored deep in my mind.
Yes, it's about a woman, blonde hair
   and eyes of blue
Whose expressions make you feel
   good inside when she looks at you.
This lovely face many times appears
   very clear in my dreams
Like unto a thirsty man her
   eyes fresh as a mountain stream.
Her body, another unexplainable
   art, created by nature's plan,
Yet the most beautiful is her mind
   overlooked by an average man.
But nature has a way to make
   us small or great.
I feel nature cursed me, for meeting
   Nancy was too late,
We'll never know about the sands
   of time if we lose or win
I do have a laugh on nature
   because Nancy is my friend.

MY NANCY

Evenings find me searching for a pleasant
   memory to carry me through the night.
Even after each long day, from dusk
   to dawn, time is a mental flight.
But I have a memory through which
   time failed to let it grow
And it haunts me as I see her face
   in my vision as its beauty glows.
Her eyes tell me we would never
   be strangers in any land,
And should the time arise for
   need of a friend, I'd just take her hand.
If the world became too much for me to
   bear and its escape beyond my eyes,
As a woman and friend she would lead
   me, those blue eyes spoke no lies.
This friendship, I take it not for granted,
   it is a blessed treasure to hold
I jealously guard this love for it
   cannot be bought or sold.
I do not expect this world whose
   treasures are materialistic gain
To ever understand this love
   between any woman or man.
A love that heeds to no one's
   call, the devil or his gold,
I pray to God that I may be
   worthy of this love to hold.

One day I was eating in this restaurant in Roscommon. This one older lady that was cooking seemed to stand out from the rest of the help because she always seemed extra busy. I asked the waitress if she knew the lady well. "Yes, I know her very well. Everybody in the neighborhood depends on her. She takes care of her two daughter's children, another kid that was abandoned in the neighborhood, plus any other one that happens to stumble in. Nobody will pay her anything, except Nancy. The rest just take advantage of her and won't do anything to help." The waitress continued on, "Matilda probably won't ever get any reward for bein' the neighborhood mother until she gets to heaven."

TAKING GRANDMA'S PLACE

Some winter mornings you lie awake
    waiting for the ring of the alarm
Knowing very well this time of year
    your day begins before dawn.
It soon will be time for the first meal
    to be prepared for the day
Also doing many chores for others
    without praise or pay.
Dressing the kids for school, and most of
    them not your own,
When tired in body and mind you wonder
    why you have such a home.
Being a lost child like me, guess you
    are paying interest on Grandma's love
Pleasant are the memories of her warmth and wisdom,
    when life had given me a shove.
Matilda days will come and some
    will slowly go
But I know you will be to others
    their joy not woe.
Completely prepared, you have taken Grandma's
    place in this world of strife,
This world is changing at a very
    fast noticeable pace.
Life no longer is a living art, it has
    become a race,
This world of what we want it to be
    would take in changing forever.
But like Grandma your just rewards
    are waiting for you in heaven.

In Upper Michigan, Mary and I found this abandoned farm that we really liked and were thinking about buying. It was off of a main road, and you had to go through a stretch of woods before you got to the open ground where the buildings were. This particular morning I had arrived early to watch the sunrise and see how it looked as the sun hit the various hills around the old home. The poem merely reflects what I witnessed that morning.

We found out later that a mining company owned the land and would not sell under any circumstances.

A NEW DAY

In Marquette County I was up
  before dawn
A short time before nature's lights
  came on.
Ears and eyes alert, being very quiet
  was an art.
I had stolen into nature's bedroom
  like a thief in the dark,
I watched an owl as it slipped quietly
  into his home.
A sly fox quickly retreating from
  its nightly roam,
Some birds chirped as a nervous
  squirrel chatted loud,
Unnoticed, a partridge and her chicks
  walked by me very proud.
The sunrise let its light and warmth
  in without a sound,
Yet it let nature know it had not
  let her down.
Her whole kingdom was busy coming
  very much alive
I had witnessed it all right before
  my two eyes.
I had not been seen and inside I
  was very glad
Watching nature's children being
  contented with what each had,
Not one act of hate was seen at the
  beginning of this day
It would truly be wonderful if people
  wake up this way!

John Trewhell was an Englishman who lived in Palmer, a little town slightly south of Ishpeming in Michigan's Upper Peninsula. His wife was a Finnlander, and about all the other residents around there were either Finnlanders or Swedes. I asked John how a lone Englishman ended up among all those Finnlanders, and he said, "Hell I don't know, guess they just didn't want me in England."

John was in excellent health for a man in his 80s. He had been an iron ore miner back when the pick and shovel were the primary tools. They made him retire from the mines when he was 70, and that pissed him off because he would rather have kept working.

I rented a small house that sat out behind John's big house and I got to know him pretty well. One day he asked me if I would take him over to Negaunee. He didn't say why he wanted to go and I didn't ask, but I did have some things to pick up myself. We started out toward Ishpeming, but at the road intersection he told me to turn and take the back roads in. When we got in Negaunee, he said, "Drive down there by the supermarket."

I pulled up in the parking lot and said, "Where you headed, John?"

"I'm goin' to that green building over there. I'll be back in an hour or so."

"OK, John," I said with a smile in my voice. He had pointed to the local whorehouse. Well I figured if he was going to be here that long, I'd walk uptown. Before I left, I skirted around the parking lot to watch him and see if that was really where he was going. Maybe he was just pulling my leg. Sure enough he went up to the door and went in.

I walked uptown and ran into Ron Ross. He was working construction in the area, so we visited awhile. Later, I walked back down to the supermarket to get the few things I needed. When I came out, John was back. "Are you ready to go now?" I asked.

"I'd like to get a beer first." He went in and got a half dozen to take home.

John said that he figured retirement would be better than this, that there were more worries now than before. Damn kids didn't seem to remember anything they had taught them. His wife wouldn't talk to me much at first. Typical Finnlander I guess; they have to stare at you

214 Poems and Memories

for awhile and size you up before they converse. She was in her eighties and a little frail, but seemed to have the same unpleasant feelings about life as he. Occasionally they would get in arguments about this or that.

I told them that they had all the blessings in the world and that Palmer was their world. They were the example to the others, and people looked to both of them to set a fine example. "Shucks," I said, "pretty soon your grandkids will be coming to you for advice."

They both replied, "Don't remind us of that."

Guess John figured I would keep my mouth shut about his trip into Negaunee, as it became a weekly favor he asked of me.

GREEN MEADOWS

Here I sat, a blank mind,
  with paper and pen in hand
Trying to make known an affection
  of a wonderful woman and man.
Our first meeting John looked me
  over with an open mind,
To know his concerned thoughts
  I would have paid a pretty dime.
John walked nine country miles
  to court his to be wife,
No one dare question their love
  in those days of simple life.
In those times they didn't know
  disrespect or what cheating meant
Their travels in life neither one's
  love has ever bent.
Yet you two have been blessed
  with all this world can give
You have had love and companionship
  of each other for years.
Joys, woes, friends and enemies,
  they have all come your way;
The fulfillment of raising children,
  witness their growth each day.
Eighty-one years has mellowed you both
  with wisdom and age
Unknowingly you are now on
  the world's stage.
A living example for one
  and all to see
Rewards are now just beginning
  for you to be.

The small maple tree had grown some since we bought the farm and had become John's favorite tree to climb. He was about eleven now and had been up in the tree more this year than I remember before. It kinda reminded me of my childhood when I liked to be off by myself to think things out. Settin' up there John could survey the world below and figure what he was gonna or not gonna do, the whole nine yards.

I had seen him up in that tree late one afternoon so at supper time I said, "John, what ya gonna do when you grow up?"

He replied, "I don't know, you'll have to ask my thinkin' tree."

THE THINKING TREE

It is just a small maple tree
   nothing special about it that one could see
But there it stood all by itself
   I notice that all the leaves had left,
All that stood were its bare limbs.
   There was a seat in one of its bends
Just right for a little boy on it to be,
   from this seat the whole world to see.
It was from this perch I could see
   my boy dreamed of what he wanted to be.
This tree held stories worth a world's gold
   of all the dreams to it had been told,
Hidden behind its leaves in summertime
   he must have left quite a few yarns behind
I asked John what he wanted to be,
   "You'll have to ask my thinking tree."

My boy Stanley was just turning 16 and at the time in his life when he was big enough to go out in the world and do as he wanted. He perceived himself big as a mountain, and the teenage path to manhood was doin' his own thing. It seemed like he always wanted to put his feet on the other side of the line, and I could see danger in that. He was hardheaded as hell, and it seemed like I couldn't get through to him so I wrote this poem.

ALMOST A MAN

Son you have reached sixteen years of age
   you have approached manhood a few years away,
Dreams in the past you will soon try
   answers to your questions soon will be alive,
I hope Mom and I will live to see
   when you are as proud of her and me.
At this age things seem to be confused,
   it's very hard for a young man to choose.
Here is one thing, there is no doubt,
   when problems get you down and out,
Have a talk with God, because He really knows,
   not one door will He ever leave closed
When you get older and are blessed with a child,
   just remember Mom and me once in awhile.
In your world we will be far behind,
   because you will just begin your climb
Set your pace so you won't be late,
   narrow it down to a gentle gait.

The cafe was located in Calumet in Michigan's Upper Peninsula. When Mary and I walked in, I was amazed at how busy it was for such a little town. Usually I try to eat something about every four hours, but it was well past that and I was really hungry. Guess I was a little fidgety because I don't mind waiting five minutes or so for a waitress, but it was goin' on 15. I started gazin' around at the other customers, wondering where they had all come from. This one lady alone at another table kinda caught my attention. She appeared to be in her 50s and was what I would describe as the perfect image of what a mother should look like. Now everyone would naturally have their own impressions on this, but to me she would be the perfect example. She carried an expression of one who had experienced life's ups and downs, and yet beneath it all was a kind of gentleness and the patience to see it all through.

Before we left the cafe, I went over and talked to her. I told her about my impressions, and that I was going to write a poem about her. She looked at me with the what-the-hell-ya-talkin'-about look in her eye, but she did give me her name, Mrs. George Barnett, and the small town she was from. Sometime later I did send her the poem, but it was returned, wrong address or she had moved.

A CERTAIN KIND OF WOMAN

On my arrival in the town of Calumet
    I noticed old buildings that had fallen down,
The rubble told me once this was a busy
    and wealthy town.
Prosperous days are thoughts of yesteryear
    in the minds of some of the old,
Yet to those who stayed, their dreams
    are the treasures they now hold.
Stopping at a cafe, hungry for a meal,
    wishing the waitress was on time,
Looking at people sitting about, with
    eating firmly on my mind,
A woman came in focus sitting in
    a booth, she was alone.
She was a perfect picture of a certain
    kind of woman, she wasn't forlorn.
Hard times of living and moments of

joy were written on this woman's face,
Her expressions told she was glad
   to have been in life's race.
Roads traveled in this life,
   face lines told, she did more than her part.
Her eyes told of kindness and patience
   in making a living an art.
My thoughts went back to the early
   days of my hurried youth
It brought back teaching of compassion
   love and truth.
As I spoke to her and the way to me,
   her answers gently came
Doubts in her mind made me feel
   humble and yet glad to be a man.
Some women I know have helped this
   world with its favored sin and shame
With the devil's beauty gone they damn
   one and all for the blame.
Though this woman, and those like her,
   have one look and one name
Hardships of life they so graceful carry
   is very hard to explain.
I hope in my future travels
   across God's great earth
I am blessed to meet more like
   her who gave life its birth.
These women are the ones who
   seem to give all they have to others,
To you Mrs. Barnett, and those of this
   world, you are simply known as mothers.

In 1980 I was working about forty miles south of Terre Haute, Indiana, on a powerhouse construction project. Becky Johnson was a common laborer, and even though she was spared such work as diggin' ditches and such, she did work hard on cleanup and lugging the 25 gallon water jugs around. She was not a very attractive girl and a lot of the guys shunned her, but from time to time I would stop and visit.

I was curious why she was out here in the first place, so I asked her to come out for supper one night to see if I could find out more. She knew it was just an invitation to supper and nothin' else, so she said, "hell yes."

She told me she was supporting her two kids and doin' a good job of it too. Becky had a positive attitude about life, but from her experience, was not fully trustful of men. Recently she had met a young fella from Kentucky. He worked on the project too, and I guess they were seriously going together. I got the impression she was looking for someone to help raise her kids and not necessarily just someone to bed down with. I don't know whether they finally got married or not.

FIGHTING FOR A LIFE

In the year nineteen fifty-two a
   joy came to this world with a cry
Five days before Christmas, Becky Johnson
   lay contented by her mother's side.
In the cool and warmth of
   Jefferson County she became a beautiful girl
Impatient to see and try what her ears
   had heard about this world,
Sincere as she was Becky married
   a love which done her wrong.
These were cloudy days, and
   eternity passed before the misery was gone
Being a earthly woman doing a job for
   men, so some say,
Yet to Becky the only way she could
   care for the two loves she knows today.
As I looked deep into her brown
   eyes old fears linger there,
Still searching for a true love she
   hopes is somewhere.
Like us all we know not
   what the tides of time will bring
But I believe in love and some day
   she will find the real thing.
I only hope she stays strong and not
   turn to the ways of wine,
As an earthly person she can't
   handle this curse the devil will have her mind.

When Dr. Cummings and Dr. King decided to open the little hospital
in Stanwood, Michigan, they needed a third doctor. They advertised
in a medical journal for another doctor, and Dr. Salvati, fresh out of
medical school, responded and filled the position.

David Salvati, to become a doctor, had overcome an obstacle most of us would have considered overwhelming. Born of well-to-do parents in upper New York, he had two major interests in life, horticulture and becoming a doctor. While in school for his degree in medicine, and still in his early 20s, cataracts caused almost total blindness. David learned braille and continued his studies until his parents took him to an eye surgeon in New Orleans where the cataracts were removed. He could now see well enough to continue his training.

At Princeton, Iowa, he finished his internship and also worked in the local greenhouses. Although he didn't have a degree in horticulture, he became involved in experiments and research on vegetable plants. By doing this, he also earned some extra money to help out with his education as he knew he had been a burden to his folks.

Dr. Salvati was our family doctor to start out with, and then Mary had a chance to work for him for five years as a receptionist and helper, so we got to know him much better and became good friends. In fact, he was the one to convince Mary she should return to school and get her high school diploma. Both he and his second wife Kathy attended Mary's graduation and purchased her class ring.

Along with his doctor's practice, David owned and operated a farm. He had produced a large family, and along with pursuing his own interests in vegetables, he wanted his children to experience the outdoors and the responsibilities of life which a farm could provide.

Bob and Marie Morris were neighbors of Doc's. Bob had been an iron worker and now had all kinds of health problems and not much money, so he used to help out on Doc's farm. Bob's wife, Marie, would also help watch Doc's kids after the divorce from his first wife. Doc looked after Bob's health and put Marie's daughter through nurse's training.

At butchering time, Doc would usually give Bob a half of a hog for helping out, and this year it would start a reaction no one would have expected. A firm in St. Louis, Michigan, mixed a fire retardant chemical (PBB) in with a livestock feed additive which then was shipped to numerous grain elevators. The grain elevator in Stanwood was where Doc got his feed mixed, and although he didn't know it, his hog feed was laced with PBB and in turn so was the half hog he gave Bob. When word got out what had happened, Doc had his feed tested to find out it was contaminated. Not too long after that Bob Morris passed away, and Doc figured that PBB ingested from the pork he had given Bob hastened his death. Doc was pissed and started getting involved as an activist for the many farmers affected. Livestock and people were coming up with unexpected illnesses, and the big companies didn't seem to be doing much to assume liability. The farmers had livestock that was quarantined, and they couldn't sell it but had to feed it. Farm families that drank milk from their contaminated dairy herds and ate meat from livestock they produced had high concentrations of the chemical in their bodies and a multitude of different health problems. Babies delivered in that time frame seemed to have more problems and there was a higher rate of miscarriages. For that reason, Doc gave up delivering babies. He sent his expectant mothers to another doctor. It was getting too much for him. He continued to prod the State to put pressure on the companies involved to take more responsibility for the problem even though it would cost millions to rectify. He also continued to communicate with other health specialists and laboratories to prove that many of the health problems were associated with the PBB.

During this time frame, Doc began to fear for his life. This PBB problem involved millions to the companies, and he was afraid that somebody was out to get him or his family and some things happened to indicate this might have been the case. He stayed overnight at our house a lot and always had guard dogs at the new place he had moved to.

Over a period of several years, the PBB crisis seemed to sort itself out, and I heard that new food labeling was a result of Doc's efforts with the government. Finally Doc moved his practice to Virginia and served the coal miners. From there he moved to Kingsport, Tennessee, had a heart attack and died in his mid-50s.

Doc's practice came to a halt when he was about 47. Since his first cataract operation he had several more. Each time to see and be able to work, he wore thicker glasses. They looked as thick as Coke bottles. He even wore contacts under the glasses. Finally, the doctors told him they couldn't operate anymore. There was too much scar tissue on his eyes.

Even though David Salvati was our family doctor, it was a long time before I needed his service. My problem started when I was a kid and jumped over a barbed wire fence. Well, almost over. A barb caught on my pants and put some holes in them and a couple in my scrotum. That all healed up OK, but now a growth had started where the holes had been. Doc examined the growth and said he could remove it without any problem, and he did. In the process I got a good look at Doc's hands and understood why he had given up general surgery. In a farm accident he had lost one and a half fingers off his right hand in a corn picker, and both hands certainly looked rough. Considering the area he was working, I was more than a little concerned, but I could sense confidence and compassion in this man.

HANDS

An artist usually paints a portrait
   most people in reality never see,
He has possession of mind and eyes for understanding
   where beauty ought to be.
His brush has captured scenes of nature's
   beautiful waters and lands,
Yet it seems God never gave him the ability
   to paint a pair of perfect hands.
Most artists I have read about
   wholeheartedly do agree,
To imprison such a scene on canvas or stone
   is a feat that is yet to be.
Sculptors and artists are unable to capture
   the bad and good of one's heart.
We must admit to have either one
   our hands play an important part.
I don't claim to have powers to see
   mysteries of the great beyond,

Nor possess a mind of the wise to judge
   the right or wrong;
But I do have the understanding
   of the touch of a hand.
Its feel will quickly tell me
   the character of the man.
Having a discomfort of its nature
   I will let its reason lay.
A man of medicine intensely looked upon me
   his eyes spoke of a trying day.
His gentle hands so careful worked,
   with patience caused me no doubt.
Enlarged eyeglasses and stubbed fingers told,
   he knew what pain was about.
His touch told me of compassion,
   yet strength of certainty was there.
The movements of his fingers showed
   his integrity was not impaired;
His unrestricted motions told of a clean
   and clear conscienced man.
Most mortals need a written record
   I need only to feel those hands.

One day I was over at our friend Dr. Salvati's house, when he lived on 100th Ave. with his wife Cathy. Cathy's sister, Michelle was visiting from Bay City at the time, and that day she looked out the big picture window and said, "That is an ugly tree." I'd never particularly paid any attention to that tree until she said something about it. It was kind of a drab olive green color, but I said, "What do ya mean an ugly tree, I've never seen an ugly tree."

"You look at that one. That is an ugly tree," and she pointed her finger at it.

"Michelle, I'm gonna have to write you a poem about that tree."

THAT TREE

Wanderers of the seas have
   given fortunes for a tree,
Nomads of the desert their last
   holding for a shady breeze.
Woodsmen have cursed her
   when she was stubborn to fall,
To others who have comfort from
   her gifts no thoughts at all.
Yet without the tree, life
   on earth would be out of place,
Our eyes would never see the magnificent
   beauty of her changing face.
Trees small and large turn the
   winds with astonishing power,
They are a haven of rest at
   times a savior of the hour.
Upon your ears these words
   may have once been told
Yet as your eyes focus upon a tree
   look at the treasury she holds.
Its true beauty is in the eyes of
   the beholder, even at a glance,
But judge not the blessing of a
   tree as an unsettled romance.

Mary met Eyvonne Shaniquitte when she worked for Dr. Salvati at the Stanwood Hospital. Evyonne was living on their family homestead in section twenty-nine (that sat on the border between Lake and Mecosta Counties). Mary took a likin' to Eyvonne. She could see they were kinda poor, and Eyvonne was always questioning Mary on how to grow a garden, can vegetables, and generally make a go of it on their homestead. Eyvonne's brother had bought back the old family homestead, and she and her four kids and father lived there. Her brother stayed in Detroit, and I guess Eyvonne's husband had run off.

I went with Mary up to visit them, and it became evident to us that they were poorer than we figured. The house looked about ready to topple down. They had no inside plumbing, just an outhouse for a bathroom, and they carried water in from an old pump outside. I guess about their only income was the father's social security, him bein' in his 80s. They were living as folks had back in the 20s and before, just tryin' to make it.

What I noticed most was the kids. They were the most happy-go-lucky bunch you could imagine, just didn't seem to realize they were lacking anything.

Her father, John Curtis, had been a musician most of his life and was a fine old gentleman. He could play about any string instrument, but concentrated on the fiddle. Being in early Vaudeville, he traveled a lot and could play any kind of music from classical to country. He could play by ear or read music and was really good but never made the big time. After Vaudeville he just ended up playin' for dances or wherever there was a need for music. He could even make his own instruments, that's the kind of talent he had. We talked about country music, which I really liked, and he and the kids were mutually curious about Mary and I.

As years went by, we lost track of Eyvonne and her family. We heard later that Mr. Curtis had died and Eyvonne had left the homestead and moved to Oklahoma.

SECTION TWENTY-NINE

In the backwoods of Lake County, section twenty-nine,
    an old man and his daughter were seeing hard times.
Her children watch me as children do when invited in,
    their questions answered who I was and where I had been.
I wouldn't put these folks down, I had lean years like this,
    it carried me back to a time I'm glad I didn't miss.
In palaces and mansions, looking over seashores and
      mountains high,
    the welcome I received at this humble home, money
      couldn't buy.
The old man and I spoke of things bad and good
    of what we did and what we should,
With his fiddle and bow he played songs of yesteryear;
    it brought back days of his youth to me thoughts so dear.
Life here was an uphill pull, this I saw so plain,
    I was ashamed as I remember when I had complained.
Love does so many wonderful wonders in life
    Those smiles told me they knew not of their strife.

Joe Avery had asked me a year before to write this poem. "I would like to have somebody write a poem about my daddy," he had said. When I asked why, he said, "Well, he keeps tellin' me it doesn't bother him the fact that someday he's gonna die, but it does concern him how he's gonna go."

One day I set out to drive down and talk to the old man. He lived about fifteen miles north of Greenville, Michigan, on M-91. When I arrived at the place, I could see that in the last couple days there had been quite a fire. The house had burned. I got out of the car and stood there by the tree for awhile. Things were still smoldering. Finally, I decided I'd walk around and survey the damage, then go into town and find out what had happened from Joe. Out from someplace popped the old man. Guess he had been watching from behind the trees where I couldn't see him.

I talked to Joe's father for quite some time. Of course the main thing on his mind was his burned up house, but eventually the conversation wound around to the topic of dying and I listened to his concerns.

LIFE'S LAST CHAPTER

Driving through the rolling countryside
   watching the beautiful farms go by,
Stopping to rest by an old oak tree
   I felt a pair of eyes staring at me.
They looked worried, through a wrinkled face,
   I saw ashes of what was an old home place.
His features told me of lessons he learned,
   life had been hard, what he had was earned.
I spoke to him, but he just smiled
   he said come on over set awhile.
This home was a monument to me he began,
   yes, I rebuilt it with my own two hands.
One hundred twenty acres is all I got
   working it with the boys is an awful lot,
We have had good and bad times here.
   all of its memories I hold very dear.
I am not sorry of the life I have lived,
   but at times I wonder how I'll leave here.
Some leave this world in awful pain,
   others go easy, some think it's a shame.
Accidents carry a lot of us away
   then again for some it's just their day.
In my time I've walked down a lot of roads
   leaving doesn't bother me it's how I'll go,
I shouldn't talk like that some say
   don't know why it's going to be my day.
I've had a pal all through my life
   yes, son, I'm talking about my wife.

If I go first what will she do,
   that's what really bothers me through and through.
You would think at my age of seventy-six,
   how I leave I would have solved it every bit.
We mortals will never know this quest
   the Lord knows for us what is best
Yet I can't get it out of my mind,
   but I'll know when it comes.

I remember old Huey Long when he was governor of Louisiana. I read when he got up in front of Congress and said, "I got people in my state who are hungry, people who don't have shoes on their feet and clothes on their back. Some don't have a place to stay, and you are telling me we are rightly distributing the wealth of this country. I'm telling you right now somebody's tellin' a damned lie." Seems like he was right, but got shot for it. All Huey Long wanted was what Alaska has today for his state of Louisiana.

When I was young, more than once I saw a kid lie about something to get out of punishment, and in the process some innocent kid would get his ass whipped.

These political people make all sorts of speeches with glossy words, and a lot of them are lying right through their teeth. That applies to Republicans and Democrats. I see little difference in the whole bunch.

LIES

Nations have risen and fallen
   because of a lie;
Righteous families are destroyed
   because of jealous hearts and evil eyes.
Liars have made fortunes
   in a short time;
We giggle with joy when we think
   by a lie we are justified.
We dance with glee when
   a lie incorrectly equalizes,
Professional liars deceive many
   with their intent.
Do liars know more than what
   God's ninth commandment meant?

What I really see here in this country is a country that could have wealth far beyond anyone's expectations if only the golden rule was applied. As far as I'm concerned, there shouldn't be a privileged class, king or peon, they should all be treated the same. They go to bed, they get up, the only natural difference is the talent that God let some possess. Our laws and our society have created a privileged class, and that is wrong. I'm not against rich people, just those who misuse their wealth.

TIRED

Tired of seeing:
  children socially learned
  three "R's" is the need.
Tired of seeing:
  youth pressed beyond
  their time.
Tired of:
  money ruling people destroying
  families before they begin.
Tired of:
  our labors in body and mind
  used in ways not intended.
Tired of:
  our lawmakers in ignorance changing
  the once righteous Constitution.
Tired of:
  our leaders being led by the
  devil and his friends.
Tired of:
  greedy and glory seekers
  especially within our own ranks.
Sad in:
  heart that our ways come before
  the ways of Jesus Christ.

My oldest boy Robert and his wife lived in Jacksonville, Florida, when she was pregnant with their first child. We kept up regular correspondence with them, and I sat down and wrote this poem before the child was born. I tried with limited knowledge to put myself in Robert's shoes for the blessed event. I guess I came pretty close to reality because after the baby was born Robert asked how I was able to foresee such a chain of confusion. Apparently all hell broke loose on the way to the hospital. They got on the wrong streets with uncooperative traffic lights and a drawbridge that was up.

THE BLESSED EVENT

The birth of a child takes a long time,
   at first you are satisfied in your mind.
But as time is halfway drawing near
   you are hustling for blankets and a crib.
You name the girl a hundred times or more
   then someone has to say, "suppose it's a boy!"
Your friends wish you both health and good cheer,
   you are wishing the baby was already here.
You lay in bed awake all night
   making plans for the faithful flight,
Your beloved lays there in peaceful rest,
   just as if she knew what was best.
One night when everything is calm
   your wife gently rings the alarm
In a wild dash you forget where you are,
   she waits in the car calmly as a cat.
Your bewildered hurry for this blessed event,
   what has happened, where had all the plans went?
Your car turns down the wrong streets,
   in your confused mind it's yourself you meet.
She gently walks down the long hall,
   doesn't seem to mind at all.
What seems like forever and a year
   the nurses come and says it's here.

We were living on a place down by Dryden when I met Harry. He was an alcoholic and had a hard life as a kid. I didn't get the details of his life from him, but instead from others who knew him and his family. Harry didn't deny anything that I'd heard, but some things he didn't want to talk about, so I let them be.

Harry's father was a very hard man. He was an old German that believed if the kid wasn't willing to learn the old man's way of doing things, then he should knock it into the kid's head. Harry was a little guy and always seemed to get the shit end of the stick in the family. The sisters all left home; only the younger brother Paul stayed and did not marry.

After Harry's first divorce, he moved in with Paul who kinda looked after him. Harry's kids went with their mother but would come back and visit Harry, and when they left they would carry off anything of value. Even their mother would try to come back and take more of Harry's stuff until Paul put a stop to it. Harry finally met another gal, one from Alabama, and she thought she was gonna get a pot full of money, but she didn't and divorced him too. As far as I know, Harry died a happy, unwed man.

HARRY

In Lapeer County, he was born and raised,
   where he plowed the fields in a beautiful maze,
A happy childhood, something he never had;
   loved by his mother, taunted by his dad.
Small in size he had the hardest of chores
   he was the oldest of the girls and boys.
The load wasn't heavy, as long as Mother lived,
   her death left only memories of love she did give.
Denied a true love even by his wife
   his children help not in the ways of life,
They all took him for what he had;
   caring not as they destroyed their dad.
Only one stood by him through it all,
   God bless his younger brother Paul.
At times he did turn to the wine
   to ease the pain of broken heart and mind
Over seventy years he has walked this earth
   heartbreaks and misery have been his berth.
Still searching for love in this earthly life,
   I received word he had taken another wife.
All I can say at this stage of life's day
   love is all he has left, the rest has gone its way
But only fools seek of this world for gold,
   love is the most precious of treasures to hold.

While working down in Alabama, I discovered this small town restaurant that had both good food and good service. Mary had been down and stayed for awhile, and she agreed with me on the quality of this place. We had eaten there together several times.

This one waitress, whose name I won't mention, usually waited on me. She proved excellent service and I tipped her well. The trouble was it was difficult to get her to say anything, and when she did she would not look at you. She normally would be staring down at her shoes when she talked. Sometimes I get a little pushy, so one day I said, "Your shoes don't need polishing, why do you keep looking at them?" I was just trying to get her to talk a little more. She said something, I don't remember what, and finally I said, "Why don't you go to supper with me some evening?"

She looked up, "Ya know, if I did that those old women and old men would talk about us both."

She knew I was married, guess that was the concern, "Hell with it, let them talk. We'll give them something to talk about."

"I can't do that," she replied, "but I will go to supper with you, only we'll do it out of these people's eyes." That kinda bothered me 'cause I wasn't tryin' to get in this girl's britches.

We were sitting in this cafe in a small neighboring town called Gunnersville and I asked her, "Why didn't you want to be seen with me?"

"Obviously you don't know all the stories about me. My husband was convicted of incest with our daughter and is in prison. I divorced him, but that's all those people want to see now is me steppin' around." I could see that she figured if I took her to supper, the old town biddies would figure I would be taking her to bed too. Maybe they would have thought that, even if she hadn't had this thing in her past. It seemed to me people in the South had more of a tendency to gossip and were more open about their secrets too.

SOCIAL CURSE

There are moments in one's life
    thoughts go back in time
When for no reason this someone
    hangs heavy in your mind.
Things you both had wished to do
    society would put down
Yet what will ease life's pains
    while society has you in bounds?
Society has never paid for
    the dues that come our way
It appears society takes and
    makes us an economic slave.
Society successfully makes us ashamed
    because we wish to be ourself,
Through laws and religions it makes
    us believe tradition is all that's left.
When alone we think of nature's
    pleasures that are within reach,
We damn one's self for the way
    we have let society teach.
Yet, as I write this note about
    society and its enslaving this land,
My thoughts are heavy of a beautiful
    woman to who I know understands.

Watching TV and the various sporting events, all emphasis is on the winner. As a lineman, I have seen men come to the trade that weren't meant for it. When the lightning is flashing and the lines are slapping together, it is not a job for the faint-hearted or you will lose your ass and somebody else's too. How many of us have been mismatched in marriage? Why can't we get on the right road to begin with? Still, when the challenge is met, I admire those that can smile when they've lost.

LOSERS

Everybody likes a winner
    they seem to have all in control
A brighter smile sparkling eyes,
    the right words, the right clothes.
Joys they express in winning
    are easily seen in their pride,
A race for the goal for them
    is won with an easy stride.
But what about the loser
    the one who failed to win?
The steps were the same in
    his determination not to bend.
His aim was just as high
    in trying to win the race,
The effect twice as hard, knowing
    he must not slack his pace.
My bet is with the loser
    because of the way he tried;
So don't tell me about your
    winners or the things they have done,
For in my eyes it takes a better
    person to smile in a race they haven't won.

Just west of Houghton Lake is a little place called Merriat. We had
parked the line truck between two spans, and I had walked one span to
this pole and the other lineman had worked in the other direction. I
was up on the pole and finished my work when a car pulled up to this
house. No one knew I was up there, so I just watched. It was clear to
me the old man had lost his wife, and the young couple had just
brought him back to visit the old home. I got to thinkin' if I don't stop
travelin' so much, I could end up like that.

LOST ROOTS

I saw an old man
   come back to his home today.
Yes, a young couple drove him
   right up to the doorway
As he got out his eyes were taking note
   of everything to be told,
He didn't see me
   I was on top of a power pole.
He quickly walked over the small yard
   looking at fresh plants,
Taking a deep breath with hands
   in the back pockets of his pants.
The house was old, weathered,
   and bent just like him,
He seemed pleased to be back
   from where he had been.
Yet I saw in his lined face
   and wrinkled eyes the truth,
His lonely life was now
   depending on the two youths.
I knew he was thankful
   for kindness they did show,
But he would rather be planting
   a garden row by row.

Memories and visions
    passed my mind and eyes,
For I was looking at a man
    glad it was him, not I.
A house is a building where you stay
    from time to time,
A home is where you live
    body, heart and mind.
To leave it you take away
    all of your roots,
And it's not long before you
    are like a worn-out boot.
Yes, it is sad to leave behind
    your very own home,
Second thoughts that pass tell you
    that it's best to roam.
Traveling may broaden your mind
    as you go from place to place,
But it isn't very long before,
    you are in a rat race
Trying to find a substitute
    for things that you left behind,
Telling yourself sweet lies
    to try and ease your mind.

It had been seven years or so since I had left the shipyard. I had been working in Florida for a week or so before the strike hit, and on my evenings I would go back over to the shipyard to see old friends. Old man Coppledge was glad to see me. The first time he said, "Climb up on that vessel and take her up the river."

"Well, I'll ride her up, but not by myself. Hell, if I did you'd probably have me thrown in jail, and I'd have to spend the rest of my days down here." He kinda grinned. I rode with another guy, but up on the bridge I directed the tugs and did those things I'd been practicin' before I moved north. I had originally intended to become a river pilot, and I guess now I was revisitin' those ambitions. Even as I was goin' through the motions of a career left behind, I realized that I would never move Mary and the kids back down here. I felt confident my decision to go north had been right.

MOTHER NATURE'S WISDOM

Northeast Florida where the St. John River flows,
　many times on her banks I've watched the winds blow.
To the wide ocean her jetties, stretching out like arms,
　like a mother reaching for her child to keep it from harm.
After a Mark Twain of years I'm standing on her shore
　marveling at her beauty, as I had in years before.
From the ocean comes a ship, I was to be its guide,
　once again I was to pilot a vessel through the river's sides.
Up Jocob's Ladder over the gunwales I climb,
　from the bridge I heard the tugs pull their lines
Each command I gave was answered with its whistle's toots,
　it felt good to be back to familiar roots.
Even from this ship I could clearly hear the wind,
　it was Mother Nature's call I knew she would win.
Familiar places in the south were all I came to see,
　but the northland had become too much a part of me.
Travels in this land I knew were over and done
　back to the northlands I came on the run,
For only here can I find happiness and rest,
　Mother Nature knew all along for me what was best.

This poem came to mind as I was pushin' the old Cadillac towards Dothan, Alabama. It was the oil static line work and I knew that I would be staying in town. My mind drifted back to our work around Alpena, Cheboygan, and Black River in Michigan. What a great life that was for a guy that liked the outdoors. Hell, we lived out there in the power line right-of-ways, just spread our sleeping bags out under the stars, caught fish, shot a rabbit or squirrel, and cooked 'em right there. We even had a young deer occasionally. I suppose the snow-mobiles and developers have civilized that country by now.

MY KEEPER

Leaving a part of the country I have learned to love,
  for its wonderful memories I have thanked God above,
Fate has moved me with her wanton hand,
  roads guide me to another part of this land.
I have no worries about going to another place,
  unlike most people I am in Mother Nature's grace.
She has so lovingly and carefully looked after me,
  in ways of life she makes it so simple to see.
Her new dress of many colors she now has on,
  just for me to see this frosty morn.
She is tempting me in her flirting ways to stay,
  just like a woman determined to have her way.
Many times she has fed me as if I were a king,
  I know if I were to ask she would give anything.
I have slept in her bed many a night,
  singing me songs, as she tucked me in tight,
Watched over me, kept me from all harm,
  I know she saw to it I was never wronged.
I know wherever I have to live
  Mother Nature will be right there to give.
It's her gift I have had so many times
  this wonderful Grace has given me a worry-free mind,
A gift I will never be able to repay,
  if I tried it would insult her, I know her way.

It was in seventy-eight, I believe, and I hadn't written my mother for quite awhile. So along with an Easter card I sent this poem. Times were rough for her and Adolph, her husband. They lived in the

Springfield district of Jacksonville, Florida, and things there were changin'. The old folks that they knew were either moving out or had died, and integration was movin' in. Now Adolph was not prejudiced, but my mother certainly was. She didn't think there ever was a good black man born. I'm not sure why she was prejudiced 'cause my grandmother wasn't. Anyway, I knew they didn't have enough money to move, so I offered to let them move up and stay with us. They decided not to.

My next oldest boy Henry had been kinda looking after Helen and Adolph, so when Adolph died he called up to tell me about Helen. "Grandma is in a daze since Adolph died. She wanders around the neighborhood lookin' in garbage cans, and she don't need to do that."

I sent Robert down to pick her up, and I got busy with a crash remodeling program to get a room ready for her upstairs. In fact, it still took another week after she got here to get it finished. It wasn't long after she arrived that she started complaining about this and that. I told her that I understood that this was a big change from Florida, but there were some things I couldn't change. I told her there just wasn't anyplace five blocks down the road where she could visit other older people. What I really wished she could do was teach my daughter Marsha and my wife Mary how to crochet. She could whip out even the fanciest doily in a couple days and put together a dress in half the time it would take Mary. I thought maybe if she would share her talent that would get her mind off the things that were bothering her. It didn't work, the complaining got worse.

One day Mother said she was dissatisfied staying with us and would I find her another place to stay. "No," I said, "but I will have Mary or Marsha take you around to look for someplace you would like to stay." Marsha took her looking, and she finally settled on an old folk's home in Millbrook, about fifteen miles east of here. I took her over myself and said, "Is this where you want to stay?"

"Yes."

When Mother became an invalid and bedridden, she was moved to Greenwich Home where she finally passed away of old age. I didn't go visit her very often 'cause every time I did she got all upset. My mother was a good woman, but she had one bad habit. She liked to live in a dream world. Even as a young woman she would daydream about how she would like things to be and would try to live out the dream. It was a way to escape problems and it got worse with age. Guess my visits just reminded her of reality and that pissed her off. I decided I would avoid bursting the bubble and stay away.

One of the cousins complained to Thelma, and she called up and asked why I wasn't visiting my mother more. I said I wanted to but didn't want to upset her. "Thelma, you know that Helen lives in a dream world."

"Yes, but Teddy you hadn't ought to let her do that."

"Thelma nobody can change your heart, and nobody can change mine, and I sure as hell can't change hers. There's no reason to sit here wringin' the rag about this makin' a family issue out of something that don't amount to a row of beans. Helen can do exactly like she wants to do. There are certain things that people aren't gonna do that Helen wants them to do. That's the whole thing in a nutshell."

That was the only bad part of the relationship with my mother, and I wish it could have been better, but still I think it went the way she wanted it to. Old people sometimes just get real set in their ways, almost childlike.

A NOTE TO MOMMY

Mommy I'm writing you a word that's long overdue,
   writing to you in a way you never knew.
I'm not the boy I was when I left home
   I change as I witness this world I roam,
For I learned of this world in a very short time
   wishing I could have grown up, yet kept my childish mind.
Of some memories I'd like to tell a lie,
   yet those memories now never seem to have been alive.
In all of my successful failures and sin
   only one regret I have of this world I'm in;
I wished my second had been my first wife,
   her love has made a contented man in this life.
I have been with people older than time,
   what was said and done didn't satisfy my mind,
Which goes to show there is no doubt
   young and old both have things to learn about.
We often think of our children as coming home,
   back to the sheltered love away from the lust to roam.
But I know the tide is turning at your feet
   the trials of living are harder each day to meet,
What I am saying in this very short note
   we have a place you can hang up your coat
Just let us know what's really on your mind.
   A letter will do and I'm sending you the dime.

The old Morley grocery store has been converted to a community education center. It is available for persons of all ages who didn't finish their education for one reason or another. It provides the opportunity to get some education for their future. I wrote this poem for those who do not comprehend the necessity of an education.

A SECOND CHANCE

Butterflies are beautiful
   in their various colors and shades,
They fly about as if performing
   in scattered parades.
Attracting attention as they
   freely go their flighty way,
You would never think some
   species have life for only a day.
Unlike the butterflies, humans
   need to be taught to have a keen mind,
To fail this requirement of society you
   will noticeably be behind.
At this very moment as you sit
   in this old retired grocery store,
Your wealth in society will
   depend on your educational score.
Those who teach have given you
   a better means and second chance,
This possession of knowledge should be used
   wisely as a decision in an unsettled romance.

SMILES

The prettiest sight that I see
　is a smiling face looking at me.
Some say I am crazy charmed by a smile,
　to see a true one I would walk a mile.
A newborn knows of no wrong
　theirs is a true smile it has no harm.
Our ways change, as older we grow,
　we smile to hide of things untold.
I tell you boys when I go
　I leave the world with a happy soul,
No worries about possessions I leave behind
　they are all with me right in my mind.

SEARCHING

We all have had our
   sleepless nights,
When keeping awake was a
   mental flight;
Through your many memories
   with a diligent search,
Trying to pacify your heart
   on this restless earth.
Such a night was upon me
   without a sound,
A fresh fallen snow
   held all life in bound;
Disruptions were none for
   the time was here,
With paper and pen, another
   poem for someone's ear.
Happiness in life is people's
   aim, possession is the call,
Yet something is missing
   they don't know why;
The warmth they search
   for money cannot buy,
These types of people bored
   deep into my mind,
With all they have not one
   friend can they find.

WALKING WITH MEMORIES

At times I like to walk through my past.
　　Joyful I recall the warmth I received that will last.
Grandma, Jake, my wife, children, and a girl,
　　these are the ones to me mean the world.
Grandma taught me of God's love and grace
　　she showed me His presence in each place,
Told me of things I would wonder about,
　　this life, this world and the only way out.
Jake holds a very special place in my heart
　　things he told and showed me made life an art,
Mother Nature's ways he so clearly made me see,
　　without his wisdom where would I be?
The one who has chosen to walk with me in life,
　　an eternal love I have for my wonderful wife.
Her love she has proved time and time again,
　　a love she gives, not the kind you have to win.
Like most children ours are the very best,
　　our patience with them has been a test.
They grow up and learn about the world on their own
　　but like all life they will return home.
The girl was one in my travels whom I met
　　who has problems and answers yet to get;
We talked of life and the way we wanted it to be,
　　a very wonderful with such lovely ways to see.
The loved ones I speak about mean much to me
　　they make life's road a pleasant place to be,
Though I walk in life with them a short while
　　always remembering love and warmth in their eye.

Ted, Gordon Galloway, and Mary — May 1995

ABOUT THE AUTHOR

Gordon Galloway graduated from Michigan State University, served in the Air Force with a Vietnam tour and spent over 20 years flying fighters with the Michigan Air National Guard. He has been a farmer in Michigan since 1966 and is also an airline Captain with American Eagle in Chicago.

Founder of Deerfield Publishing Company, Gordon has discovered that he doesn't have to go farther than his own neighborhood to find fascinating stories to tell and that maybe many of those people in our everyday life are more deserving of celebrity status than some we read about in the headlines.

Wheels to trace their roots, with more stories to tell.

ADDITIONAL COPIES

To obtain **HILLBILLY POET** send
$10 plus $1.25 postage to:

Deerfield Publishing
Box 146
Morley, MI 49336

ALSO AVAILABLE

SCARS OF A SOLDIER — Vernon Heppe's true story by GORDON
GALLOWAY— a Michigan farm boy with an eighth grade education is drafted into
the Army during WWII and becomes a man on the Pacific battlefields of Kwajalein,
Leyte, and Okinawa. Wounded four times, he received both the Silver and Bronze
Star. With a keen sense of humor, Vernon tells about growing up on the farm and his
adjustment to becoming a soldier. He describes combat in vivid detail and the
memories that remain.

Send $10 plus $1.25 to Deerfield Publishing

COMING SOON

If you liked **HILLBILLY POET**, Deerfield Publishing will soon have an
additional book available that you will certainly enjoy. Through a series of short
stories, Ted Aldridge has highlighted other memorable events in his life. The
stories make excellent reading and offer plenty of humor and an even closer look at
this fine individual. Send us your name and address and we'll let you know when
each new Deerfield book will be available.